Whole Language:

Beliefs and Practices, K–8

Gary Manning and Maryann Manning, Editors

nea PROFESSIONAL LIBRARY
National Education Association
Washington, D.C.

Printing History
    First Printing: July 1989
    Second Printing: January 1990
    Third Printing: August 1990
    Fourth Printing: September 1992

Note

The opinions expressed in this publication should not be construed as representing the policy or position of the National Education Association. Materials published by the NEA Professional Library are intended to be discussion documents for teachers who are concerned with specialized interests of the profession.

Library of Congress Cataloging-in-Publication Data

Whole language : beliefs and practices, K–8 / Gary Manning and Maryann
    Manning, editors.
        p. cm. — (NEA aspects of learning)
    Bibliography: p.
    ISBN 0–8106–1482–0
    1. Language experience approach in education. 2. Language arts
(Elementary) 3. Reading (Elementary)—Language experience approach.
I. Manning, Gary L. II. Manning, Maryann Murphy. III. National
Education Association of the United States. IV. Series.
LB1576.W4866   1989
372.6—dc19   89–3156
                                                                  CIP

Whole Language:

Beliefs and Practices, K-8

The Editors

Gary Manning and Maryann Manning are Professors in the School of Education at the University of Alabama at Birmingham. They are the authors of several NEA publications: *Reading Instruction in the Middle School, Improving Spelling in the Middle Grades,* and *A Guide and Plan for Conducting Reading (K-12) In-Service Workshops.* They are also two of the coauthors of *Reading and Writing in the Primary Grades,* and they are the developers of *Reading K-12: The NEA In-Service Training Program.*

CONTENTS

INTRODUCTION

by Gary and Maryann Manning

The last decade or so has been a time of significant growth in understanding how students develop as readers and writers. In the past, classroom teachers used some sensible practices in teaching reading. They had sound intuition, they were trusted and supported, and they acted accordingly. In addition, they learned about reading and writing instruction from several reading authorities who had remarkable insight into the nature of student learning. Jeanette Veatch, for example, made teachers aware of individualized reading and provided a number of ideas for helping students develop as readers. May Hill Arbuthnot informed and excited teachers about the wonderful world of children's books. Roach Van Allen acquainted teachers with the importance of students' writing their own stories as well as being surrounded with meaningful print. And Mauree Applegate held teachers spellbound with her suggestions about English.

In the late sixties and early seventies, however, abandoning their intuition, many teachers flirted with or became committed to the skills movement. Some watched and even approved as the behaviorists chopped the act of reading into bits and pieces of isolated skills, placing those scraps on a skills continuum. Teachers continued to observe as tests were developed to assess student "mastery" of the bits and pieces. When the expected proficiency was not forthcoming, additional worksheets, workbooks, and drill activities were produced to ensure student mastery of these so-called essential skills that were promised as the solution to the nation's reading problems.

After watching students struggle over digraphs, diphthongs, and other isolated skills, we, like countless others, became disenchanted with this view of language learning. We noticed several things—students could bubble in the right answer on a test measuring skills; they could complete stacks of dittos, but often could not read or tell about what they read; others could read, but chose not to because it was not a pleasurable activity for them.

Fortunately, teachers have now recaptured their intuition about language learning, and their knowledge about student learning continues to be clarified and extended. Through sound scientific research and theory, outstanding educators have shown how students develop as readers and writers. Ken and Yetta Goodman, for example, have been of special help to us and continue to be a source of information and inspiration as we grow in our understanding of literacy development. Many others have also assisted us in our thinking; several of these authorities are included in this anthology. In addition, we are grateful to the classroom teachers with whom we work regularly. As we interact with teachers in their classrooms, we learn from them, and, most importantly, we learn from the students themselves.

"Whole Language" refers to a set of beliefs about language learning. Several of these beliefs were presented in *Reading and Writing in the Primary Grades*, which we coauthored with Roberta Long and Bernice Wolfson (Washington, D.C.: National Education Association, 1987):

1. Reading and writing should be a natural outgrowth of oral language development.
2. Children construct their own knowledge from within.
3. Reading is comprehension, that is, creating meaning from text.
4. Communication is the main aim of writing.
5. Learning to read and write is a social process.
6. Risk taking and making mistakes are critical to reading and writing well.

Misunderstandings will arise about any view of language learning; some are beginning to surface about whole language. For instance, we listened recently to a sales representative give a report of a commercial whole-language phonics program; we also heard another speaker share ideas about the teaching of sight words in whole language. Educators must not let the benefits of a strong theoretical base be lost by treating whole language as another new term or gimmick for teaching reading and writing.

This anthology includes the ideas of many of the leading authorities on whole language. It contains chapters in several areas: the meaning of whole language, the skills movement and its lack of sound theory on how students construct knowledge about reading and writing, reading and writing development, and teacher autonomy. Each chapter begins with a brief overview. Although not every facet of whole language is discussed, references are provided for readers who would like additional information.

1. WHOLE LANGUAGE: WHAT'S NEW?

by Bess Altwerger, University of New Mexico, Albuquerque; and
Carole Edelsky and Barbara M. Flores, Arizona State University,
Tempe

*According to Bess Altwerger, Carole Edelsky, and Barbara Flores,
"Whole language is not practice. It is a set of beliefs, a perspective."
Comparing it with other views of literacy learning, these authors emphasize that whole language is not a whole-word approach with the focus on
"getting the words." Rather, it is one of constructing meaning from text,
using cues that include words, syntax, semantics, and pragmatics. Neither
is whole language teaching skills in context. One of its goals is to have students "become skilled language users," not just learners of separate language skills. Among the practices congruent with a whole-language view,
the authors list journal writing and reading aloud to students.*

*Altwerger, Edelsky, and Flores also point out that whole language is
not another term for language experience. Advocates of that approach,
such as Roach Van Allen and Jeanette Veatch (who have made great contributions to better reading and writing programs), "do not state that
reading consists of separate skills," but they do imply that students learn
about reading from studying skills lessons. Finally, the authors note that
whole language is not another round of open education. It rests on a solid
theoretical base, which should prevent it from suffering the same fate as
open education.*

This chapter appeared in The Reading Teacher, *vol. 41 (November
1987): 144–54. Copyright © 1987 by the International Reading Association. Reprinted with permission of Bess Altwerger and the International
Reading Association.*

More and more educators are warming to a new idea in education—
Whole Language. Wherever we go, we hear statements which support
Whole Language at the same time as they reveal questions or outright
confusions about it. So while we are delighted with the increasing popularity, we wonder what it is that is popular: the idea of Whole Language? The label? Innovation per se?

Educational innovations have not fared well in the United States.
Open Education was a recent casualty. It was widely distorted so that
open space was substituted for openness of ideas, learning centers for
learning-centeredness. The final irony is that it was judged a failure even
though (because of the distortions) it was never implemented on any

broad scale (a few exceptions still exist—e.g., Prospect School in Vermont, Central Park East in New York City, and scattered classrooms elsewhere).

Whole Language is too good an idea to suffer such a fate. Widespread understanding of the substance, rather than widespread adoption of the label might be one way to prevent this possibility. Though Goodman's monograph, *What's Whole in Whole Language* (1986), will certainly help, we see a need to address the specific points of confusion and particular questions we are frequently asked about Whole Language. But first a brief description.

WHOLE LANGUAGE: WHAT IS IT?

First and foremost: Whole Language is *not* practice. It is a set of beliefs, a perspective. It must become practice but it is not the practice itself. Journals, book publishing, literature study, thematic science units and so forth do not make a classroom "Whole Language." Rather, these practices become Whole Language-like because the teacher has particular beliefs and intentions.

Whole Language is based on the following ideas: (a) language is for making meanings, for accomplishing purposes; (b) written language is language—thus what is true for language in general is true for written language; (c) the cuing systems of language (phonology in oral, orthography in written language, morphology, syntax, semantics, pragmatics) are always simultaneously present and interacting in any instance of language in use; (d) language use always occurs in a situation; (e) situations are critical to meaning-making.

Since language in use is taken to have at least the features listed above, the implication is that anyone using language (a baby, an adult, a second language learner) is using all systems in making meaning to accomplish purposes.

The key theoretical premise for Whole Language is that, the world over, babies acquire a language through actually using it, not through practicing its separate parts until some later date when the parts are assembled and the totality is finally used. The major assumption is that the model of acquisition through real use (not through practice exercises) is the best model for thinking about and helping with the learning of reading and writing and learning in general.

Language acquisition (both oral *and* written) is seen as natural—not in the sense of innate or inevitably unfolding, but natural in the sense that when language (oral or written) is an integral part of the functioning of a community and is used around and with neophytes, it is learned "incidentally" (Ferreiro and Teberosky, 1982; Lindfors, 1987).

Certain practices are especially congruent with a Whole Language framework. The overriding consideration regarding classroom reading and writing is that these be real reading and writing, not exercises in reading and writing (see Edelsky and Draper, in press, and Edelsky and Smith, 1984 for a full description of authenticity in reading and writing). Beyond that, Whole Language classrooms are rich in a variety of print. Little use is made of materials written specifically to teach reading or writing. Instead, Whole Language relies heavily on literature, on other print used for appropriate purposes (e.g., cake mix directions used for really making a cake rather than for finding short vowels), and on writing for varied purposes.

Because language is considered a tool for making sense of something else, the "something elses" (science, social studies topics) have prominence. Social studies and science topics receive a big chunk of the school day, providing contexts for much of the real reading and writing. Assessment is focused on constant kid watching (Goodman, 1985) and on documenting growth in children's actual work rather than on comparing scores on work substitutes.

Whole Language is thus a perspective on language and language acquisition with classroom implications extending far beyond literacy. Many descriptions of Whole Language appear in the literature (e.g., Edelsky, 1986; Edelsky, Draper, and Smith, 1983; Goodman, 1986; Goodman and Goodman, 1981; Harste, Woodward, and Burke, 1984; Newman, 1985).

Nevertheless, as we indicated, questions persist about what Whole Language is and what it isn't.

QUESTIONS ABOUT WHOLE LANGUAGE

We will address the following:

1. Is Whole Language another term for the whole word approach?
2. Is Whole Language a new way of saying "teach skills in context" with an emphasis on comprehension skills?
3. Is Whole Language a method? A "slant" that can be given to phonics programs, basals, or language arts software?
4. Is Whole Language a new term for Language Experience?
5. Is Whole Language a new term for Open Education?

These are all reasonable questions, having a foundation in current practice, recent history, or prevailing beliefs. Therefore, as we present each question, we will first ground that question with its own sensibleness before presenting a Whole Language answer to the question.

11

- *Is Whole Language a new term for the whole word approach?*

It could be . . .

Equating Whole Language with whole word may stem from a conception of reading as a matter of "getting the words." The Great Debate (Chall, 1967) was presented and continues to be thought of as a debate between two distinctly different conceptions of reading—look/say and phonics. Actually, the two are simply variations on a single theme—a phonics approach to "getting the words" and a look-say or whole word approach to "getting the words." Each has strong roots in behaviorism (i.e., getting the words means *saying* the words).

Conventional wisdom and school paraphernalia support the notion that reading is "getting the words," indeed that language development amounts to *knowing* words. Vocabulary exercises and tests are an important part of many language arts series, reading instruction and assessment programs. Moreover, vocabulary is one means of social class gatekeeping. Much, then, in the general and school cultures supports the idea that reading amounts to "getting the words" and that there are only two basics ways to "get words." It is reasonable to assume that Whole Language might be one of them.

But it isn't

The Whole Language view of reading is not one of getting the words but of constructing meaning (see the development of this view in the writings of K. Goodman (Gollasch, 1982). Word boundaries and lexical features are indeed used as cues, but meaning is created with many other cues too—syntax, semantics, pragmatics (including the reader's purpose, the setting, what the reader knows about the author's purpose). To believe that reading means getting words assumes that words have constant meanings; yet words like *Mary*, *lamb*, *had*, and *little* in the following examples derive meaning from the clauses which follow them.

1. Mary had a little lamb
   Its fleece was white as snow.
2. Mary had a little lamb
   She spilled mint jelly on her dress.
3. Mary had a little lamb
   It was such a difficult delivery the vet needed a drink.
(Example adapted from Trabaso, 1981.)

The varied meanings of *Mary*, *had*, *little*, and *lamb* provide evidence that as we read, we create tentative texts, assigning tentative within-text word meanings which must often be revised based on later cues.

12

A belief in reading as getting and *saying* the word implies that we have to know a word orally in order to read it (get its meaning). In fact, we learn words through reading just as we learn them through conversing. (How many of us learned words like *Penelope* and *orgy* through print and were later surprised to discover they did not rhyme with *antelope* and *morgue-y?*)

A vocabulary item is not part of a list of words in our brain but a set of potentials (e.g., meaning potentials, word class information, morphological possibilities, possible metaphorical usages) related to other sets of potentials, embedded in a variety of schemas. It is the set, the ranges, and the schema-type storage that permit us to relate the two lines in examples (1), (2), and (3) so that we create different meanings with them.

A belief that reading means getting words also assumes that word meanings, once "gotten," are added up to produce a text meaning. In fact, the whole far exceeds the sum of the parts. Print provides a text potential (Harste, Woodward, and Burke, 1984; Rosenblatt, 1978, 1985). When we read, we turn that potential into an actual instance, creating details of meaning that must be inferred from but do not appear in the printed cues.

The meaning, that is, can *never* be *in* the print. Whole Language focuses on texts-in-situations, creating meaningful texts by filling in. A whole word approach, by contrast, has a completely different focus, is based on a completely different conception of reading, and entertains faulty premises concerning words and word meanings.

- *Is Whole Language another term for teaching skills in context?*

It could be . . .

A popular view of language use (oral and written) is that it consists of isolatable skills (e.g., decoding skills, pronunciation skills, comprehension skills of finding the main idea, using details), separately learnable and separately teachable (DeFord, 1985; Harste and Burke, 1977). This is part of a more general assumption: If it is possible to identify subskills or subactivities in the proficient performance of any complex activity, then those subactivities should be taught separately. Tests of separate skills invade education to such an extent that they ensure that the idea of separate skills remains a given.

A similarly "small parts" viewpoint is common regarding *context*. Context is often seen as a background "part" *rather* than the crucial medium for as well as the inevitable creation of language use. Sometimes context is reduced to meaning merely the verbal setting (e.g., the story as background for the sentence, the sentence as background for the word). Such small parts conceptions of comprehension and context could

13

be readily applied to a new idea like Whole Language, which in fact relies heavily on *context* and *comprehension*.

Other sources add to the confusion. Beginning Whole Language educators, who do not yet know new ways of talking about their changed views, provide more grist for the skills-in-context mill. So do thoroughly Whole Language teachers who use such descriptions as survival strategies in order to teach according to their Whole Language beliefs in districts permitting only skills instruction. Thus, people have much evidence from the talk of others as well as from their own viewpoints regarding what constitutes written language and context for believing Whole Language is simply teaching skills in context with an emphasis on comprehension skills.

But it isn't

Again, the Whole Language view is that reading/writing are whole activities, that any separate skills or subactivities used outside the total activity are different from that subactivity used within the total activity. Moreover, the subactivity is not merely the behavior. It has a role to play in the total activity; it interacts with other subactivities; it engenders consequences. If the role, relationships, interactions, and consequences are taken away, what is left is only the behavior—meaningless in itself. It would be as if separate pedaling, handlebar holding, steering, and brake-applying did not need to be integrated, as if they could simply be added together to produce bike riding.

In authentic written language use, cues from one system have an effect on cues from other systems. Thus syntax influences phonology, permitting a reduced vowel when *can* is part of a verb (*the garbage /kən/ go over there*) but not when it is a noun (*the garbage /kæn/ is over there*). Syntax influences graphophonics so that the unit (initial *th* + vowel) is voiced for function words (*this, their*) but voiceless in content words (*thing, thistle*). Semantics controls syntactic parsing in such sentences as *flying planes can be dangerous*. Pragmatics is what permits variation in orthography (*lite/light*; *through/thru*).

It should be noted that the direction of influence is from high to low: Information from the higher system is required in order to make a decision about the lower. This is just the opposite of the basic skills hierarchy which begins at the supposed beginning—the smaller units and lower levels.

A major Whole Language goal is to help children use, not sever, these interrelationships among cuing systems. The means for achieving that goal is to engage children with authentic texts (versus textoids, as Hunt, in press, calls them) and in authentic reading and writing. A Whole

14

Language framework insists that we become "skilled language users" *not* that we "learn language skills." Altwerger and Resta (1986) have shown that many proficient readers cannot do skills exercises, while many poor readers can. That is, the activity of performing divisible subskills may have little or no relation to the indivisible activity of reading. It is the latter activity which interests Whole Language people.

- *Is Whole Language a method? A program? A "slant" for basals or phonics or other packaged programs?*

It could be . . .

A tendency to assume that the essence of something is the surface behavior rather than the underlying meaning is legitimized, in the case of Whole Language, by erroneous information from authoritative sources. Documents such as State Reading Guides describe Whole Language as "one of many *methods*." Publishers of instructional materials advertise Whole Language basals and Whole Language phonics programs. Additionally, many educators, anxious to avoid offending or taking a theoretical stand, justify their avoidance by claiming to be eclectic. Link a preference for eclecticism with errors in education documents and advertising pitches from publishers and it is easy to see how Whole Language comes to be (mis)understood as a method or another kind of basal series.

But it isn't

Whole Language is first of all a lens for viewing, a framework that insists that belief shapes practice. Equating it with a method is an error in level of abstraction. Each of the following is an example of one of many methods: writing chart stories with children, conducting spelling drills, holding writers' workshops. None of these are underlying viewpoints. The following are theoretical viewpoints: skills, Whole Language. Neither of these is a method.

Moreover, there are no essential component practices for a Whole Language viewpoint. Some practices are easily made congruent and are therefore typical in Whole Language classrooms (e.g., journals, reading aloud to children, silent reading, literature study, publishing books, content logs, content thematic units). However, none of these is essential. It would be possible, though impoverishing, to emphasize science projects and exclude literature, yet still have a Whole Language classroom. One could focus entirely on art, music, and drama (writing to publishers to obtain releases for play readings, writing off for catalogues of art openings, staging the school's own gala arts fair), or on a political issue within the community and never write any personal narratives and still have a Whole Language classroom. What *is* essential are component principles

15

or beliefs, including those listed in the earlier section describing Whole Language.

If thinking of Whole Language as method or component parts is a problem in mixing levels of abstraction, wishing to offer a little of everything, to be eclectic, constitutes magical thinking. How idyllic, how "nice" it would be to have no conflict in underlying positions, no basic contradictions. But there *are* basic contradictions (e.g., the idea that reading consists of separate skills contradicts the idea that reading does not consist of separate skills). There is no eclecticism at the level of underlying beliefs whether these beliefs are acknowledged or not. Like a liquid, practice takes the shape of whatever belief-container it is in (Browne, 1985).

Some materials, however, written for the instruction of separate reading or writing subskills conflict with Whole Language beliefs by definition. "Holistic" or not, phonics materials and basal series all entail simulations (quote-reading or quote-writing), either eliminating some subsystems, artificially highlighting others, or ensuring that the learners' purpose must be compliance with an assignment. Thus, the basic Whole Language belief—acquisition through use not exercise—is violated. The only way basal readers or phonics programs could be congruent with Whole Language beliefs would be for children to use them as data—for example, as documents in an historical study of changes in school culture. They could not be used for practicing or learning supposed subskills or written language, including comprehension as a subskill, and be congruent with Whole Language beliefs. (In Whole Language, if there is reading, there is comprehension; if there is no comprehension, there is no reading. Comprehension is not a subskill.)

Whole Language teachers *are* eclectic in the sense of having a large repertoire of materials, modes of interacting, ways of organizing classrooms, etc. Indeed, they are particularly sensitive to the need to vary their approaches with different children for different purposes. However, eclecticism usually means something else in the contexts in which we have heard it—something more like typical practices borrowed from conflicting paradigms, but unwittingly "biased" by one unacknowledged, unexamined single underlying paradigm. In contrast, Whole Language teachers try to be conscious of and reflect on their own underlying beliefs; they deliberately tie practice and theory.

- *Is Whole Language a new term for Language Experience Approach?*

It could be ...

The two certainly share some ties in practice. Written statements

16

about Whole Language (Calkins, 1986; Edelsky, Draper, and Smith, 1983; Goodman, 1986; Newman, 1985) and written statements about the Language Experience Approach (Allen, 1976; Ashton-Warner, 1963; Peterson, 1981; Veatch et al., 1973) advocate an abundance of books written by children about their own lives. Both Whole Language and Language Experience paint images of rich classroom environments; both emphasize the importance of literature. Both treat reading as a personal act, arguing for the need to accept and work with whatever language varieties a child brings to school. Visitors to Whole Language classrooms indeed see children writing books, working with literature, using a variety of symbol systems. Moreover, with the recent popularity of the term Whole Language, many teachers using dictation during their reading instruction time now call this Whole Language, thereby confusing framework (Language Experience Approach; Whole Language) with method (taking dictation). Thus, there are similarities in statements, in practice, and a frequent mislabeling of practice that would give people good reason for thinking Whole Language is a synonym for Language Experience Approach.

But it isn't

One primary difference concerns premises about the relation of oral and written language. Language experience presumes that written language is a secondary system derived from oral language. Whole Language sees oral and written language systems as structurally related without one being an alternate symbolic rendition of the other. Moreover, written language learning need not wait for oral language acquisition. According to Whole Language research, people can learn vocabulary, syntax, and stylistic conventions directly through written language (Edelsky, 1986; Harste, Woodward, and Burke, 1984; Hudelson, 1984).

Dictation provides another symptomatic difference. Language Experience teachers plan frequently for taking dictation from students. Whole Language teachers may take dictation but less frequently and usually only when prompted by the child's request. The underlying reasons for this disparity are critical, revealing an example of evolution in, not merely competition between theories. At the time Language Experience Approach (as a theory) was being developed, the implicit notion about the writing act was that it amounted to taking dictation from oneself, that composing occurred prior to transcribing. By the time Whole Language *theory* was being developed, the conception of writing had evolved to viewing meaning-making as occurring *during* the act of writing (Smith, 1982). Taking dictation deprives language learners of a key context for making meaning—the act of writing. It also deprives them of the opportunity to make a full range of hypotheses.

17

While Language Experience Approach statements and recommended practices do not state that reading consists of separate skills, they do assume that reading entails knowledge *about* reading and that this set of "subknowledges" is derived from skills lessons and practice (Allen, 1976). Additionally, Language Experience statements (Allen, 1976; Peterson, 1981; Veatch et al., 1973) include recommendations for using programmed materials and teaching about parts of language. Thus, after a child's experience is put to use in dictation, the transcription is often used to teach word attack or phonics skills.

In contrast, Whole Language acknowledges that metalinguistic knowledge is part of written language competence. Progress in theory development and research now allows Whole Language to dispute that such knowledge is best gained through fragmented exercises.

One unfortunate similarity is poor translation. The literature on both Language Experience and Whole Language (let alone actual classroom events) sometimes offers an inadequate vision of how some abstraction might look in real life. For example, in Language Experience statements, important abstractions like *reflection* and *dialogue* are trivialized by being put to service in the teaching of punctuation.

The Whole Language literature has its own share of contradictions. Children are supposed to write for their own purposes; yet activities (that word is used advisedly) are suggested wherein children end someone else's story (see recent issues of *Livewire*). Whole Language considers literature a way of knowing and also a critical medium for participating "in the club" of readers and writers (Smith, 1984). Nevertheless, literature is sometimes presented as a "strategy" for teaching reading.

The main distinction, however, between Whole Language and Language Experience is that the latter appealed to no developed theory regarding the nature of language, language acquisition, or the reading process. It made some use of structural linguistics; its references to child language consisted primarily of naive views of vocabulary acquisition (appealing to studies of size and type of vocabulary and of frequently used lexicon).

We must emphasize here that in the 1950s through the 1970s, the Language Experience Approach was the most progressive comprehensive view (i.e., stated assumptions and suggested practice) of written language teaching and learning. As we point out its theoretical inadequacies, we have to remind ourselves that it was developed in the late 1950s, before the advent of Goodman's (1969) revolutionary research on the reading process. That Allen and others did not account for literacy events, speech events, speech acts, or a sociopsycholinguistic model of the reading process reflects historical limits on knowledge rather than individual failure of vision. Even though Language Experience was not accompanied by a paradigm shift regarding written language (the required information was not available), it may have been a necessary precursor to Whole Language.

- *Is Whole Language a new term for the Open Classroom?*

It could be ...

Whole Language and the Open Classroom of the 1960s and 1970s certainly bear a family resemblance. Recent comprehensive, respected statements on Open Education (Gross and Gross, 1969; Lucas, 1976; Neill, 1960; Nyquist and Hawes, 1972; Silberman, 1970) advocated something like the Language Experience Approach for literacy instruction. Dewey, more Whole Language-like than his followers, however, thought literacy should only be taught in connection with its use as a tool for something else (Lucas, 1976). Similarities between Language Experience and Whole Language have already been described in the preceding sections. But these are not the only likenesses.

Both Open Education and Whole Language note the active character of learning; both center on "the whole child." Both see learning as rooted in firsthand experience and genuine problem solving. Both concern themselves with more than language and literacy, more than thought or learning in the abstract but with thought-in-interaction, with learning-in-life. Significant content provides a curricular focus in Whole Language as well as Open Education. With so many resemblances, no wonder Whole Language is seen not as a cousin, but as an identical twin of Open Education.

But it isn't

We are deliberately avoiding, for these comparisons, using poor examples of Open Education practice. For example, in the name of Open Education, some classrooms were organized so children rotated, in rigid time blocks, among so-called Learning Centers at which they worked on Ditto sheets (round tables must have seemed more "open" than rectangular desks). Instead, we want to compare only the prototypical statements and practice in Open Education with the prototypical statements and practice in Whole Language.

An appearance of similar behavior may mask underlying differences. For instance, as we said, Whole Language emphasizes content; so did Open Education of the 1960s. However, the supremacy of "process" over content (perhaps as a vulgarization of the Open Education idea that there is no body of knowledge essential to everyone) became so strong in Open Education that curriculum content could be anything at all, with little attention paid to its disciplinary or social significance. While for

19

Whole Language, the "process" (generating questions, handling data, abstracting, categorizing, etc.) is critical, it does not overshadow content.

The role of the teacher is also similar but different. Bussis and Chittendon (1972) describe a highly active Open Classroom teacher rather than a passive reactor. Many Open Education statements paint the teacher as an ingenious, spontaneous facilitator, provisioner of the environment, and resource person. So do Whole Language statements (e.g., Edelsky, Draper, and Smith, 1983; Newman, 1985).

The distinction here is one of degree. Whole Language statements and workshops offer less on provisioning the environment, highlighting instead how teachers can intervene and fine tune interaction, keeping it theoretically "honest" and congruent with beliefs about language acquisition. In particular areas Whole Language teachers are more likely to actively participate as colearners, to construct meaning together with students rather than simply facilitate. Whole Language teachers also often act like coaches, demonstrating, explaining, and cheering so children can more effectively develop their own writing, drama, or science projects.

Classroom organization differs. Open Classrooms are frequently organized around some secondary structure—Learning Centers or committees, for example, where the grouping structure determines the schedule. Scheduling in Whole Language classrooms is more closely tied to the task (e.g., writing workshops, science project work).

The view of the learner varies. Despite the stress placed by Dewey (and Neill, 1960) on communities, the emphasis in Open Education was the learner as an individual, individually choosing topics of study, or, more likely, selecting from among the options the teacher offered at Learning Centers. Whole Language views the learner as profoundly social. Thus practice congruent with Whole Language includes participating in a community of readers during small group literature study, peer writing workshops, group social studies projects with built-in plans for collaborative learning.

Both Open Classroom and Whole Language educators oppose standardized testing. The difference in bases for their opposition is instructive. Open Classroom proponents claim that standardized tests fail to test what teachers are teaching (e.g., self-directedness, problem solving). The tests, in other words, are *insufficient*.

Whole Language educators, on the other hand, argue that the tests fail to test what the tests themselves claim to be testing (i.e., reading). That is, they are *invalid*.

This is a significant difference. It permits highly sophisticated Open Classroom educators (see Meier, 1981) to acknowledge invalidity but to concentrate their criticism on class and ethnic bias. In contrast, while Whole Language educators acknowledge such biases, they concentrate on a different fundamental problem with reading tests: i.e., the tests can *never* test reading even if class bias could be eliminated (Altwerger and Resta, 1986; Edelsky and Draper, in press).

This discrepancy in rationale for opposing standardized reading tests stems from a distinction in origins of Open Education and Whole Language. Whole Language takes its direction from a particular view of language acquisition and of the reading process. Embedded in that view is a concern with a theoretical definition of the notion of authenticity as applied to reading and writing. It is that definition which allows Whole Language educators to argue that standardized tests are invalid.

This theoretical view of language undergirding Whole Language but absent from Open Education and its embedded Language Experience Approach to literacy instruction (because it was developed later) is the most important difference between these two innovations.

The last distinction we will mention concerns political vision and political context. Open Education's vision includes the belief that it is possible for truly democratic classroom communities to exist within non-democratic larger contexts. Moreover, experience in such classroom communities according to Open Education, should foster a lifelong demand for similar democratic contexts.

The rebirth after several decades of Open Education in the United States in the 1960s came at a time of both relative prosperity and widespread criticism of inequities endemic throughout society. Whole Language, on the other hand, is gaining momentum at a time when the homeless are increasing, when government social programs have suffered many cuts, when freedom to criticize is threatened by right wing groups such as Accuracy in Media and Accuracy in Academia.

The political vision woven through Whole Language beliefs grows out of this context. Its goal is empowerment of learners and teachers, in part through demystification (demystifying everything from what proficient readers actually do to how city water rates are actually determined). The Whole Language framework recognizes that large exploitive contexts have an impact on individual classrooms and relations within them; that increased democracy within individual classrooms must accompany work on understanding and changing larger contexts.

CONCLUSION

We have tried to show that Whole Language is not a phonics program or a whole word approach. Neither is it a revitalized Language Experience Approach or another round of Open Education. If its newness is not recognized, we fear it will suffer the fate of these two past innovations.

21

Language Experience was vulgarized to become a collection of flash cards hung on a shower hook. The idea of Open Education was distorted to mean an open pod. Lately we have seen Whole Language misrepresented by a whole word perspective (at a recent conference, there was a booth selling Whole Language pocket charts for sight words). It is already widely equated with a program of component parts explained in old terms that render it "nothing new."

But those who have had the courage to examine old beliefs, who have struggled, collaborated, sought and given support in working with the ideas of Whole Language know the excitement of discovering its newness for themselves. We invite all educators to join in this difficult, exhilarating, empowering work.

REFERENCES

Allen, Roach Van. *Language Experiences in Communication*. Boston, MA: Houghton Mifflin, 1976.

Altwerger, Bess, and Virginia Resta. "Comparing Standardized Test Scores and Miscues." Paper presented at the International Reading Association annual convention, Philadelphia, PA, April 1986.

Ashton-Warner, Sylvia. *Teacher*. New York, NY: Bantam, 1963.

Browne, Caryl. Personal communication, 1985.

Bussis, Anne, and Edward Chittendon. "Toward Clarifying the Teacher's Role." In *Open Education*, edited by Edward Nyquist and Gene Hawes. New York, NY: Bantam, 1972.

Calkins, Lucy. *The Art of Teaching Writing*. Exeter, NH: Heinemann, 1986.

Chall, Jeanne. *Learning to Read*. New York, NY: McGraw-Hill, 1967.

DeFord, Diane. "Validating the Construct of Theoretical Orientation in Reading Instruction." *Reading Research Quarterly*, vol. 20, no. 3, 1985, pp. 351–67.

Edelsky, Carole. *Writing in a Bilingual Program: Habia Una Vez*. Norwood NJ: Ablex, 1986.

Edelsky, Carole, and Kelly Draper. "Reading/'Reading'; Writing/'Writing'; Text/'Text.'" In *Reading and Writing: Theory and Research*, edited by Anthony Petrosky. Norwood, NJ: Ablex, in press.

Edelsky, Carole, Kelly Draper, and Karen Smith. "Hookin' 'em in at the Start of School in a 'Whole Language' Classroom." *Anthropology and Education Quarterly*, vol. 14, no. 3, 1983, pp. 257–81.

Edelsky, Carole, and Karen Smith. "Is That Writing—or Are those Marks Just a Figment of Your Curriculum?" *Language Arts*, vol. 61, no. 1, 1984, pp. 24–32.

Ferreiro, Emilia, and Ana Teberosky. *Literacy before Schooling*. Exeter, NH: Heinemann, 1982.

Gollasch, Fred, ed. *Language and Literacy: The Selected Writings of Kenneth S. Goodman, Volumes 1 and 2*. London, England: Routledge and Kegan Paul, 1982.

Goodman, Kenneth. "Analysis of Oral Reading Miscues: Applied Psycholinguistics." *Reading Research Quarterly*, vol. 5, 1969, pp. 9–30.

Goodman, Kenneth. *What's Whole in Whole Language?* Exeter, NH: Heinemann, 1986.

Goodman, Kenneth, and Yetta Goodman. "A Whole-Language Comprehension-Centered View of Reading Development." Occasional Paper no. 1, Program in Language and Literacy, University of Arizona, Tucson, AZ, 1981.

Goodman, Yetta. "Kidwatching: Observing Children in the Classroom." In *Observing the Language Learner*, edited by Angela Jaggar and M. Trika Smith-Burke. Newark, DE: International Reading Association/National Council of Teachers of English, 1985.

Gross, Ronald, and Beatrice Gross. *Radical School Reform*. New York, NY: Simon and Schuster, 1969.

Harste, Jerome, and Carolyn Burke. "A New Hypothesis for Reading Teacher Research: Both Teaching and Learning of Reading Are Theoretically Based." In *Reading: Theory, Research, and Practice, 26th Yearbook of the National Reading Conference*, edited by P. David Pearson. St. Paul, MN: Mason Publishing, 1977.

Harste, Jerome, Virginia Woodward, and Carolyn Burke. *Language Stories and Literacy Lessons*. Exeter, NH: Heinemann, 1984.

Hudelson, Sarah. "Kan yu ret an rayt en ingles: Children Become Literate in English as a Second Language." *TESOL Quarterly*, vol. 18, no. 2, 1984, pp. 221–38.

Hunt, Russell. "A Boy Named Shawn, A Horse Named Hans: Responding to Writing by the Herr von Osten Method." In *Responding to Student Writing: Models, Methods and Curricular Change*, edited by Chris Anson. Urbana, IL: National Council of Teachers of English, in press.

Lindfors, Judith. *Children's Language and Learning. Second Edition*. Englewood Cliffs, NJ: Prentice-Hall, 1987.

Lucas, Christopher. "Humanism and the Schools: The Open Education Movement." In *Challenge and Choice in Contemporary Education*, edited by Christopher Lucas. New York, NY: Macmillan, 1976.

Meier, Deborah. "Why Reading Tests Don't Test Reading." *Dissent*, vol. 28, no. 4, 1981, pp. 457–66.

Neill, A. S. *Summerhill: A Radical Approach to Child Rearing*. New York, NY: Hart Publishing, 1960.

Newman, Judith. *Whole Language: Theory in Use*. Portsmouth, NH: Heinemann, 1985.

Nyquist, Edward, and Gene Hawes, eds. *Open Education: A Sourcebook for Parents and Teachers*. New York, NY: Bantam, 1972.

Peterson, Ralph L. "Language Experience: A Methodic Approach to Teaching Literacy." *Georgia Journal of Reading*, vol. 7 (Fall 1981), pp. 15–23.

Rosenblatt, Louise. *The Reader, the Text, the Poem*. Carbondale, IL: Southern Illinois University Press, 1978.

Rosenblatt, Louise. "Viewpoints: Transaction Versus Interaction—A Terminological Rescue Operation." *Research in the Teaching of English*, vol. 19, no. 1, 1985, pp. 96–107.

Silberman, Charles. *Crisis in the Classroom: The Remaking of American Education*. New York, NY: Vintage Books, 1970.

Smith, Frank. *Writing and the Writer*. New York, NY: Holt, Rinehart and Winston, 1982.

Smith, Frank. "The Creative Achievement of Literacy." In *Awakening to Literacy*, edited by Hillel Goelman, Antoinette Oberg, and Frank Smith. Exeter, NH: Heinemann, 1984.

Trabaso, Mary. "On the Making of Inferences during Reading and Their Assessment." In *Comprehension and Teaching*, edited by John T. Guthrie. Newark, DE: International Reading Association, 1981.

Veatch, Jeanette, Florence Sawicki, Geraldine Elliott, Eleanor Barnette, and Janis Blakey. *Key Words to Reading: The Language Experience Approach Begins*. Columbus, OH: Charles E. Merrill, 1973.

2. LANGUAGE ARTS BASICS: ADVOCACY VS RESEARCH

by Peter Hasselriis and Dorothy J. Watson, University of Missouri, Columbia

Peter Hasselriis and Dorothy Watson refute the back-to-basics movement with six important theoretical principles for a language arts program: (a) linguistic order is constructed internally by the learner through social interactions; (b) students' prior knowledge before they listen, speak, read, and write determines the meaning they construct; (c) risk taking is essential in language learning; (d) learners develop as speakers, listeners, readers, and writers by engaging in those processes; (e) listening and reading are constructive processes as are speaking and writing; (f) engaging in language is "rewarding and motivating in itself"; and (g) language learning is rooted in the home. The authors also identify six practices based on these theoretical principles: (a) respect the strengths and knowledge of the learner in curriculum planning; (b) help students realize the value of errors because error making is necessary for the construction of knowledge; (c) make provisions for a large amount of time for students to discuss, read, and write; (d) use texts that have meaning for readers; (e) help students value their own progress rather than use behavioristic systems; and (f) inform parents of the theory of whole language and the activities congruent with the theory.

Readers who wish more information will find the following publication, edited by Dorothy Watson, helpful: Ideas and Insights: Language Arts in the Elementary School *(Urbana, Ill.: National Council of Teachers of English, 1987).*

This chapter appeared in Contemporary Educational Psychology, *vol. 6 (July 1981): 278–86. Copyright © 1981 by Academic Press, Inc. Reprinted with permission.*

The back-to-basics thrust in teaching the language arts has been marked by a great deal of emotion and misinformation. On an emotional level it appears to be a reaction against what is viewed as a move toward permissive, open, child-centered schools and classrooms. Intellectually, it appears to be characterized by a view that there are serious problems with what young people are being taught and that those problems can be solved by implementing teaching materials and methods that were held to have been taught in past years and that are no longer being taught. These "basics," moreover, are held to be necessary for gaining control over broader goals. (The ability to spell words correctly is held to be basic to writing, knowledge of phonics generalizations is seen as basic to reading, and miscue-free oral reading is viewed as basic to other reading proficiencies.)

We propose to describe the basics as they are perceived by those who are suggesting that schools go back to them. We will then describe the basics as we perceive them and supply a base of research and theory that describe and categorize those elements of language which appear to be truly fundamental, supplying at the same time, examples of teaching practices that are supported by the research.

LANGUAGE ARTS BASICS: ADVOCACY

Back to the basics advocates appear to view reading as a product consisting of discrete skills which must be mastered in sequence. They call for elementary school teachers to stress instruction in phonics and in other aspects of reading that tend to be fragments of the total act rather than integrated activities having comprehension as their principal focus. In a "basic" reading program there is a great deal of teacher direction and materials that incorporate repetitive drill. Much time is spent on teaching "skills," which, when mastered, will enable students to read at a designated "grade level."

Basic programs in the other language arts appear to have a similar focus. Students diagram sentences, choose correct words to be placed in blanks, underline parts of speech, and work on other such skills that will enable them to write when they are mastered.

Oral language is handled similarly. Back-to-the-basics advocates view regional dialects as "incorrect" language that needs to be corrected. Students are therefore asked to complete exercises in which they must choose the correct word for a sentence. Most of us have worked through a lifetime's supply of such sit-set, lie-lay kinds of exercises.

Back-to-the-basics programs, reflecting what many strident voices in society are demanding, place a great deal of emphasis on penmanship and spelling, again emphasizing skills which must be mastered in order to assure proficiency at higher levels.

Language arts teachers are under pressure to teach grammar and the classics. Grammar instruction is considered to be traditional grammar in which the emphasis is on identifying parts of speech. Such study is expected to help students become proficient readers and writers. Students' required reading is strictly prescribed and generally consists of works that are neither contemporary nor controversial. *Ivanhoe*, *Silas Marner*, *Julius Caesar*, and *Macbeth* are examples that come to mind.

25

LANGUAGE ARTS BASICS: RESEARCH

From our perspective the back to the basics movement is more of a nonmovement than a movement—a nonmovement in which we find instructional fragmentation of a static bloat of unnecessary information. In order to change a nonfunctional nonmovement into a vigorous course of action, we need, first of all, to identify the real basics as the students themselves and their language. With this clarification we can immediately reject skills, drills, mastery programs, and the technology of the uninformed curriculum makers, for they have nothing to do with students and their language. Fortunately, when we abandon the "back-to-the-basics" curriculum we are not cut adrift, floundering about for wise information on which to build our program and to invite our students. Rather, when we discard the technocrats' baggage we find energy and spirit to investigate the information provided by language theorists and researchers.

We have chosen the following researchers/theorists/educators to help us describe an active, real basics program for at least three reasons. First, they are known and respected for their professionalism and clear studies; second, their views are consistent and compatible; and third, they probably would not take offense to being dubbed kid watchers (Goodman, 1978) and listeners rather than subject(s) experimenters.

From Vygotsky (1962, 1978), Halliday (1978), Smith (1977), Britton (1970), Y. Goodman (1978, 1979), and K. Goodman (1979) we hear again and again that our attention must indeed be directed to students and to their language. These theorists tell us that we must look at students in their entirety: their motivations, interests, stories, songs, games, jokes, and jargon. We must explore the potential meaning symbolized in the string after string of words that are heard, spoken, written, and read in diverse settings, societies, and cultures. That is, we must investigate how language users make meaning and under what circumstances they make it.

Following are seven if-then statements that direct us toward some basic instructional procedures. These procedures are followed by further arguments and suggestions for activities that are consistent with the theoretical principle presented.

If-Then Statement I

If we know from theorists that linguistic order is created internally, cannot be imposed upon the learner, and is constructed by the learner through social interactions in which the user's *intent* is clear—then it is basic that we

1. reject unnatural activities, assignments, and materials that impose

26

the bloat of unnecessary information on the learner and that have no hint of meaning off the page, out of the kit, nor outside the classroom in which they are found;

2. replace contrived isolated and impersonal drill with expanded, personal and social activities in which students can hear and read the situation as well as hear and read the speaker and author—in order to construe meaning.

Discussion. Advocates of skills-oriented basal readers, phonics workbooks, spelling lists, programmed instruction, and the like seem to share a view that teaching involves showing students examples of the "right" way to use language. Unfortunately, such views not only place meaning and the unique differences among students as users of language in the background, but they also pay no regard to the pragmatics; that is, the context of the situation in which language is used.

Because language functions in situational contexts which dictate form, activities such as language experience stories, spontaneous conversations (including written conversations), role playing, scripted and extemporaneous drama allow learners to get a feel for the intent. That is, they understand why language is being used in the particular way it is being used.

If-Then Statement II

If we know from theorists (Y. Goodman, 1979; K. Goodman, 1979; Smith, 1977; Britton, 1970) that we often underestimate and underrepresent students' knowledge and their ability to use language, and that what learners experience and know *before* they listen, speak, read and write powerfully affects their ability to construct meaning—then it is basic that we

1. reject a deficit view of the student's language in which attention is on the half-empty rather than the half-full container;

2. come to know and respect the learner's store of knowledge and use this information as a guide in planning curriculum;

3. use our energies and knowledge in planning a learning-by-doing curriculum in which students become comfortable with new ideas, concepts, and unfamiliar labels before they are asked to read and write about them.

Discussion. Often a deficit view of students comes about from educators looking at standardized test scores rather than looking at students. In a study conducted by Allen (1978) we learn that only 42 of the 255 items on a popular reading test are designed specifically to find out how well the pupil can comprehend text. Scores on the subtests were, for the most part, not indicative of the actual reading proficiency of students. Such tests are widely used and often direct the curriculum. For example, students who score below 80 percent on the Sound Discrimination subtest are to have remediation in sound recognition, even though we know that children and adults constantly demonstrate an ability to read despite low scores on the Sound Discrimination subtest. Assessments of this sort rarely give information upon which teachers can build curriculum. Activities that allow children to show, tell, and demonstrate their abilities are far more informative.

A student who thinks Loretta Lynn exemplifies the state of the art in vocal tone production will run from Luciano Pavarotti as if Pavarotti were rabid. There is an elitism in many schools that would place Loretta Lynn, Harlequin Romances, and many other forms of art that are highly regarded and sincerely respected by many persons at the negative end of a "cultural" continuum. Luciano Pavarotti and Shakespeare would probably be placed quite readily on the positive side. Constructing curricula and lessons exclusively around Pavarotti and Shakespeare would typify what many critics seem to expect schools to do, thereby leaving students with a heightened conviction that school is so far removed from their world—the real world, as they see it—that putting a great deal of physical or psychic energy into it is a waste of time. If the critics, schools, researchers, and students start communicating with one another we will begin to observe schools in which students are using language in ways that they perceive to be both valuable and enjoyable. We will, moreover, begin to observe astonishing amounts of improved writing, speaking, listening, and creative thinking.

If-Then Statement III

If we know from theorists that risk taking is a necessary part of all language learning—then it is basic that we

1. reject any program that is devoted to simplistic exactness, prescription, and mastery;

2. encourage informed risk taking by urging students to explore and ultimately control language by using it in large amounts at all appropriate times;

3. teach students that they can learn as much from getting it wrong as from getting it right.

Discussion. Goodman (1967) calls reading a psycholinguistic guessing game in which the reader interacts with the text, and, based on what the author has written and on the reader's prior knowledge, he takes a guess—a risk—and reads. [Editors' Note: For a visual presentation of a second grader's (Edie's) risk taking, see Figure 1, page 283, *Contemporary Educational Psychology*, July 1981.]

The point to be made here is that Edie's risk taking was encouraged;

the teacher did not stop her after each miscue to give her a basic skill strategy. Rather, Edie was allowed to construct meaning by interacting with the full text.

If-Then Statement IV

If we know from theorists that students learn to speak, listen, read, and write by engaging in a great deal of speaking, listening, reading and writing—then it is basic that we

1. carefully scrutinize our curriculum and exclude all dry and dispirited activities that take time away from practicing oral language and literacy;

2. provide as part of the curriculum (not as a reward, as "enrichment," or an elective) significant amounts of time to discuss, read, and write;

3. become kid watchers and listeners and as a result of watching and listening guide our students toward successful reception and production of language.

Discussion. Schools need to implement whole-school emphasis on language development and to explain to all teachers why this should be done. Every class should be organized in such a way that students spend the majority of their time engaged in conversations, panels, and discussions and in reading and writing whole stories, poems, books, and plays. Teachers should serve as models in such programs as Sustained Silent Reading (McCracken, 1971) and in all other "languaging" activities.

If-Then Statement V

If we know from language theorists that when students read and listen they are constructing (not reconstructing) meaning just as surely as they are constructing when they are speaking and writing—then it is basic that we

1. reject evaluative procedures that demand a template answer or cloned response that is an instant replay of the speaker's or author's message;

2. place students in situations in which they can construct meaning from meaningful discourse; construction from nonsense is nonsense;

3. enjoy diversity of interests, texts, language, and encourage students to acknowledge and use their background of experience to translate and understand everything they hear and read.

Discussion. Educators are encouraged to ask students to explore language within the discipline of general semantics. General semantics

29

stems from the work of Alfred Korzybski in the 1930s and has been popularized by such persons as S. I. Hayakawa, Stuart Chase, Wendell Johnson, and in more recent years, Neil Postman, and Charles Weingartner. Closely aligned with the thrusts of general semantics are the National Council of Teachers of English's concerns with "uses and misuses of language" as these are examined by its Committee on Public Doublespeak. *Language and Public Policy* and *Teaching About Doublespeak* are NCTE publications on this topic.

General semantics examines language within a context of social interaction and, thus, helps students become acquainted with the multitude of ways in which business, government, education, and others use language to persuade, manipulate, and otherwise influence people. General semanticists would argue that an evening spent studying how language is used in traffic court might be of much more value than spending the same amount of time doing workbook exercises on subject–verb agreement.

At any event, students need to use language in truly functional ways. If they are asked to write, it must be evident to them that what they are writing is valuable, either to themselves or for an important outside purpose. (A message needs to be sent, for example, a record kept, a thought captured before it's forgotten, or an order written and sent.)

If-Then Statement VI

If we know from language theorists that having control of language (being able to use it, play with it, learn through it) is amply rewarding and motivating in itself—then it is basic that we

1. exclude external rewards such as stars, coupons, M&M's, and extravagant praise from our language arts program;

2. help students enter into language using situations in which they can succeed and consequently be rewarded and motivated to use more and more language;

3. value and help students value their own as well as the work of other learners.

Discussion. Children begin to value language when they see that adults value language. Students need to experience a teacher who is experiencing language—that is, a teacher who is reading and writing right along with his/her students. When a principal comes into a classroom and reads during the silent reading period, the students know that reading is special—even the principal does it.

When students see their poems and stories in print (anything from a class paper to a polished school district publication), they know that their language has been taken seriously and is valued.

If we know from language theorists that home is where the language start is—then it is basic that we

1. know something of the language, experiences, and values of the family and community;

2. share with parents information gained from research on language development;

3. suggest whole-language activities such as silent reading time, singing, playing, talking, and writing together that will complement and support the school curriculum.

Discussion. Teachers who explain to parents the basis of invented spelling (Read, 1975; Chomsky, 1979), miscues in reading (Allen and Watson, 1976), the difference between real composing and superficial grammar drills, and the harm in attempting to eradicate dialect find the experience rewarding and in return for their efforts are supported by informed parents. The teacher who refused to identify her students by "a reading level" was told by her colleagues that the parents would demand to know their children's ranking. When the teacher outlined the problems, restrictions, and uselessness of such categorizing the parents expressed their relief; they were tired of big sisters reminding little brothers that they were "dismally below level."

CONCLUSION

Back-to-basics advocates lobby for schools that are product centered, with the products being mastery of skills, correct and neatly done drills and exercises, standard dialect, perfect penmanship, and other forms of conformity.

As we have shown, language researchers and theorists have given us a basis on which to lobby for schools that are student centered. Language activities in such schools will be characterized by respect for learners, their language, their motivations, and their strengths. Such language will be functional and valued at all times by students, parents, and teachers. Ironically, it will turn out to be language that is also more "correct," and, thus, more statisfying to those among us who appear to be certain that form is more "basic" than content.

REFERENCES

Allen, P. D., and Watson, D. J. *Findings of research in miscue and analysis: Classroom implications.* Urbana, Ill.: ERIC/NCTE, 1976.

Allen, V. Riddle: What does a reading test test? *Learning*, November 1978.

Britton, J. *Language and learning*. Miami: Univ. of Miami Press, 1970.

Chase, S. *Roads to agreement*. New York: Harper & Row, 1951.

Chomsky, C. Approaching reading through invented spelling. In L. B. Resnick and P. A. Weaver (Eds.), *Theory and practice of early reading*. Hillsdale, N.J.: Erlbaum, 1979.

Dieterich, D. *Teaching about doublespeak*. Urbana, Ill.: National Council of Teachers of English, 1976.

Goodman, K. S. Reading: A psycholinguistic guessing game. *Journal of the Reading Specialist*, May 1967, pp. 126–135.

Goodman, K. S., and Goodman, Y. M. Learning to read is natural. In L. B. Resnick and P. A. Weaver (Eds.), *Theory and practice of early reading*. Hillsdale, N.J.: Erlbaum, 1979.

Goodman, Y. Kid watching: An alternative to testing. *National Elementary School Principal*, June 1978, pp. 41–45.

Halliday, M. A. K. *Learning how to mean: Explorations in the development of language*. London: Edward Arnold, 1975.

Halliday, M. A. K. *Language as social semiotic*. London: Edward Arnold, 1978.

Hayakawa, S. I. *Language in thought and action*. New York: Harcourt Brace Jovanovich, 1939/1972.

Johnson, W. *People in quandaries*. New York: Harper and Row, 1946.

Korzybski, A. *Science and sanity*. Lakeville, Conn.: Int. NonAristotelian Library, 1933.

McCracken, R. A. Initiating sustained silent reading. *Journal of Reading*, May 1971, pp. 521–524, 582–583.

Postman, N., and Weingartner, C. *Teaching as a subversive activity*. New York: Dell, 1969.

Rank, H. *Language and public policy*. Urbana, Ill.: National Council of Teachers of English, 1974.

Read, C. *Children's categorization of speech sounds in English* (NCTE Res. Rep. No. 17). Urbana, Ill.: NCTE, 1975.

Smith, F. *Comprehension and learning*. New York: Holt, Rinehart and Winston, 1977.

Vygotsky, L. S. *Thought and language*. Cambridge, Mass.: MIT Press, 1962, (originally published in 1934).

Vygotsky, L. S. Learning and development. In M. Cole, V. John-Steiner, S. Scribner, and E. Souberman (Eds.), *Mind in Society: The development of higher psychological processes*. Cambridge, Mass.: Harvard Univ. Press, 1978.

3. EXAMINING INSTRUCTIONAL ASSUMPTIONS: THE CHILD AS INFORMANT

by Jerome C. Harste and Carolyn L. Burke, Indiana University, Bloomington

Jerome Harste and Carolyn Burke provide insights about written language with a description of a first grader's literacy development as shaped by the influences of instruction. Alison already knew a great deal about written language before entering first grade, as indicated by examples of her reading and writing from ages three to six. Her teacher's practices, reflecting personal beliefs, do not acknowledge experience with language outside school or provide opportunities for the child to use what she knows. Thus, Allison is required to focus on letters of the alphabet, correct spelling, and standard handwriting. The authors show how the student's confidence as a writer is diminished by the teacher's instructional practice.

Whole-language teachers have an alternate set of beliefs supported by scientific theory of child development. Unfortunately, they are too often prevented from using practices congruent with their views of language learning because of state- and school-mandated curricula as well as other authoritatively imposed guidelines. The assumptions about learning written language held by Alison's teacher are held by far too many teachers of young students, administrators, and politicians. As Harste and Burke urge, teachers must be encouraged to increase their understanding and to examine their own beliefs about language learning in risk-free environments so that they and their students may benefit.

This chapter appeared in Theory Into Practice, *vol. 19 no. 3 (Summer 1980): 170–78. Copyright © 1980 by the College of Education, the Ohio State University. Reprinted with permission.*

A great deal can be learned about the validity of language activities in a classroom by looking at the assumptions that lie behind those activities. While the activities may appear on the surface to be varied and creative, a closer examination often reveals that they reflect unfounded assumptions about language growth and development, which may in fact debilitate rather than facilitate the process of language literacy.

A case in point is the first grade classroom of Alison, age six. As we will illustrate later in this [chapter], Alison had already had a variety of experiences with written language when she began first grade. While her teacher was well intentioned, the reading and writing activities which she provided did not build upon Alison's range of experience. We would like to share with the reader some examples of these activities, as we think they are typical of the language activities found in first grades. They may even be better than those found in many classrooms, though we wish to argue that they are not good enough, because of the unfounded assumptions that lie behind them.

IDENTIFYING THE TEACHER'S ASSUMPTIONS

One of the first activities which Alison completed is that shown in Figure 1. When questioned at home about why she had elected to draw the bottom half of her body, Alison responded, "It's okay, teacher said so. Someone asked and teacher said we didn't have to draw our 'whole self' if we didn't want to."

On first blush, we might think, "A creative response to a good instructional activity." But is it? After all, this was an activity designed to help children learn to control the reading/writing process. Did it do for language what it did for art? In order to answer this question it becomes necessary to examine the activity more closely. We need to identify what teacher-held assumptions underlay the creation and selection of this activity.

This is readily done by identifying the set of written language principles relative to learning which undergird this activity as opposed to other activities which might have been selected. We can easily think of both more open and more closed activities which were available options to the teacher. For example, the teacher did not elect to give the children a sheet of paper, ask them to draw a picture of themselves and then write or pretend to write an autobiographical story to share (a more open activity), nor did the teacher focus the children's attention upon an isolated letter or letter-sound correspondence pattern (a more closed activity). An analysis, then, of this activity and of the teacher's responses to it, suggests the following assumptions relative to written language learning:

Assumption 1: One of the first tasks in learning to read and write is to be able to discriminate visually the letters of the alphabet.

This is best taught by activities such as underwriting which force the child to attend to the distinctive features of each letter.

Assumption 2: Language activities designed for children should be manageable to insure completion and hence success.

One way to accomplish this is to use simple whole texts which contain a limited number of basic vocabulary items (Here I am. My name is . . .).

Assumption 3: Errors should be marked to give corrective feedback and to stop bad habits from forming. (See the teacher's correction of *s* in Figure 1).

Assumption 4: Initial language activities should be personally meaningful to the child.

This is best done by focusing on topics of interest to the child. (In this activity, the topic self).

Assumption 5: Children do not need as much support in art as they do in writing.

The incorporation of art allows for self-expression and creativity.

The question now becomes, "In order to make these assumptions, what does one have to believe?"

The more obvious belief underlying Assumption 1 is that children need to be able to note differences between the various letters of the alphabet in order to learn to read and write. Less obvious perhaps is the implicit belief that first graders do not already possess this ability to discriminate the letters of the alphabet, i.e., that visual discrimination of letters must be formally taught. Each of these beliefs merits investigation. The rampant popularity of a belief is never criterion for acceptability, but rather for testing.

A listing of further beliefs which we have identified as inherent in this single instructional activity is given below.

• Access to the reading/writing process hinges on mastery of the distinctive features of print (see Assumption 1).

• The word is the key unit in language (See Assumption 2).

• Words selected for initial instruction must be chosen on the basis of frequency of usage (see Assumption 2).

• Errors must be pointed out by a guiding adult as children do not have information which they can use for self-correction (see Assumption 3).

• The goal of early language learning is an error-free performance on basics as without this children will never be able to access the process (see Assumption 3).

• Activities which make personal sense support the child's access to basic literary processes (see Assumption 4).

• This means, in as far as language learning is concerned, that topics should be chosen carefully so that children find them personally meaningful but the actual language introduced must be carefully selected and controlled by the teacher (see Assumptions 2 and 4).

• Art is an easy activity for the child (natural); reading and writing are hard activities (unnatural) (see Assumption 5).

• Art is learned; reading and writing must be taught (see Assumption 5).

- Creativity must wait upon control. Because children have already learned the basic forms of art, i.e., they have control of the basic conventions, creativity can be expected. Once children control the conventions of written language, they can and will become creative written language users as well (see Assumption 5).

One might argue that this analysis is a highly speculative process, and infers much from a single instructional activity. To illustrate the reoccurrence of the identified language learning principles in subsequent activities, three additional activities completed during the first week of school are described.

The activity illustrated in Figure 2 is closely tied to that discussed in Figure 1. In this instance, children were given ditto master copies of story parts of which the page shown is one. The children were asked to arrange the pages in order, paste them to the blank pages of a stapled book, draw a picture to fit the text, and overwrite the script on each page. Though this assignment involves more procedures, what has been said relative to beliefs inherent in the first activity, holds for this activity too. The significant creative decisions related to the written language—the writing of the story—have been made by the teacher. The student is left to simply recreate the decreed text order and to copy the print. Only the art is left open to creative efforts of the student.

The activity which generated the product illustrated in Figure 3 initially appears somewhat different, but closer examination indicates that it too shares the beliefs reflected in the first two assignments. This assignment is a parent-teacher notice which the children were asked to copy from the blackboard and take home as a reminder of an upcoming meeting. In this instance, the teacher gave each child a sheet of lined paper with his/her name on it. Children were asked to underwrite their name twice, and then copy the message that had been written on the blackboard.

An analysis of the beliefs which guided this activity suggests that all of the original beliefs hold, and that a further clarification has been obtained. Presumably the teacher is concerned with how Alison spatially controls the writing of her name and feels that practice is needed. Often this concern for the child's inability to stay within the lines is predicated on the belief that handwriting signals muscle and eye coordination and that such coordination is prerequisite to learning to read and write.

Figure 4 illustrates this teacher's application of the language experience approach to teaching reading. Rather than transcribe what the children actually said, Alison's teacher transformed each new suggestion into a common pattern for the purpose of teaching the word *we* and controlling the complexity of the syntactic patterns used. After the teacher had

Figure 1. Underwriting (Alison, Age 6.4)

Figure 2. Overwriting (Alison, Age 6.4)

Figure 3. Copying (Alison, Age 6.4)

Figure 4. Class-Contributed "Language Experience Story" (Alison, Age 6.4)

composed this text, each child was given a ditto copy of their class-contributed "language experience story" and asked to circle the word *we* each time it appeared. While the instructional activity has changed, the underlying assumptions governing the activity remain intact from the first three lessons.

An analysis such as we have been doing is intended to indicate that what Alison's teacher believes about the reading and writing process strongly affects both her choice of instructional activities and her handling of such activities. Her behavior is orderly, consistent and predictable. This is so in spite of the fact that she maintains she is eclectic and applies "a variety of approaches to the teaching of reading." Despite supposed surface structure variety in activities, her invariant assumptions continue to show.

From data such as this, we have come to believe that looking at teacher behavior in terms of the beliefs held and assumptions made is a more cogent and powerful one than looking at behavior in terms of the supposed approach being used (Harste and Burke, 1977). This teacher presumably changes approaches, but because she has not changed beliefs, her classroom practice is unaffected (as is, in all likelihood, the outcome of her instruction, but that's another equally important and complex issue which we will not develop in this [chapter].)

These data support the position that the teaching of reading and writing is theoretically based—that each of us as teachers has a theory of how to teach reading and writing in our heads which strongly affects our perception and behavior. We define theory simply as a set of interrelated beliefs and assumptions through which perception and behavior are organized. What this means practically is that in order to change behavior we must change beliefs. To that end we now turn to an examination of language encounters which Alison has had prior to and outside her school related experiences.

IDENTIFYING THE LANGUAGE LEARNER'S ASSUMPTIONS

Reading. Alison, we wish to argue, has been a user of written language for a long time now. One of the earliest instances of Alison's use of written language occurred when she was three years old. At the time, Alison and her family were on the way to the zoo. As they approached the beltway which would take them to the zoo, Alison's father, pointing to an overhead sign signaling "West 465," asked, "Alison, what do you think that says?"

Alison responded, "It says... uh... 'Daddy, turn right here to go to the zoo.'"

While some might argue this isn't reading, we wish to disagree. Alison has made a decision which puts her in the semantic ball park. She assumes that the print out there relates to the activity in which she and her family is engaged. And she's right in all but the pickiest sense. Alison's response demonstrates her expectation that written language will be meaningful. We do not know how or when children come to this important conclusion. All we know is that children as young as three have already made it, and that somehow readers who end up in remedial classes have lost or lost faith in it.

We believe it is through the expectation that written language will make sense that control is gained. Once the sense-making intent of written language has been perceived, ideation and hypothesis-making become the process forces of control. To further illustrate this point we can share another one of Alison's early encounters with print. This encounter occurred on a "dessert trip" to Baskin-Robbins. She was four years old at the time.

After eating her ice cream cone, Alison looked around the room attempting to find a trash can in which to deposit her napkin. After exploring logical locations, she found it, studied the wooden flap engraved with the word *push*, performed the required action, and deposited her napkin. Alison's mother, who had been observing her problem-solving behaviors, now asked, "Alison, what does that say on the trash can?"

"Push," came the response.

"How do you know?" was her mother's next question, to which Alison took her index finger and ran it over the *p*, the *u*, the *s*, and the *h* in turn, and responded, "Because it's got all the right letters!"

It was from knowing what written language does that Alison had grown in her control of the form. From earlier cognitive decisions such as that illustrated in the trip to the zoo, which put her in the semantic ball park, she could and did test language hypotheses which put her—to carry the metaphor another step—not only on base, but gave her the metalinguistic control to speak about the game itself.

The importance of this process of on-going hypothesis testing is best illustrated by yet another language story. Alison was four years, one month at the time. In this instance she was shown a Wendy's cup and asked, "What do you think this says?"

Alison responded, running her finger under the word *Wendy's*, "Wendy's" and running her finger under the word *hamburgers*, "cup." Alison paused a moment after producing her response, as if in reflection, and added, "That's a long word with a short sound!"

In this instance, the hypothesis which Alison has formulated relative to graphic-sound correspondence is an incorrect one. Yet, her very mention of it signals us to the fact that she has also formulated the correct alternative and was attempting to orchestrate this decision with the sense-making intent she knew existed. Need we help her? Not in a traditional corrective sense. All we need is to ensure that she have continuing encounters with the process, for each encounter will allow her to test out the validity of her current hypotheses and to reconstruct a new set at a level far above our assumptive imaginations.

Alison was reading before she went to first grade. Her teacher, through the use of standardized tests, has placed her at the preprimer level. At home she reads such texts as *It's The Easter Beagle, Charlie Brown* (Schulz, 1976). She's likely not to encounter equivalent print settings in school until fourth grade.

Why the discrepancy? It's those assumptions again. The tests Alison has taken in school strip language of its context, forcing her to deal with letters and words not only outside a supportive linguistic environment, but also outside a supportive context of situation. Without the latter Alison has neither a point of anticipation, nor a point of contextualization.

Written language learning is a social event of some complexity and written language use reflects the orchestration of this complex social event. Both the complexity and the orchestration support the development of user control. Knowing Alison as the reader she is would leave her production of a backward *s* in writing (as illustrated in Figure 1) a puzzlement unless one gives up the assumption that control of form is prerequisite to the language process. It is because Alison is, and has been, a reader and writer that she has a growing control of its form, not vice versa.

Writing. Alison is, and has been as impressive a writer as she is a reader. Her explorations of written language began long before what was produced became representational in any adult sense. What Alison reaffirmed in her movement into writing is that children must encounter the language process in its complexity in order to learn control. As with reading, it was Alison's early access to what written language does that allowed her control.

At four years, three months, Alison encountered a wordless book and made up an appropriate story. The next evening in wanting to reread the book she asked, "What was that story I read last night?"

"Well, I'm sure I don't know. If you want to remember your stories, you need to write them down. Then you can reread them whenever you want to."

Alison's story in Figure 5 about Daddy coming home and taking the family to McDonald's was placeheld using the letters of her name simply reshuffled in order. For months, whenever she encountered this book, she would get her paper out and faithfully read this text with minor variation:

One day Daddy came home and he said, "'Hi family, I'm home," and he's gonna take us to McDonald's. I'm gonna have a fun meal.

This sample illustrates Alison's public announcement of her discovery of the finite symbol system in written language; namely, one continuously re-orchestrates the same set of letters to produce an infinite set of words. Alison, as was always the case, demonstrated this growth using print of high personal worth—in this instance, her name. As in reading, adult recognition of the process often seems to hinge on how representational or conventional the product is. This is unfortunate, for it leads to the dismissal of early efforts as not worthy of attention.

Alison is, clearly, a writer in this instance, orchestrating aspects of this particular social event much as would any writer. She has grasped much: the meaning relationship between picture, text and her world; directionality (both top-down and left-to-right); the function of print in this setting; the organizational scaffolding of a story; the use of structure components to placehold meaning. Each of these decisions are signals of developing written language literacy. The fact that her writing is not yet representational (the symbols she uses to placehold McDonald's or Daddy do not look identifiable as such to our literate eye) is not nearly as significant as are these other factors.

Alison's orchestration of these multiple decisions is clear evidence of her sophistication. In light of all that she has managed to do, why should the questions most frequently generated about her accomplishments be, "Did she spell correctly?" and "Did she make her letters right?"

At four years, eight months, Alison placeheld all written messages using a cursive script such as that illustrated in Figure 6. While a first look at Alison's product at this juncture might indicate that she knew little about writing, such a conclusion would turn out to be assumptive and false. What this product represents is simply Alison's testing of alternate available hypotheses. Although we cannot know for sure what is being tested, we can feel fairly comfortable in light of her earlier behavior in saying that she has tentatively set aside some of what she already knows (her knowledge of letterness and the finite symbol system of English) to test other aspects of the process. Alison has not had a setback. Current models suggest linear growth with more and more aspects brought under control in an incremental fashion. Data such as this clearly challenge such extant notions of development.

If one views each instance of written language use as the orchestration of a complex social event, then what the initiate written language user is faced with is a problem of some magnitude. As varied elements in this event are perceived, new hypotheses are generated and tested. The hypotheses are concerned with pragmatics (what are the rules of language

41

use relative to a particular context), semantics (how can I say what I mean), syntax (how do I get the flow of my message captured on paper), graphics (how do I represent what I wish to say), and the orchestration of these systems (how do I draw on all these systems simultaneously). Within each of these areas there are, of course, a range of hypotheses which need formulation and fit. Additional hypotheses arise as more and more elements are orchestrated. What looks like regression, given the assumptions underlying one theory, signals growth from another theoretical perspective.

Growth, while constant, looks sporadic because of the primitives which undergird our assumptive yardsticks. Current yardsticks divert attention away from growth toward "developmental stages" which attempt to calculate growth by marking surface level features of conventional form. Such a focus draws our attention away from the universals of written language literacy which operate across language users at all ages and express themselves in a variety of forms. Our thinking becomes limited to a step-wise regression to perfection.

As an instance, let's take spelling, often measured as a simple yes-no decision. Alison has used the conventional spelling of her name since she was three years old, as is illustrated in Figure 7. Yet her most interesting signature is not her first or last, but one she experimented with during a two week period shortly after she turned five years of age. At this point, Alison wrote her name adding a *u* in the middle. When asked why she added the *u*, she replied, "Because I wanted to." After several weeks of experimenting with this signature, she abandoned it in favor of the spelling her parents had elected at birth.

Isn't it fascinating? Everything Alison had discovered about print compelled her to say that there ought to be a *u* in her name. And there well could be. It was one of the options her parents could have taken when they selected the original spelling of her name.

Alison feels comfortable with what she's discovered about how print operates. Like all of us, she's satisfied and interested in her latest discovery and tries it on for fit. Similar trends will be seen in the writing of all of us—a favorite word, a favorite syntactic pattern, a favorite organizational style. The issue is not so much what is being tested or how much conventional congruency is achieved, but that the universality of growth, and fit, and continued growth is expressed.

At five and one-half Alison made a finger puppet out of paper and was asked to make a smiling face and to write about something that made her happy. She produced the product illustrated in Figure 8. Without apparent warning, Alison moved so naturally from the writing illustrated in Figure 6 to that represented in Figure 8 that her behavior quite shocks us. She has been writing in this latter fashion ever since.

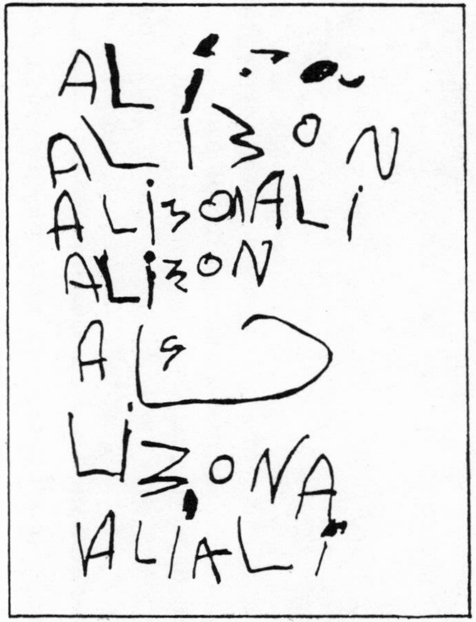

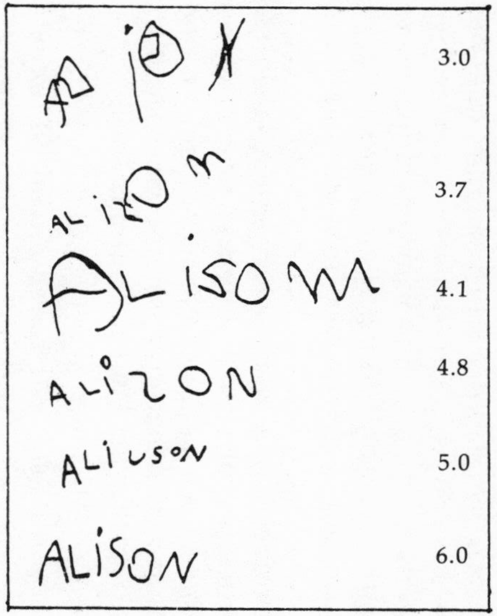

Figure 7. Signatures (Alison)

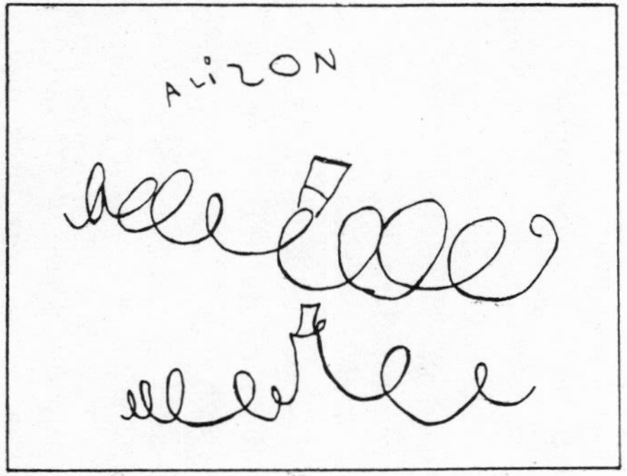

Figure 6. Cursive Story Script
(Alison, Age 4.8)

Figure 5. Story to Wordless Book
(Alison, Age 4.3)

Alison's What Makes Me Happy ("Mn I C FLOMRS"—When I see flowers) is an impressive display of rule-governed and orchestrated behavior. The message is the product of an integrated processing of pragmatics (used appropriate language in this setting), semantics (said something which makes personal sense), syntax (managed to capture the flow of her thought on paper using the standard conventional form of wordness), and graphics (abstracted out salient letter-sound relationships which undergird written language and placeheld these relationships with letter forms). Given such a magnificent breakthrough, we find it quite frustrating that the only comment made by one professional with whom we shared this piece was that her "Ws were upside down"

On her sixth birthday, Alison wrote her grandmother a letter thanking her for the present which she had received (Figure 9). Once again her knowledge of written language is extensive, showing a complex mapping of letter-sound relationships, syntax, and meaning. When her writing in this instance is compared with that done on the puppet, it becomes clear Alison also has some awareness of the function of written language in alternate settings. That is, her letter sounds like a letter while the message on her puppet was a response to the implied lead, "What makes me happy..." Note also Alison's conventional spellings of *loved* and *your*, indicating that she is not only using a phonetic mapping in her spelling, but a visual memory of what these words look like. Alison orchestrates these elements so smoothly that they go easily undetected as the magnificent achievements which they are. The fact that such phenonema are sorted out so readily by children at such an early age leads us and others to conclude that "writing is natural" (Goodman and Goodman, 1976).

Alison's behavior here is a vivid display of the interrelatedness of reading and writing. It is through having encountered the words *loved* and *your* in reading that Alison fine-tunes her writing strategies. Alison simultaneously orchestrated spelling the way it sounds, spelling the way it looks, and spelling the way it means. All of the growth illustrated in the examples above occurred prior to Alison's entrance into first grade, yet the growth was untapped in the instructional activities which Alison's teacher provided for her.

On the occasion of Alison's return from school with the written product shown in Figure 10, she was given a piece of paper and asked to write, "Here is my house and family," the very script which she had underwritten on the school worksheet. Alison, we lamentingly report, burst into tears and said, "I can't write." After comforting she was told, "Sure you can, you've been writing a long time now."

"But I don't know how to spell and write good," came the still tearful reply.

44

"Oh, yes you do. You're only in first grade. If your writing looked like ours, there would be no reason for you to be there. You know we can read anything you write."

With this Alison produced the text illustrated in Figure 11.

You, we hope, will say with us, "How sad that Alison had to have this moment of doubt."

Her assumptions did not match the instructional assumptions being addressed and hence she decided she was wrong. In this instance instruction was a debilitating rather than a facilitating experience.

CONCLUSION

Data collected from Alison and some 67 other three, four, five, and six year olds (Harste, Burke, and Woodward, 1977; Woodward, in progress; Harste, Burke, and Woodward, in press) leads us to conclude that many of the instructional assumptions currently made are faulty at best and debilitating at worst. In no instance—and our data has been collected from high, middle, and low SES, black and white, boys and girls, small town and urban inner-city—would the assumptions underlying Alison's instruction have been appropriate ones from which to operate instructionally.

The error in the instruction provided by Alison's teacher was that the instructional assumptions were never tested through the provision of open-entry student activities which could provide alternate data and lead the teacher to challenge her own beliefs. All of the activities given to Alison by her teacher effectively forced Alison to operate within the teacher's assumptive bounds; never providing her the opportunity to demonstrate what decisions she as a language user was interested in and capable of making.

What we recommend instructionally for both teacher and pupil is open-entry language activities where constraints are allowed to evolve in a risk-free language environment, where each (both teacher and pupil) can go beyond their assumptions. In many ways the real issue which this [chapter] addresses is whose written language assumptions should be tested—the teacher's or the language user's.

It's not that assumptions are bad. It is in fact our professional right and responsibility to make and have them. But it's also our professional responsibility to self-examine them. It is only in knowing ourselves and what assumptions we hold that we can begin to challenge them and grow. What is true for the language learner is true for the language teacher.

Figure 8. Finger Puppet (Alison, Age 5.6)

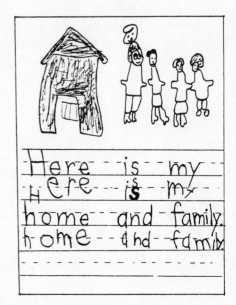

Figure 10. Underwriting
(Alison, Age 6.4)

Figure 9. Letter to Grandmother
(Alison, Age 6.0). ''Dear Grandma,
I loved your present. Alison.''

HoRos Mi Hos ADND FoMLE

Figure 11. Uninterrupted Writing
(Alison, Age 6.4)

NOTES

Harste, C., Burke, L., and Woodward, A. "Children's Initial Encounters with Written Language." Maris M. Proffitt Research Grant, 1977.
Harste, C., Burke, L., Woodward, A. "Children, Their Language, and World: Initial Encounters with Print." NIE Research Grant NIE-G-79-0132, 1979.
Woodward, Virginia A. "A Longitudinal Case Study of Five Children's Initial Encounters with Print." NCTE Research Grant (in progress).

REFERENCES

Clay, M. *What Did I Write?* London: Heinemann Educational Books, 1975.
Goodman, K. S., and Goodman, Y. "Learning to Read is Natural." Paper presented at conference on theory and practice of beginning reading instruction, University of Pittsburgh, 1976. (Mimeographed)
Halliday, M. A. K. *Learning How to Mean.* London: Edward Arnold Ltd., 1975.
Harste, J. C., and Burke, C. L. "A new hypothesis for reading teacher education research: Both the teaching and learning of reading are theoretically based." In P. D. Pearson (Ed.) *Reading: Research, Theory, and Practice.* 26th Yearbook of the National Reading Conference, Mason Publishing Co., 1977.
Harste, J. C., Burke, C. L., and Woodward, V. A. "Children's language and world: Initial encounters with print." In J. Langer and M. Smith-Burke (Eds.) *Bridging the Gap: Reader Meets Author.* Newark, Delaware: International Reading Association, in press.
Read, C. "Children's categorization of speech sounds in English." (Res. Rep. No. 17). Urbana, Ill; National Council of Teachers of English Committee on Research, 1975.

4. DEMONSTRATIONS, ENGAGEMENT AND SENSITIVITY: THE CHOICE BETWEEN PEOPLE AND PROGRAMS

by Frank Smith, University of Victoria, British Columbia

Frank Smith believes that teachers must show students that literacy is useful, enjoyable, and attainable. At the same time, he points out that in this century linguists, psychologists, computer specialists, and other external agents are increasingly influencing "what and how teachers should teach." He also notes that the influence of programmatic approaches to reading instruction is growing. Teachers are told to follow program guidelines; instructional decisions are made in advance by the program developers even though these "experts" have no personal knowledge of the student who is supposed to profit from the program. Smith thinks that the basal programs dominating today's schools fracture literacy experiences for students.

A dilemma that must be confronted, according to Smith, occurs when schools use highly structured programs and at the same time produce high standardized test scores. He provides two explanations for this phenomenon: (a) structured programs often teach the same isolated facts and skills that tests measure; therefore, the higher test scores do not represent higher reading ability, just higher test scores; and (b) effective teachers, who are required to use formal programs, also use meaningful reading activities such as an independent reading program with time for reading and time for talking about what they read. Students in the latter situation become better readers with the credit going to the programmatic approach being used rather than to the teachers' sensitive instruction.

Another reason for the high test scores, not mentioned by Smith, is the influence of socioeconomic status. There is a high correlation between social class and reading achievement scores. As a result, schools serving students from high socioeconomic backgrounds will have high test scores regardless of the program used. Consequently, attention must be diverted from the narrow focus on test scores as indicators of achievement. Other more significant factors need attention in order to help students of all backgrounds develop as readers who do, in fact, read.

Readers who wish to know more about Smith's views will enjoy his Understanding Reading, *2d edition (New York: Holt, Rinehart, and Winston, 1978), and* Insult to Intelligence *(Portsmouth, N.H.: Heinemann, 1986).*

This chapter appeared in Language Arts, *vol. 58, no. 6 (September 1981): 634–42. © by the National Council of Teachers of English. Reprinted with permission.*

In an earlier article in this [issue of *Language Arts*] entitled "Demonstrations, Engagement and Sensitivity: A Revised Approach to Language Learning" (Smith [September] 1981), I discussed the proposition that children's brains learn constantly. Everything demonstrated by children by act or by artifact is likely to be learned by them. Educators should not ask why children often do not learn what we believe they are taught, but rather what they might be learning in its place. Teachers may not teach what they think they are teaching.

In [this chapter] I shall consider some implications of the view that children are always likely to learn what is demonstrated to them. In particular I shall argue that the critical question confronting teachers of language arts today is not how writing, reading, and other aspects of literacy should be taught, but what we want children to learn. This is not a question for research to resolve; the relevant evidence is available. Rather the question requires a decision, upon which the future of teachers and of literacy may depend.

The decision to be made is whether responsibility for teaching children to write and to read should rest with people or with programs, with teachers or with technology. This is not a matter of selecting among alternative methods of teaching children the same things. Different educational means achieve different ends (Olson and Bruner 1974). The issue concerns who is to be in control of classrooms, the people in the classroom (teachers and children) or the people elsewhere who develop programs. Different answers will have different consequences.

The argument will cover the following points: (1) that programs cannot teach children literacy (though they may be extremely efficient at teaching other things); (2) that programs and teachers are currently competing for control of classrooms; and (3) that teachers will lose this contest if it is fought in terms of those things that programs teach best. Of course, I must be more explicit about what I mean by "programs." But first I shall briefly restate some relevant points from the [earlier article].

THE EVER-LEARNING BRAIN

Analysis of the enormous complexity and essential arbitrariness of the conventions of language that all children master who succeed in using and understanding the familiar language used around them led to the proposition that children's brains strive to learn all the time. Children cannot tolerate situations in which it is not possible for learning to take place. Boredom or confusion are as aversive to brains whose natural and constant function is to learn as suffocation is to lungs deprived of the opportunity to breathe.

49

Learning occurs in the presence of *demonstrations*, and what is learned is whatever happens to be demonstrated at the time (or rather the learner's interpretation of the demonstration, the way the learner makes sense of it). Learning never takes place in the absence of demonstrations, and what is demonstrated is always likely to be learned. Demonstrations are continually and inevitably provided by people and by products, by acts and by artifacts. A teacher bored with what is being taught demonstrates that what is taught is boring. A reading or writing workbook containing nonsensical exercises demonstrates that reading and writing can be nonsensical. Demonstrations can also be self-generated; they can be constructed by imagination and reflection in the privacy of the mind.

Learning is an interaction, a concurrent event rather than a consequence of a demonstration. Learning is immediate and vicarious, the demonstration becoming in effect the learner's own learning trial. I termed this interaction *engagement* to indicate the intimate meshing of the learner's brain with the demonstration.

Engagement with a demonstration will occur if there is *sensitivity*, defined as the absence of expectation that learning will not take place. The expectation that learning something will be difficult, punishing, or unlikely is itself learned and can be devastating in its long-term consequences. Like all other learning, the expectation that learning will not occur is established by demonstrations.

To learn to read and to write, children require (1) demonstrations of how reading and writing can be used for evident meaningful purposes, (2) opportunities for engagement in such meaningful uses of reading and writing, and (3) freedom from the unnecessary undermining of sensitivity. Obviously teachers are able (or should be able) to provide such demonstrations and opportunities for engagement. The question is whether programs can also meet the three requirements.

THE NATURE OF PROGRAMS

Programs appear in a number of educational guises—as sets of materials, workbooks, activity kits, guidelines, manuals, record sheets, objectives, television series, and computer-based instructional sequences. The history of instructional programs is probably as long as that of education itself, but they began proliferating during the present century as experts in other fields (such as linguistics, psychology, computer science, and test construction) and other external agents increasingly asserted views about what and how teachers should teach. The assumption that programs could achieve educational ends beyond the capacity of autonomous

50

teachers grew rapidly in North America with the educational panic that followed Sputnik in 1957 and the coincidental development of management systems and operational techniques for the solution of logistical problems. (A senior official of the International Reading Association once announced gratefully that the National Aeronautics and Space Administration would help to eliminate literacy by contributing the technology that had delivered men to the moon.) The pervasiveness of programmatic approaches to education is now expanding further and faster as the development of microcomputers makes a new technology available for the delivery of prepackaged instruction.

Despite their manifold variety in education, programs have a number of common elements, the most critical being that they transfer instructional decision-making from the teacher (and children) in the classroom to procedures laid down by people removed from the teaching situation by time and distance.

Children and teachers can be programmed in the same way that computers are programmed, with all goals and activities specified in advance and procedures provided for every decision to be made. Unprogrammed decisions made by computers are regarded as random behavior likely to divert or derail the entire program, and the same attitude is taken in the programming of teachers and children. At least one commercial reading program specifically admonishes teachers not to answer questions asked by children which the program has not anticipated. Some programs are explicitly "teacher proof"; others merely warn teachers not to improvise or to tamper with their procedures. No program, however "individualized," asserts: "This program should only be used by a sensitive and intelligent teacher capable of exercising independent judgment about whether it makes sense to use this program with a particular child on a particular occasion." Instead there is an assumption that the program will be more sensitive and intelligent than the teacher, that instructional decisions will be better made in advance by individuals who do not know and cannot see the child who is supposed to be learning from the program (and who in turn cannot see, know, or question them).

Educational programs share a number of other characteristics, all deriving from the fact that they strive to make decisions in advance on behalf of teachers and children. All of these common characteristics constitute constraints or limitations on what the program can achieve, yet paradoxically they are frequently claimed to be virtues of the program. For example, it is a critical limitation of programs that they cannot demonstrate what reading and writing are for. Teachers can demonstrate the utility of literacy by ensuring that children observe and participate in written language activities that have a purpose—stories to be written and read for pleasure, poems to be recited, songs to be sung, plays to be act-

51

ed, letters to be sent and received, catalogs to be consulted, newspapers and announcements to be circulated, advertisements to be published, signs to be posted, schedules to be followed, even cribs to be concealed, all the multiplicity of ways in which written language is used (and taken for granted) in the world at large. None of these purposes can be demonstrated by programs, which can only demonstrate their own instructional intentions. Reading and writing are *human* activities, and children learn in the course of engaging in them. Programs must assume that children will learn to read and write before actually engaging in these activities, which means that programs demand learning for which no utility is evident.

The virtue claimed for programs in face of the fact that their instruction is decontextualized and bereft of evident purpose is that they are "skill-based," that they teach basic or sub-skills with an implied promise that isolated fragments of skill and knowledge will one day fall into place and the learner will suddenly become able to participate in the new and hitherto unexplored activities of reading and writing. Because programs are more concerned with exercises than purposes, their activities bear little resemblance to any normal, motivated, selective act of reading or writing. Therefore program developers tend to depend on theories that reading and writing are inherently unnatural and difficult (e.g., Mattingly 1972; Liberman and Shankweiler 1979), to be learned by rote rather than by the meaningfulness which is the basis of spoken language learning (Smith 1977).

All programs fractionate learning experience. Because learners cannot be left free to wander at will through (and out of) the program—which would then not be a program—tasks have to be broken down into small steps without evident relationships to each other or to reading and writing as a whole. Because learners can have no intrinsic motivation to perform such tasks—there is no evident reason for doing one thing rather than another—the order in which tasks must be approached and mastered is narrowly prescribed. This is totally unlike the way in which infants are immersed in the environments of meaningful spoken language, to be progressively understood in the manner which makes most sense to each individual child. The virtue claimed for the highly artificial and arbitrary sequencing of programmatic learning is that it is systematic and scientific, although it could equally well be characterized as a systematic deprivation of experience. The responsibility assumed by prescribing the exact nature and order of experience that each individual child requires in order to reach an understanding of reading and writing is awesome, analogous to restricting a child's exploration of the visual world to glimpses of predetermined events paraded past a slit in an enveloping curtain.

Also because of the purposeless and decontextualized nature of programmatic instruction, the program itself must decide whether the learner is right or wrong. When language is employed for meaningful uses, the context provides clues which not only indicate what the language is probably about and how it works but also whether the learner is right or wrong (Smith 1975). There are only two kinds of mistakes in such meaningful language, those that make a difference and those that do not. A mistake that does not make a difference does not make a difference. A mistake that makes a difference becomes self-evident and is the basis of learning. But with meaningless programmatic instruction every deviation from the literal path is an "error" although the only difference it can possibly make is that it is not permitted by the program. Mistakes are to be avoided rather than accepted as opportunities for learning. Nevertheless, learners are constantly moved towards difficulty because tasks that they can accomplish without error are regarded as "learned" and no longer relevant. The virtue claimed for these constraints is that learning can be promoted, monitored, and evaluated every step along the way. There is "quality control" of both the learner and the teacher, no matter how insignificant the mistake or irrelevant the learning task.

As programs have become increasingly more systematic, greater restrictions have been placed on both the time and possibilities available to teachers to introduce activities of their own. Programs dominate classroom activities. The virtue claimed for this limitation is that programs become total "management systems" for delivering instruction to children. Instruction is seen as a manufacturing process, with the learner as raw material, the teacher a tool, the instruction as "treatment," and a literate child as the product delivered at the end. Few program developers are as frank as Atkinson (1974) who admitted that his own elaborate computer-based program began with phonic drills because these could be most easily programmed on the computer. The importance of comprehension in reading (but not in learning) was acknowledged by the characteristic programmatic strategy of treating comprehension as a set of skills to be acquired rather than a state which is the basis of all learning (Smith 1975).

Because programs are by their very nature piecemeal, unmotivated, standardized, decontextualized, trivial, and difficulty-oriented, it would often not be apparent what they were supposed to be teaching if they were not clearly identified. Teachers often say they are teaching reading or writing (or spelling or comprehension) because this is the label attached to the program that happens to be in use. And programs are typically not modest in their claims, particularly those that insist upon being the most rigorous. A widely promoted program of "direct instruction" claims that "any child can learn if he's taught in the right way," the right way being the "carefully developed and unique programming and teaching strategies" of the system. To continue quoting from the promotional materials, "The teacher knows exactly what she has to teach. And how to teach it. All the steps for presenting a task, evaluating student responses, praising and correcting the children are carefully outlined." Having made every decision in advance, including when it is appropriate to praise, the program claims that "the teacher can concentrate fully on teaching" though what is left to be taught (apart from the program) is not specified. A more frankly commercial program combines mutually incompatible vogue words with hyperbole to claim that "The needs of the gifted, the average and the perceptually handicapped child are all met through (the program's) psycholinguistic approach.... Pupils are introduced to reading through the multisensory-motor method . . . combined with intensive audio-visual activity." Also not untypically, this program claims to be indebted to eminent neurologists who had emphasized "the central role played by the integrative areas of the brain" and "the functional grouping of neural units in learning," as if the activities laid down in the program had some kind of unique neurophysiological status.

THE RELEVANCE OF RESEARCH

Another egregious characteristic of programs in education is their claim to be based upon research. The more elaborate and restrictive the program, the more its developers are likely to assert that its content and successes are validated by empirical evidence while instruction that is based on teacher insight and experience is likely to be dismissed as naive, intuitive, and primitive. "Child-centered" is used as a derogatory label.

However, despite all the claims and assumptions there is no evidence that any child ever learned to read because of a program. And probably there never could be such definitive evidence because no child (one would hope) is ever exposed to a "controlled" situation of only programmatic instruction without other access to written language in its manifold purposeful manifestations in the world. On the other hand, there is abundant empirical evidence that children have learned to read without benefit of formal instruction, either before they came to school or by interaction with teachers who were independently self-directed (Clark 1976; Torry 1979). Often such children have few social or intellectual advantages; they are precisely the children for whom programmatic instruction is supposed to be particularly appropriate.

Research has yet to look closely at the manner in which children frequently learn to read and write without or despite formal instruction,

54

nor indeed at what children actually learn as a consequence of such instruction. Instead research has tended to concentrate only on whether children learn whatever fragmented skills particular programs happen to teach. The research paradigm often contrasts an experimental group which receives a particular program with a "control" group which does not. Both groups are then tested on the specific instruction and the experimental group naturally does somewhat better. Alternatively, one program is compared with another, generally to show minimal difference between them (Bond and Dykstra 1967; Stebbins et al. 1977; House et al. 1978). The advantage of whatever such programs actually teach seems to wash out after Grade 3 (Williams 1979; Chall 1967) when matters of comprehension begin to assume inescapable proportions.

Considerable research remains to be done on how exactly children succeed in learning to read and write, but it will not be done by researchers who believe that such learning is a matter of mastering programmatic reading and writing skills. Instead there is a great need for longitudinal and ethnographic studies of how children come to make sense of print and its uses, such as those of Goodman (1980), Ferreiro (1978), and Heibert (1981), demonstrating for example that preschool children can understand functions and the general character of print long before they receive formal instruction.

Much more research could be done into what children can and must learn about reading and writing without recourse to programs, into how programs do and should relate to this prior knowledge, into what teachers who succeed in helping children learn to read and write actually do, into what exactly children who have learned to read and write have learned (from teachers and from programs), and also into what children who have failed to become readers and writers have learned. On the other hand, the fact that research demonstrates that readers have particular skills which nonreaders do not have should not be interpreted to mean that nonreaders will become readers if drilled in those particular skills, which may be a consequence rather than a cause of reading. Such has been found to be the case for knowledge of letter-names (Samuels 1971) and for familiarity with the conventional language of reading instruction (Downing and Oliver 1973-74).

TEACHERS VERSUS PROGRAMS

With their inevitably limited objectives, programs teach trivial aspects of literacy and they can teach that literacy is trivial. Children are learning all the time. Rather than demonstrate the utility of written language, programs may demonstrate that reading is nonsense and ritual, that writing is boring, that learning is threatening, that children are stupid, that teachers are puppets, that schools cannot be trusted and that children's own interests, cultures, and insights into language can be ignored. Teachers can demonstrate all these things too, but programs do so more efficiently.

The proliferation of programs in education today is unnecessary, irrelevant, and dangerous. Programs are unnecessary because millions of children have learned to be literate without the contemporary technology of instructional development and there is no evidence at all that the employment and enjoyment of literacy have increased with the growing reliance upon programs. There is no evidence that children who have difficulty becoming literate do better with impersonal programs (although they may exhibit irrelevant and limited learning from what the programs teach). Rather it is the children who have the least success in learning who most need personal contact, to be reassured of their ability to learn, and of the utility of what is to be learned. I am not saying that teachers cannot on occasion make independent use of material provided with programs, but that teachers should not be used by programs.

Programs tend to be irrelevant by their very nature. They demonstrate tasks rather than purposes. There is widespread anxiety today because many students leave school with poor writing and reading abilities. But the real tragedy is that competent readers and writers as well as the less able leave school with a lifelong aversion to reading and writing, which they regard as purely school activities, as trivial and tedious "work." Students of poor ability who are interested in reading and writing will always have the possibility of learning. But those who detest the activities are lost; they have learned from the wrong demonstrations.

Programs are dangerous because they may take the place of teachers. The issue is more critical today than ever before because more people seem to believe that the way to improve education is to operationalize it even further, and because the technology now exists to make teachers redundant. It is widely believed, especially among those who promote computer-based instruction, that children can "do all their learning" at a console, that microcomputers are cheaper than teachers (which is a fact) and that they are more efficient than teachers (which is true for what such devices teach best). It is perhaps ironic that dissatisfaction with the performance of teachers has tended to grow as education has become more systematized, yet the "solution" to the perceived decline in literacy and teacher effectiveness has continued to be the increase of program control at the expense of teacher autonomy.

Teachers are an endangered species. While being given less and less freedom to teach, they are being held more and more accountable. And in the comparison with technology teachers are being put at a crucial disadvantage. Teachers are not evaluated on whether children enjoy reading and writing, on how often and extensively children independently engage in reading and writing in their everyday lives, nor even on how fast they learn when the learning is relevant to their own individual interests. Instead children and teachers are evaluated on what the programs teach best, on standardized, decontextualized, fragmented "skills." The majority of reading tests favor programs, since they are restricted to measuring the same kinds of things that programs teach best, isolated facts and skills that can be dealt with one standardized step at a time.

The problem is also that while programs make teachers look ineffectual, teachers (and children) make programs look good. A teacher tells a child to spend an hour on worksheets and at the end of the day there will be time for independent reading. At the end of the year the child can read and the teacher gives all the credit to the worksheets. The way most teachers are trained not only leads them to be dependent upon programs but to give programs the credit for success, though not the blame for failure.

THE MARTIAN TEST

Imagine a Martian space traveler sent to earth to investigate the nature and utility of the reading and writing that earthlings find so important. Suppose the Martian decided that classrooms would be the best places to gather information. What would the Martian conclude reading and writing to be from the materials available and from the activities of teachers and children under the influence of programs? Could a reasonable report be sent back to Mars? As I said in my earlier article, the problem may not be that children do not learn in school but that they learn all the time. And like the Martian they will learn exactly what is demonstrated. Should we expect children to be any less misled than the Martian?

CONCLUSIONS

The critical issue confronting education today is not which programs are best for teaching children to read and to write, but what children will learn. Teachers can teach that literacy is useful, enjoyable, and attainable, provided they are left free to teach in an unprogrammed manner. Programs will teach something else—that literacy is what programs demonstrate.

I am not arguing against technology, I think microprocessors and every other aspect of contemporary technology should be important tools for learning—like typewriters and calculators—but not control devices for teaching. Children should learn to use technology but not to be used by it. The question again is, "Who is in charge?"

Many people can think of teachers who override programs and who engage children in productive language learning. Many teachers believe they themselves are exceptions. And of course such teachers exist. My concern is that they may be losing the possibility of teaching. Programs are being thrust upon them, not only by school and political administrations but by parents and the media, all seemingly convinced that programmed education is a universal panacea. It will not help if teachers also believe that programs can only be benign.

Teachers as well as literacy are threatened. And only teachers can resist the threat. They can resist by asserting their crucial role in teaching literacy against all who assert otherwise. In the present decade, the most important educational function of teachers may well be outside the classroom rather than within it.

REFERENCES

Atkinson, R. C. "Teaching Children to Read Using a Computer." *American Psychologist* 29 (1974): 169–178.

Bond, G. and Dykstra, R. "The Cooperative Research Program in First-Grade Reading." *Reading Research Quarterly* 2 (1967): 5–142.

Chall, J. S. *Learning to Read: The Great Debate.* New York: McGraw-Hill, 1967.

Clark, M. M. *Young Fluent Readers.* London: Heinemann Educational Books, 1976.

Downing, J. and Oliver, P. "The Child's Conception of 'A Word'." *Reading Research Quarterly* 4 (1973-74): 568–582.

Ferreira, E. "What Is Written in a Written Sentence? A Developmental Answer." *Journal of Education* 160 (1978): 25–39.

Goodman, Y. "'The Roots of Literacy." In *Claremont Reading Conference Forty-Fourth Yearbook,* edited by M. P. Douglass. Claremont, CA, 1980.

Hiebert, E. H. "Developmental Patterns and Interrelationships of Preschool Children's Print Awareness." *Reading Research Quarterly* 16 (1981): 236–260.

House, E. R.; Glass, G. V.; McLean, L. D.; and Walker, D. F. "No Simple Answer: Critique of the Follow-Through Evaluation." *Harvard Educational Review* 48 (1978): 128–160.

Liberman, I. Y. and Shankweiler, D. "Speech, the Alphabet and Teaching to Read." In *Theory and Practice of Early Reading* (Vol. 2), edited by L. B. Resnick and P. A. Weaver. Hillsdale, NJ: Erlbaum, 1979.

Mattingly, I. G. "Reading, the Linguistic Process, and Linguistic Awareness." In *Language by Ear and by Eye,* edited by J. F. Kavanagh and I. G. Mattingly. Cambridge, MA: M.I.T. Press, 1972.

Olson, D. R. and Bruner, J. S. "Learning Through Experience and Learning Through Instruction." In *Media and Symbols: The Forms of Expression, Communication and Education,* edited by D. R. Olson. Chicago: National Society for the Study of Education, 73rd Yearbook, Part 1. 1974.

Samuels, S. J. "Letter-Name versus Letter-Sound Knowledge in Learning to Read." *Reading Teacher* 24 (1971): 604–608.

Smith, F. *Comprehension and Learning*. New York: Holt, Rinehart and Winston, 1975.

———. "Making Sense of Reading—And of Reading Instruction." *Harvard Educational Review*, 47 (1977): 386–395.

———. "Conflicting Approaches to Reading Research and Instruction." In *Theory and Practice of Early Reading* (Vol. 2), edited by L. B. Resnick and P. A. Weaver. Hillsdale, NJ: Erlbaum, 1979.

———. "Demonstrations, Engagement and Sensitivity: A Revised Approach to Language Learning." *Language Arts* 58 (1981): 103–112.

Stebbins, L. B.; St. Pierre, R. G.; Proper, E. C.; Anderson, R. B.; and Cerva, T. R. *Education as Experimentation: A Planned Variation Model: Vol. LV-A An Evaluation of Follow-Through*. Cambridge, MA: Abt Associates, 1977.

Torrey, Jane W. "Reading That Comes Naturally: The Early Reader." In *Reading Research: Advances in Theory and Practice* (Vol. 1), edited by T. G. Walker and G. E. MacKinnon. New York: Academic Press, 1979.

Williams, J. "Reading Instruction Today." *American Psycholgist* 34 (1979): 917–922.

5. 'BURN IT AT THE CASKET': RESEARCH, READING INSTRUCTION, AND CHILDREN'S LEARNING OF THE FIRST R

by Anne M. Bussis, Educational Testing Service

Anne Bussis deplores the current emphasis on isolated skills in the teaching and testing of reading. She shares the case study of a student who was able to read meaningful text, but could not do well on isolated skill tasks. As Bussis states, "Instructional programs in schools in the United States focus on 'essential' reading skills; yet these skills have no demonstrable relationship to learning how to read books, and they impose definitions of reading and standards of reading progress that are contrary to common sense." Current research accepted by most social scientists suggests that human beings construct meaning in order to make sense out of their experiences. Students often become confused when they are asked to focus on isolated skills that do not make sense to them. On the other hand, when teachers ask students to read books that convey useful information and/or provide pleasure, they are able to construct meaning and come to know that reading is a worthwhile activity.

Bussis suggests several practices that teachers can use to help students develop as readers: (a) provide for a range of appropriate reading materials; (b) set aside time daily for students to read self-selected books and to write on self-selected topics; (c) read aloud quality literature; and (d) talk individually with students and listen to them read.

This chapter appeared in Phi Delta Kappan, *vol. 64 (December 1982): 237–41. © 1982, Phi Delta Kappan, Inc. Reprinted with permission.*

The King's Shadow is a book about a little king who was terribly afraid of his own shadow. In the opening lines of the story, the king asks his three wise men what to do about the shadow, and they respond as follows:

"Chop of your shadow's head," said one.

"Boil it in oil," said another.

"Burn it at the stake," said a third.

When Tim came to the third line, he quickly read, "'Burn it at the casket. . . .'"

Tim is one of many children whose classroom learning was documented for a two-year period (grades K-1 or 1-2) by teachers and researchers in the Collaborative Study of Reading of the Educational Testing Service (ETS). This program of research was funded by the National Institute of Education, the Ford Foundation, and ETS.

Substituting *casket* for *stake* is a puzzling error when considered in isolation, but it was fairly typical of other of Tim's renditions that went astray. His substitutions fell into a pattern; they tended to resemble anagrams, containing some or all of the letters of the text but in scrambled order. (With the exception of the first letters, *casket* is an anagram of *stake*.) This pattern was prominent in Tim's reading from May of first grade through November of second grade, and it is illustrated by the following additional examples. He read *want* for *what*, *blump* for *blurp*, *off* for *for*, *white* for *while*, *places* for *palace*, *last* for *least*, *still* for *silly*, *tried* for *tired*, *screeching* for *searching*, *left* for *felt*, and *Green Cold Superpie* for *Green Cloud Supreme* (the name of a dessert).

Aside from this scrambled-letter characteristic, many of Tim's errors also seemed both prompted and constrained by his anticipation of the story line or of the grammar of a sentence. Most of these mistakes occurred when Tim was reading a relatively unfamiliar book that challenged his capabilities; by and large, they did not daunt his efforts. He would continue reading, and he usually grasped the basic meaning of the text quite well.

Errors of a more debilitating nature surfaced when Tim's teacher asked him to stop and sound out words analytically. This was certainly not an unreasonable request, for Tim had been exposed to intensive instruction in letter/sound correspondence during the previous year in kindergarten, and his first-grade teacher had reinforced that instruction throughout the fall. The kindergarten program had emphasized various sounds of individual letters, of digraphs, and of consonant blends. When asked to apply this knowledge, Tim tried to oblige but invariably failed. He would reverse sound sequences or say he couldn't remember the correct sound; he produced whole words rather than a requested blend; and, if he did manage to articulate a sound sequence that closely approximated the text word, he usually did not recognize what he had said well enough to adjust to the proper enunciation.

In short, Tim seemed unable to process words in the letter-by-letter analytic fashion required by phonic decoding. After a particularly painful session of this nature in January of first grade, his teacher abandoned analytic decoding as a viable instructional approach with Tim. She would remind him of letter sounds from time to time or ask him the sound of a letter, but she never again required that he "'sound out'' a whole word.

Tim's first-grade teacher taught a combined class, so she kept Tim in her classroom for second grade. By the end of second grade, Tim was a competent and comprehending reader of texts that presented complex ideas and approximated adult books in vocabulary, grammar, and format. The following few lines illustrate a scientific text he read rapidly and discussed intelligently during his last tape-recorded oral reading in June of second grade.

> What did prehistoric man look like? That was the question some people had been asking even before the Paris Exhibition of 1867. Now many scientists all over Europe, including those who had once argued against De Perthe's whole theory, were eager to find the answer to that question. But they couldn't find the answer without first studying some of the clues which to this day are very rare—the actual bones of prehistoric man.*

Tim's progress in reading books was never matched by progress in his ability to perform phonic analysis, a fact periodically highlighted by the program of Individualized Criterion-Referenced Testing (ICRT) mandated by the school system. The particular ICRT system used in Tim's district breaks reading into 340 discrete "skills" and provides a card of test items for each one. This system is apparently designed to serve as the major instructional program in reading in a given school throughout the primary years, since it supposes that every child will receive instruction in every skill to the point of mastering the test items. But Tim's teacher didn't use the ICRT system for reading instruction—nor did most other teachers in the district. Rather, she tried to fit the system into her own program. She used the skill cards without giving her students specific prior instruction and then discussed with individual children the skills that they had failed to master.

Tim fared well on many skill cards, but he and his teacher nearly always had to talk about the cards that dealt with letter/sound relationships. However, since Tim and most of his classmates were reading books, the teacher wasn't too concerned about failures on the test items. She noted them in her records and, for purposes of the reading study, wrote periodic reports on Tim's performance. In February of second grade, for instance, she reported about ICRT item #165 as follows: "This was the short *i* vowel sound. The exercise shows two pictures of things that have identical vowel sounds, and the child is supposed to pick the one word from four alternatives that has the same vowel sound. It was hard for Tim."

Tim is a normal child in every respect, including the soundness of his sight and hearing. In fact, his reading errors and strategies were quite similar to the learning behaviors of many children in the ETS study, just as they were dissimilar to the behaviors of other children. Tim's case history illustrates nothing particularly unusual about him, his teacher, his

---

All About Prehistoric Cavemen (New York: Random House, 1959), p. 74.

school, or his school district. But it illustrates superbly the kind of incongruity that typifies reading instruction in many schools.

The ingredients that combine to produce incongruity have all been presented above:

- a child who is actually reading books but who cannot answer correctly many test items related to "essential skills";
- a teaching/testing program that focuses solely on such skills, on the premise that they are prerequisites to learning to read;
- a school district that mandates the use of these tests and the recording of scores, presumably in the interest of demonstrating accountability for children's progress; and
- a teacher caught in the middle, trying to steer as intelligent a course as possible between satisfying district policy and supporting children's efforts to learn how to read.

The principal fully backed the teacher's instructional approach in this instance, but that is not always the case. Principals may express uneasiness and even disapproval, if they more often observe children reading books than teachers directing concrete, identifiable reading instruction.

It seems bizarre that emphasis on "essential" reading skills displaces actual reading in the classroom, but this is what happens far too often. And research has repeatedly shown that less competent readers receive the lion's share of the drill on skills. The pattern is predictable. Children who are least able to read text when they enter school are given the least exposure to books. Moreover, this approach "works," in the sense that reading programs that focus on skills are often modestly or highly successful in accomplishing what they claim. They enable children to perform better on tests designed to measure what the programs teach.

This circular definition of success becomes quite maddening; it causes teachers, administrators, researchers, and parents to doubt their own rationality. Given enough arguments in favor of such programs and abundant proof of what they can accomplish, we begin to doubt what we *know* about reading and to look instead to the instructional programs to tell us what reading is. In Tim's case, for example, we may begin to wonder whether fluent reading and intelligent discussion of a book really count for much without mastery of the skills. Has Tim somehow fooled us? Is he adequately prepared for work in the upper grades without a firm grasp of short *i*? We are no longer certain of what it means to read.

Let's look at the evidence—or, in this case, lack of evidence. The International Reading Association (IRA) held a special conference of researchers in 1973 to consider tests of early reading, the skills they typically assess, and the relationship of these skills to reading acquisition. The researchers held diverse theories about reading acquisition; many of them, in their own research, focused on specific components of the reading process. Although they disagreed about the merits and drawbacks of different kinds of tests, they agreed on one thing: No available evidence indicated that *any* identifiable group of subskills was essential to reading.

In 1975, as programs emphasizing basic skills continued to proliferate, the National Institute of Education (NIE) issued a call for intensive research on essential skills and skill hierarchies in reading, along with a plan for accomplishing this end. The plan reflected the deliberation of scientists and educators, most of whom were sympathetic to an instructional approach that focused on reading skills. The plan began with a statement of research objectives:

> [to] determine if there are essential skills or processing skills related to reading, what they are, how to identify and validate them, how they are interrelated, and which are causally related to reading.

The research generated by this plan failed to identify essential skills, skill hierarchies, and causal connections—just as all the prior research, considered at the IRA conference in 1973, had failed to do so.

But studies of a very different nature were also being conducted in the 1970s, and they produced promising results. The findings were so promising, in fact, that they shaped a surer rationale and a very different set of objectives for the new research plan that the NIE issued in December 1980. The 1980 plan argued that the reading process is both constructive and interactive (i.e., interpretation and perception influence one another), that it involves many strategies for constructing meaning, and that a reader adapts the process to deal with different kinds of texts.

Moreover, the 1980 plan presented these characteristics of the reading process as sound conclusions derived from reasonable evidence. It also acknowledged the failure of previous efforts to produce a coherent theory to explain reading acquisition. It attributed much of this failure to the fact that "most early research focused on decoding skills and various methods of teaching children to be good decoders." Only after educators began to realize that many children could master decoding skills and still fail to read effectively did "the focus of research begin to expand," according to the 1980 NIE research plan.

A stranger to the world of educational research, policy, and practice might legitimately wonder how we could have allowed the current situation to develop. Instructional programs in U.S. schools focus on "essential" reading skills; yet these skills have no demonstrable relationship to learning how to read books, and they impose definitions of reading and standards of reading progress that are contrary to common sense. The stranger would have a good point.

To develop a more effective approach to reading instruction, we must first understand some of the evidence on which the NIE based its 1980 statement. The most influential research is not all of a kind, nor did it spring full-blown from research efforts of the 1970s. It represents logical extensions of many years of previous investigations of memory, perception, thought, and language—all of which support a particular view of how the brain functions. This view is now so thoroughly documented that it is accepted as a "given" by most social scientists.

- The brain constructs perceptions and thoughts (instead of behaving as a sponge).
- The central function of the brain is to create meaning.
- Meaning arises through the perception and interpretation of patterns (or relationships) in events.
- Anticipation and intention influence brain activity.

Collectively, these characteristics imply that humans neither "soak up" elements in the environment nor respond directly to environmental stimuli (except in instinctive behavior). Instead, humans create symbolic representations of the environment and then act in accordance with the meanings they have constructed. Although meaning is relative in the sense that it may change somewhat from one context or culture to another, from one developmental stage to another, and from one individual to another, there seems to be nothing relative about its function in life. People in every culture and at every age strive to make their experiences as meaningful as possible. When they find themselves in situations that make little sense and that they cannot anticipate effectively, they become confused, anxious, and often hesitant to act at all.

The propensity of humans to construct meaning is one reason why books that convey meaningful information or tell comprehensible stories are so important to children. And because children—like adults—constantly construct meaning, their learning behaviors constitute a continuous source of information from which teachers can infer the meanings that children are (or are not) constructing in the classroom.

To go beyond these general implications in order to clarify the nature of reading, I must first redefine some terms that educators often use interchangeably and without much thought.

Information becomes potentially knowable and meaningful only when it stems from events that an individual actually heeds. But heeding alone does not suffice to transform information into knowledge. An individual must discern some unifying pattern in events before information becomes predictable and thus interpretable. Only when a person interprets information—however tentatively—does information qualify as knowledge. The interpretation need not be formulated in words; many experiences are represented in nonarticulate form. But an individual must note and interpret a pattern before he or she can be said to know something. In other words, information exists "out there" in the physical/social/cultural world or in physiological sensations arising from within the body. *Knowledge* exists in the mind.

This distinction between information and knowledge (and the fact that heeding is not equivalent to knowing) calls into question another popular instructional concern: time on task. Those researchers who stress time on task argue that the more time a child spends attending to instructional information (within reasonable bounds), the more he or she will learn. The problem with this logic is that the human brain doesn't always comply. An individual could conceivably attend to a particular kind of information for years without ever discerning a pattern that unifies the information or relates it to other meaningful patterns. Such a dismal outcome is not only theoretically possible but also quite probable, if the information an individual heeds consists primarily of isolated fragments of an event. Sufficient attention to information is an important and rather obvious condition of learning, but it guarantees nothing.

Written language contains information that is crucial to reading, and the beginning reader must figure out what this information means. This task involves separating irrelevant data (the size and style of print, for example) from potentially meaningful data, and then detecting patterns that make the potentially meaningful information predictable and interpretable. Since pattern detection is the crucial task and since patterns involve relationships between both similar and contrasting events, rich data are more useful to the learner than meager data. For this reason, books that present written language in its naturally occurring variations are helpful to children.

The human brain is an exquisitely designed pattern detector, and it works with remarkable ease and efficiency when it receives appropriate information. Perhaps the most impressive testimony to the prowess of the brain is the fact that infants detect and assimilate the underlying sound patterns and grammatical structures of their native language from the rich speech environment that surrounds them. When the brain must try to construct a coherent whole from fragmented data, however, its efficiency plummets to mediocre at best. Presenting children with written language in piecemeal fashion may seem a logical instructional approach to reading, but it actually imposes formidable burdens on the learner.

As children successfully detect the underlying patterns in written language, they acquire more and more knowledge. However, knowledge about writing does not equate with skill in reading, and to assume that it does will lead an instructional program off course. Reading is a singular skill. A curriculum that focuses on reading skills (in the plural) actually attempts to foster instead various kinds of formal knowledge about written language—some of it important for reading, some of it not, and much of it very difficult to learn if one is not already able to read. Such curricula test children's ability to demonstrate this formal knowledge about written language.

A *skill* supposes intention, it is affected by attitudes, and it depends on knowledge. Yet it is none of these. A skill demands the coordination or orchestration of diverse knowledge to achieve a particular result that is characterized by particular constraints or criteria. Were there no constraints or criteria, virtually any action could be called a skill. The skill of reading requires the orchestration of at least five kinds of orchestration of at least five kinds of knowledge in order to construct meaning from a text while maintaining reasonable fluency and reasonable faithfulness to the information that has been encoded in the text. This is the singular skill of reading.

Beginners execute any skill more awkwardly and less proficiently than do experts. The only way to gain the proficiency that comes with experience is to practice a skill in its overall complexity. Orchestration and coordination are brain functions that seem to be learned only through repeated attempts to perform them. Beginning readers may wish to concentrate on different aspects of the skill at times (e.g., the flow or the accuracy), and they must limit their ambitions at first (e.g., reading a few sentences or short books). But practice is what counts.

The paradox of learning a skill is that neophytes can begin to practice before they control all the knowledge that a polished performance requires. In fact, there is no other way to begin learning a skill. Practice can start as soon as an individual possesses some of the necessary knowledge and understands what the skill is intended to accomplish. The brain picks up additional knowledge in the course of practice. This explains why initial stages of practice are always both fumbling and fatiguing. Beginners are operating under the handicap of incomplete knowledge, they are still learning the crucial act of orchestration, and they are detecting and interpreting relevant patterns of information along the way. Fortunately, the human brain can handle such a complex task quite well. But the effort is tiring, and a beginner needs encouragement from others and the motivation of a desirable end result. If appropriate support is not forthcoming or if outcomes of early practice sessions continually prove dissatisfying and relatively meaningless, the learner may eventually decide that the reward does not justify the effort.

Children have two strong knowledge resources for reading acquisition. They have a tacit understanding of the grammatical structures and sound patterns of English, and they know a great deal about the everyday world. These resources help them to comprehend and to anticipate the

67

content of books. Children who have attended to such familiar forms of writing as words on signs, on cereal boxes, and on television commercials usually possess implicit knowledge of some letter/sound relationships as well.

The best way to support a beginning reader is to tell him or her what the text says. When children realize that a particular graphic configuration represents "once upon a time" or "Curious George went to the store," they can begin to detect recurring features within the configuration and to relate these to the meaning that the configuration conveys. When they tentatively apply these interpretations to other familiar lines of text, learning to read has begun. As practice proceeds, children acquire more and more knowledge about the two kinds of information encoded in writing: phonetic (i.e., letter/sound) relationships and spelling patterns.

A child who makes any progress in reading at all will, of necessity, interpret many letter/sound relationships. Much of this knowledge may remain implicit, however, and in such form may not lead the beginner much beyond the initial consonant sounds of unknown words. Explicit knowledge of the rules that govern letter/sound relationships is a prerequisite for the kind of phonetic analysis that helps to unlock whole words. Many children can use these formal rules to advantage in learning to read, but many others—like Tim—either cannot or will not.

Tim's classmate, Rita, thrived on instruction in phonics and would try to use what she knew to solve every unknown word she encountered. If she couldn't figure out a word, she would ask her teacher or someone else for help before moving on. In fact, Rita approached text as if every word were a crucial step in a straight and orderly path to meaning. She never skipped a word in her beginning practice efforts, nor would she rest with substituting a good guess for an unknown word. Rita was able to sound out many difficult words by the end of first grade, but by that time her path to meaning had also broadened. She was willing to settle for some intelligent guesses in the interest of getting on with a text, and she was relying heavily on the kind of information on which Tim seemed to focus from the very first.

Tim almost always tackled a new book as if he were eager to get on with the text. He would take a stab at troublesome words, skip them, offer substitute words, or use some combination of these strategies. He tended to read rapidly, and his reading behavior suggested that he was dealing with relatively broad spans of print. These facts alone suggest that Tim was attending to the visual configurations of whole words (i.e., their spellings), rather than to the sounds of the individual letters in each word (i.e., phonetics). And the nature of his errors bears out this hypothesis. Although only a few of Tim's errors seemed to represent

68

faulty interpretations of the sound structures of words, many of his errors reflected faulty interpretations of the spelling structures of words.

Tim was actually attending to the dominant information encoded in writing. Phonetic information may receive more publicity, but linguistic analysis has shown that written English emphasizes consistent spellings more than it emphasizes consistent letter/sound relationships. When the letter *s* is applied at the end of a word, for example, it becomes a meaningful word part—a suffix that always signals the same meaning (i.e., plurality) but that can have any one of three pronunciations (as in *cats*, *cars*, or *houses*). Written English does not indicate the particular sound of the letter *s* in a given word, because native speakers intuitively predict and accommodate to shifts in the sound of this letter. If the sound, rather than the meaning, of *s* were the more important information to convey, then the writing system would indicate plurality by three different spellings.

The spelling principle is especially useful when root words are combined with suffixes. *National* retains the root word *nation*; the suffix *-al* simultaneously signals that the word is an adjective. Although the suffix changes the sound of the first vowel (from the long *a* of nation to the short *a* of national), English speakers make this shift quite unconsciously. The more important information that the writing system has emphasized is the intimate bond of meaning between the two words. Thus we can predictably transform nouns into adjectives or verbs, adjectives into adverbs, and verbs into nouns by tacking on such endings as *-al*, *-able*, *-ive*, *-ful*, *-less*, *-ize*, *-ate*, *-ly*, *-ship*, *-tion*, *-ity*, and so on.

The semantic information encoded in writing suggests that a learner must eventually attend to the visual organization of spelling patterns if he or she is ever to become a proficient reader. Tim's history suggests that he focused on such organizational features very early in his learning. And Tim's history in this respect duplicates the histories of many other children in the ETS reading study, just as Rita's general learning progress duplicates the progress of many of her peers.

I have emphasized learning, because good teaching begins with an understanding of learning—particularly when it comes to skills. Teachers and curriculum developers cannot crawl inside children's minds and manipulate the orchestration of knowledge that is necessary for reading. But teachers can make this task easy or hard, rewarding or painful, worthwhile or nor worthwhile for students by the provisions they make in the classroom and the help that they offer.

Specific provisions and kinds of help will depend on the child. But let me suggest five general practices.

1. Provide a range of reading materials in the classroom. For the young learner, these materials might include alphabet and counting

books, picture books, informational and reference books, classics of children's literature, easy-to-read trade books, and a variety of beginning reading series.

2. Provide time each day for children to read books of their own choosing or—in the case of youngsters who are not yet reading—to look at pictures in self-selected books.

3. Provide time for children to write, preferably every day but at least two or three times each week. Young children can begin by dictating sentences or words to their teachers or to classroom aides and then copying what these adults write for them.

4. Read to the class each day, varying the selections between well-written imaginative literature and interesting informational books.

5. Work individually with children at least some of the time. Listen to each child read or discuss what he or she has read.

The first four practices give children several perspectives on the written word and encourage them to exercise intelligence in choosing, deciphering, and making sense of books and other writing. These practices do not add up to a full instructional program. But they do lend coherence and direction to otherwise diverse instructional approaches (whether phonic, basal, or language experience) in diverse instructional settings (whether large groups, small groups, or one-to-one). The practices are not my idea; rather, they are the key similarities that characterize the classrooms of the most successful teachers I know.

The fifth practice allows teachers to observe their students. If a general understanding of learning is the first principle of effective teaching, then careful observation of learners must rank a close second. In fact, the first principle presupposes the second. But observation must be of a special kind. The teacher who monitors only students' correct responses will derive relatively little data to inform his or her instructional decisions. Merely counting up errors will add nothing more. It is the nature of children's errors and their general approach to text that reveal what is happening in the orchestration and comprehension process.

"Burn it at the casket" and "Green Cold Superpie" may never be uttered again. Nor will other children manifest a desire to get on with the story or to read every word of text in precisely the same ways as Tim and Rita did. But other children will manifest intentions, strategies, struggles, and errors that are just as revealing—if they have opportunities to read interesting books. And knowledgeable, observant teachers will be informed by children's reading behaviors—if they are freed from paperwork long enough to observe.

70

SELECTED BIBLIOGRAPHY

Allington, Richard. "Poor Readers Don't Get Much in Reading Groups." *Language Arts*, vol. 57, 1980, pp. 872–76.

Bartlett, Elsa. "Curriculum, Concepts of Literacy, and Social Class," in Lauren Resnick and Phyllis Weaver, eds., *Theory and Practice of Early Reading, Vol.* 2. Hillsdale, N.J.: Erlbaum, 1979, pp. 229–42.

Bissex, Glenda. *Gnys at Work: A Child Learns to Write and Read.* Cambridge, Mass.: Harvard University Press, 1980.

Bobrow, Daniel and Allan Collins, eds. *Representation and Understanding: Studies in Cognitive Science.* New York: Academic Press, 1975.

Bussis, Anne M. with Edward A. Chittenden, Marianne Amarel, and Edith Klausner. *Inquiry into Meaning: An Investigation of Learning to Read.* Hillsdale, N.J.: Erlbaum, forthcoming.

Chomsky, Carol. "Reading, Writing, and Phonology." *Harvard Educational Review*, May 1970, pp. 287–309.

_____. "Stages in Language Development and Language Exposure." *Harvard Educational Review*, February 1972, pp. 1–33.

Clay, Marie M. *Reading: The Patterning of Complex Behaviour.* New Zealand: Heinemann Educational Books, 1972.

Conference on Studies in Reading, Panel 10 Report. *Essential Skills and Skill Hierarchies in Reading.* Washington, D.C.: National Institute of Education, June 1975.

Fader, Daniel. *The Naked Children.* New York: Macmillan, 1971.

Freedle, Roy, ed. *New Directions in Discourse Processing, Vol.* 2. Norwood N.J.: Ablex, 1979.

Goodman, Kenneth S. and Yetta M. Goodman. "Learning About Psycholinguistic Processes by Analyzing Oral Reading." *Harvard Educational Review*, August 1977, pp. 317–33.

Henderson, Edmund H. *Learning to Read and Spell.* DeKalb, Ill.: Northern Illinois University Press, 1981.

Center for the Study of Reading. *RFP Notification.* Washington, D.C.: National Institute of Education, December 1980.

Scheffler, Israel. *Conditions of Knowledge.* Chicago: Scott, Foresman, 1965.

Smith, Frank. *Understanding Reading.* New York: Holt, Rinehart & Winston, 1971.

_____. *Comprehension and Learning. A Conceptual Framework for Teachers.* New York: Holt, Rinehart & Winston, 1975.

Spiro, Rand, Bertram Bruce, and William Brewer, eds. *Theoretical Issues in Reading Comprehension.* Hillsdale, N.J.: Erlbaum, 1980.

Weber, Rose M. "First-Graders' Use of Grammatical Context in Reading," in Harry Levin and Joanna Williams, eds., *Basic Studies on Reading.* New York: Basic Books, 1970.

6. EARLY PHONICS INSTRUCTION: ITS EFFECT ON LITERACY DEVELOPMENT

by Maryann Manning, Gary Manning, and Constance Kamii,
University of Alabama at Birmingham

Maryann Manning, Gary Manning, and Constance Kamii present the effects of phonics instruction on the literacy development of the Mannings' daughter. When she entered kindergarten, Marilee had confidence in herself as a reader and writer, but she lost this sureness when formal phonics instruction was imposed. As she became preoccupied with the newly acquired phonics information, she stopped focusing on meaning in her reading and no longer thought about the expression of thoughts and ideas in her writing.

Marilee's kindergarten teacher was outstanding. Her classroom environment was developmentally sound throughout the day, except for the period of formal phonics instruction. Like many other good teachers, Marilee's teacher felt that she must follow the official curriculum, including phonics instruction, especially since she also had been told that her students must do well on tests at the end of the year.

As this chapter indicates, teachers are too often treated as workers on an assembly line; autonomous teachers should be accorded the respect and trust they deserve. In recognizing the positive contributions that these professionals can make to students' development, we also recognize the necessity of educating new teachers to practice their craft with continuous intellectual inquiry and responsible action. The authors urge support for commendable teachers, like Marilee's kindergarten teacher, and encourage natural literacy learning rather than requirements for formal and isolated phonics instruction. It is also worth noting that current research and theory often match the intuition and common sense of effective teachers of young children.

This chapter appeared in Young Children, *vol. 44 (November 1988): 4–8. Copyright © 1988 by Maryann Manning, Gary Manning, and Constance Kamii.*

Phonics is being taught in many kindergartens and most first grades in the nation to introduce children to reading and spelling. A large number of educators believe that phonics instruction is necessary for children to learn to read and spell, but many psycholinguists question the value of this instruction. The teaching of phonics has been a source of controversy since Rudolf Flesch's (1955) book *Why Johnny Can't Read*. Chall (1967) addressed the debate in her book *Learning To Read: The Great Debate*, concluding that a code-emphasis approach produced better reading achievement than a meaning-emphasis one. Since the publication of Chall's book, we have seen a movement toward greater code-emphasis approaches in beginning reading.

The subject of phonics instruction has been very perplexing to us. As classroom teachers many years ago, two of us were made to feel guilty if we didn't teach phonics skills included in the basal readers we were using. Yet the direct teaching of phonics skills, which often resulted in "mastery," did not necessarily lead to children's ability to read a text. We were also frustrated teaching the phonics skills suggested in spelling books; the instruction seemed to cause confusion for many children. We were puzzled by children who spelled words in their own ways, and by the similarities among children's errors in the same age group.

Research during the past decade has enlightened us by providing insights into how children develop as written language users. Ferreiro and Teberosky (1982) documented the constructive process in both reading and spelling, and their findings have been confirmed in Switzerland, Mexico, Spain, France, and Italy (personal communication in conversations with E. Ferreiro, A. Teberosky, and H. Sinclair of the University of Geneva, 1984 to present). Beers, Beers, and Grant (1977); Bissex (1980); Chomsky (1971, 1979); Gentry and Henderson (1978); Read (1971, 1975); Schickedanz (1986); and Zuttell (1978) have all shown how children develop as spellers and how their errors are manifestations of their efforts to work out personally a system of rules. We believe that psycholinguistic research is congruent with Piaget's theory and is but one more example of constructivism, the view that children did not internalize knowledge directly from the environment, but construct it from within by going through one level after another of being "wrong."

Still, the debate continues concerning phonics instruction for beginning readers and spellers. While proponents of phonics and psycholinguistics argue in support of their respective positions, there is very little precise information on what happens to developing readers and spellers when phonics instruction is imposed on them. To address the need for such information and to air some disturbing questions raised by our personal experience, we describe in some detail what happened to one six-year-old when she received phonics instruction in kindergarten. Marilee, the six-year-old we will talk about, is the daughter of the first two authors. She was reading predictable books before kindergarten. She was also writing: notes to the tooth fairy, letters to relatives for birthdays and holidays, greetings to friends, and notes to visitors. She had a large audience who appreciated her reading and invented spelling: her parents, relatives, and friends.

Marilee's teacher was kind, loving, and knowledgeable. However, she felt compelled to teach phonics because of mandates from the school system and the state that heavily emphasized test scores. Needless to say, these tests included items on phonics. Marilee thus received a heavy dose of phonics instruction. When we questioned this practice in parent-teacher conference, the teacher replied emphatically that if she didn't teach phonics, her pupils would not do well on the tests. The phonics instruction led to confusion for Marilee, and we will give here a few examples observed at home.

SUPER E INSTRUCTION

Marilee received instruction on *Super E*, the name given to the following rule: In certain two-vowel words ending with *e*, the final *e* is not sounded and the first vowel usually represents its long sound. When spelling words with short vowels such as *cap*, Marilee began to spend a great deal of time muttering statements like, "I know you don't use *Super E* because the vowel isn't screaming its name." Moreover, she continued to concentrate on this idea with similar words such as *hat*, *ham*, and *ten* even though she already knew how to spell these words before the instruction. Thus, the *Super E* emphasis caused her to become preoccupied with how to spell words she already knew how to spell, taking attention away from the thoughts and ideas she wanted to express in writing.

Long-vowel instruction confused her because the new knowledge did not fit into her spelling system and her stage of development. She started reciting mnemonic nonsense such as *April Apple*, *Edith Egg*, *Isaiah Indian*, *Opy Octopus*, and *Ulysses Umbrella*. She spelled *mile* as before, *mil*, but proceeded to make strange speeches such as the following : "*M* and *l* aren't vowels and *i* is a vowel. The *i* is like *Isaiah Indian* and *i* is being scrunched by the two consonants *m* and *l*, so *Super E* comes in to save him. He is the rescuer. Hurray for *Super E*." Then she added an *e*. For some time thereafter, she would simply say, "The vowel is screaming its name, so *Super E* comes in to save him." Sometimes she would say, "It doesn't matter if a consonant says its name, it's just when a vowel screams its name that you have to think."

Some observers might say that Marilee profited from the instruction. And, indeed, she did spell *mile* correctly after thinking about *Super E*. Further, she would probably have shown competence on a test measuring such knowledge. However, the time and effort spent on learning this knowledge would have been better spent on actual reading and writing.

As Bussis (1982) points out, the emphasis on "essential" skills takes the place of actual reading and writing in the classroom. Marilee and her classmates would eventually become able to spell *mile* anyway through more indirect means as suggested by Gentry and Henderson (1978) and Kamii and Randazzo (1985).

OTHER VOWEL INSTRUCTION

Instruction about the *y* at the ends of words also created a problem. Marilee said that she did not know much about *y*, but that it was sometimes a vowel. She also said that a word like *fry* had to be spelled differently from *fri* "because the teacher put it on the chalkboard." However, she still felt that *fry* should be *fri*; *fancy* should be *fanse*; *jelly* should be *jele*; *shy* should be *si*; *story* should be *store*; and *happy* should be *hape*. We could see her confusion as she wrote *hape*, finally saying, "A *y* just wouldn't be right to me."

After instruction on the double *o*, she doubled many letters. For example, she said, "*Hook* is spelled *huc*, so it must be *huuc*." In the word *school*, the spelling changed from *scol* to *scool*.

DIGRAPHS AND CONSONANT BLENDS

An area of phonics instruction that seemed to provide the greatest relief for Marilee was digraphs and blends. She had hesitated when trying to write words with *th*, *sh*, and *ch*. Before digraph instruction *bath* was *bah*, *crash* was *cras*, and *thought* was *tot*. Consonant blend instruction gave her the letters to represent sounds that she had been dissatisfied with as she wrote. She started using *br*, *gr*, *sl*, *sw*, and other blends without confusion in her writing.

The observations are in agreement with Henderson (1985), who noted that children who seem to know short vowels learn blends and digraphs quite easily. He pointed out that *sh*, *th*, and *ch* rarely cause difficulty for beginners. Marilee, like other children, learned them quickly, making few errors thereafter.

READING

Like other children, Marilee was aware of environmental print from an early age. For instance, when she first started to talk, she could find Coke signs and would say "Coke." She continued to develop as a reader and was able to read several predictable books before she entered kindergarten.

The same group of people who appreciated her early writing also appreciated her early reading. They listened to her tell about pictures and "read" from memory books that had been read to her repeatedly. After phonics instruction was initiated in kindergarten, she felt compelled to use her "new knowledge" on all words, even words she had read prior to school. She would "c-c-c-c" until she could say the next sound represented in the word. Instead of focusing on meaning, as she had been doing, she tried to "sound out" everything. She labored over words, gave up, and often asked for help. Unfortunately, she stopped relying on her own system of using a combination of initial consonants and context. In summary, it took a while before she abandoned her new phonics information and went back to focusing on meaning.

DISCUSSION AND CONCLUSIONS

We saw that Marilee sometimes used her new information and over-corrected, as in *huuc* for *hook*, and at other times thought about her phonics instruction but rejected the rule taught in favor of her own invented spelling. With the exception of digraphs and consonant blends, the instruction caused confusion and reduced her confidence in her own ability to figure things out. She also began to be preoccupied with the newly acquired phonics information rather than focusing on getting meaning from her reading, or, in the case of writing, focusing on the ideas and thoughts she wanted to express. As a result, reading and writing became less fluent, and the activities less enjoyable. Graves (1978) made a similar observation concerning writing when emphasis is placed on the surface level features of words. He said that teachers' correction of invented spelling discourages many young children from writing words they are not certain about, and this often leads to poor writing and discomfort with it.

We are not against the teaching of sound-symbol correspondence, as children need this information to become literate. What we question is the way this instruction is generally given today based on the erroneous assumptions that (1) children come to school not knowing anything about our system of writing, and (2) they learn to read and write by having isolated bits of phonics information sequentially taught by association.

All children come to school already knowing something about our system of writing (Ferreiro and Teberosky, 1982; Kontos, 1986). They are not passive vessels that remain empty until they go to school; they have already thought about the written squiggles they see on boxes, signs, the television screen, and elsewhere. Marilee happened to be at a relatively high level of development, and she was not permanently harmed by the phonics instruction she received. However, the difficulty and confusion she experienced made us wonder about the frustration and loss of confidence other children must endure, especially if they come from backgrounds that place less emphasis on broad literacy experiences at home. Marilee had already learned that attending to meaning is important in reading and writing. Phonics instruction given to children without this prior knowledge could mislead them completely about what reading and writing are all about.

Let's consider children who are at a lower developmental level in their spelling and may merely juxtapose letters they know when they write. For instance, they may write *LFTO* when asked to write *mother*. Phonics instruction may prevent these children from constructing the system at the next level, the consonantal level (Manning, Long, Manning, and Kamii, 1987). The system the child constructs at the consonantal level consists only of consonants, as can be seen in the child who writes *PNMT* for *punishment*. This level is an important achievement because it represents the first establishment of correspondences between what the child writes and what she utters. It is also an important achievement because the child constructs the next level, called the alphabetic level, out of the consonantal system. At this level, the child uses vowels and consonants and might spell the word *punishment* as *puneshmint*.

Marilee was already at the alphabetic level and learned certain things from instruction, such as digraphs and consonant blends, but did not learn from other rules. She accepted only the elements that she could fit into her natural system. Thus, she learned not by having isolated bits of phonics instruction sequentially taught by association but by constructing a system in a way that made sense to her. This is how she and other children go through one level after another of being "wrong."

Marilee's teacher defended her phonics teaching by saying that phonics instruction was necessary to produce higher test scores. Unfortunately, success or failure in this area is often judged by standardized and/or criterion-referenced tests. As Bussis (1982) suggests, many teachers teach the "essential" skills because these same "essential" skills are measured by tests. Phonics teaching often improves children's test scores, but educators must ask themselves whether their objectives are only to produce higher test scores or to develop literate and intelligent individuals. Too often, children learn to read and write but find these activities unpleasant.

A great deal is now known about children's development of thinking, reading, and writing. Unfortunately, most educators are not aware of this information. Many do not know about the developmental spelling research listed at the beginning of this [chapter], which is more than 10 years old, or Piaget's constructivism, which is more than a half-century old. Many educators, when they become knowledgeable about developmental ideas, often reconsider their ideas about formal phonics instruction, which reflects behaviorism and/or associationism. In this [chapter], we have shown what happened to one learner when her teacher taught formal phonics. Further research is needed on the precise effects of formal phonics instruction if we are to know what kind of phonics instruction will assist the beginning reader and writer.

REFERENCES

Beers, J. W., Beers, C. S., and Grant, K. (1977). The logic behind children's spelling. *Elementary School Journal, 77,* 238–242.
Bissex, G. L. (1980). *GNYS AT WRK.* Cambridge, MA: Harvard University Press.
Bussis, A. M. (1982). Burn it at the casket. *Phi Delta Kappan, 64,* 237–241.
Chall, J. S. (1967). *Learning to read: The great debate.* New York: McGraw-Hill.
Chomsky, C. (1971). Write first, read later. *Childhood Education, 47,* 292–299.
Chomsky, C. (1979). Approaching reading through invented spelling. In L. B. Resnick and P. A. Weaver (Eds.), *Theory and practice of early reading* (pp. 43–65). Hillsdale, NJ: Erlbaum.
Ferreiro, E., and Teberosky, A. (1982). *Literacy before schooling.* Exeter, NH: Heinemann.
Flesch, R. (1965). *Why Johnny can't read.* New York: Harper and Row.
Gentry, J. R., and Henderson, E. H. (1978). Three steps to teaching beginning readers to spell. *The Reading Teacher, 31,* 632–637.
Graves, D. (1978). *Balance the basics: Let them write.* New York: Ford Foundation.
Henderson, E. (1985). *Teaching spelling.* Boston: Houghton Mifflin.
Kamii, C., and Randazzo, M. (1985). Social interaction and invented spelling. *Language Arts, 62,* 124–133.
Kontos, S. (1986). What preschool children know about reading and how they learn it. *Young Children, 42*(1), 58–66.
Manning, M., Long, R., Manning, G., and Kamii, C. (1987, April). *Spelling in kindergarten.* Paper presented at the annual meeting of the American Educational Research Association, Washington, DC.
Read, C. (1971). Preschool children's knowledge of English phonology. *Harvard Educational Review, 41,* 1–34.
Read, C. (1975). *Children's categorization of speech sounds in English.* Research Report No. 14. Urbana, IL: National Council of Teachers of English.
Schickedanz, J. A. (1986). *More than the ABCs: The early stages of reading and writing.* Washington, DC: NAEYC.
Zuttell, J. (1978). Some psycholinguistic perspectives on children's spelling. *Language Arts, 55,* 844–850.

7. READING COMPREHENSION: FROM CARDBOARD KEYS TO MEANINGFUL TEXTS

by Barbara A. Lewis, University of Alabama at Birmingham

Barbara Lewis discusses several aspects of reading comprehension. She uses the analogy of learning to play the piano using cardboard keys that make no music with learning to read using isolated skills activities that make no sense. She also describes several differences between a skills view and a meaning-centered view of reading comprehension. She concludes with a brief description of a visit to a second-grade classroom where students are involved in a variety of meaningful activities.

Many teachers realize the pitfalls of a reading program with meaningless "cardboard key" activities. They are, therefore, putting meaningful texts and practices back into their reading programs.

As I observe students wading through reading comprehension lessons decontexualized from real purposes and real meanings, I am often reminded of my first months of piano lessons. The way in which I began learning about making music is similar in many respects to the way in which students begin learning about making sense of written communication.

When I was seven, my parents, unswayed by the fact that we did not own a piano, decided that it was time for me to take lessons. I don't know if they were convinced by a teacher who needed students that a piano was not absolutely necessary for a beginner, or whether they decided that the positive value of lessons would offset the lack of opportunity for real practice, but, for whatever reason, lessons began. During the first lesson, sitting at the big piano in my teacher's house and learning about the keyboard, middle C, and simple notation, I knew that this was what playing was all about. When it was time for me to leave, however, my teacher surprised me by bringing out a narrow piece of cardboard folded in thirds. When opened, it was a full-size replica of three octaves of a piano keyboard. Everyday, she said, I was to practice lessons on the keyboard, and dutifully I did just that. Each night after supper, I carefully unfolded the keyboard onto the kitchen table and thumped out my lesson. Night after night I thumped away—CC, GG, AA, G—but since there was nothing but silence, I had no way of knowing if I was playing anything that sounded like music. Soon my initial anticipation gave way to frustration. A real piano arrived six months later, just in time.

Every day millions of students are given "cardboard keys" to help them gain meaning from text. Like the cardboard keys, skills-oriented instruction provides practice without purpose, and reading without meaning.

For several decades, reading instruction has been influenced by the notion that reading is a set of skills that can be learned through instruction. This view stems from early studies of the reading process in which word identification and comprehension were named as major components, each divided into numerous subcomponents. Although several studies have identified various reasoning abilities associated with comprehension, no evidence has been found to support the idea that there is a set of skills, or a particular hierarchy of skills, specific to comprehension (Rosenshine 1980).

Nevertheless, many teachers continue to view reading comprehension as a set of separate and independent skills and use materials consistent with this view. Most commercial materials are organized so that skills are sequentially introduced and reinforced from one level to the next. For the most part, instruction of a particular skill is followed by practice in a workbook or on worksheets. The practice exercises consist of isolated, decontextualized sentences, paragraphs, and short passages. In a skills-oriented program, the emphasis of the teacher and the focus of the materials seem to be more on practicing comprehension skills than on comprehending meaningful text. While a skills-oriented view currently dominates reading instruction in the United States, more and more educators are realizing that students' comprehension suffers from such instruction.

Recent research in reading comprehension has revealed that comprehension is a process of constructing meaning. (See Anderson and Pearson 1984; Mason et al. 1984; and Rumelhart 1987, for a comprehensive treatment of a schema-theoretic view of reading comprehension.) In a synthesis of recent research, McNeil (1987) offers the following description of reading comprehension:

It is a process of using one's existing knowledge (schemata) to interpret text in order to construe meaning. Although writers structure texts for their given purposes, readers interpret and arrive at their own construction of what the text means. Comprehension includes understanding the information in the text as well as changing the knowledge used to understand the text in the first place. (p. 1)

According to this view, a reader continually makes inferences about meaning based on prior knowledge. A reciprocal action between the

80

reader and text occurs as the reader gathers clues about meaning. Hypotheses about meaning based on what the reader already knows are accepted or rejected and in turn influence how subsequent meaning is constructed. If readers do not have the necessary background knowledge or for some reason it is not activated, they will not be able to make the relationships necessary for making sense out of text. With adequate background knowledge, readers can construct meaning appropriate to the text by using their knowledge of the world as they read.

The remainder of this chapter provides an account of how one teacher uses practices that support readers' construction of meaning. She is a friend and we frequently talk about her second grade class. Recently she invited me to visit and see firsthand what she had been telling me.

The first thing I noticed as I entered her room was an abundant array of materials that varied in content and complexity. Print was everywhere and was easily accessible for use. A few well-worn "big books" were propped up in a corner, while nearby several shelves were filled with favorite children's books. *Anno's Journey*, *Jumanji*, and an old Mother Goose book stood ready as did other picture books, collections of poetry, and works of fiction. On a table, under a sign announcing "Best of the Best," was a boxed collection of paperbacks. Around the room were texts written by the teacher and the students. Lining the walls was students' work from the week before.

Several different things were going on at the same time; a hum of purposeful activity filled the room as students worked individually, in pairs, and in small groups. By the door, a stack of reference books was sitting on the edge of a platform filled with painted salt-dough mountains, valleys, oceans, and deserts. The class had been studying landforms, and as I watched, a group of students added to their forms tiny cacti, trees, and other adornments they thought necessary. Labels came next, and each mountain and valley was duly noted. Occasionally, students flipped through reference books and collaborated, when necessary, to decide which ideas they wanted to use. On the other side of the room, another group was bringing to a close its study of works by Leo Lionni. Students were writing descriptions of a favorite book and sharing them with each other. I noticed that they went to the books again and again to confirm that "best" book. When finished, they hung their descriptions under the books resting on the chalk tray and took off to do more of their morning work. In the "Question Corner," a few students were reading simple books about sea animals. When finished reading they wrote, but did not answer, three questions about something they wanted to know that the text did not answer. They dropped their questions in a question box to be posed to the whole group later for a general discussion.

81

The teacher moved among the students asking pertinent questions and responding to their work. Eventually, she sensed that it was time for a change of pace and gathered them into a large group to share a new book.

During the morning, the usual disruptions occurred that anyone who has ever been in a second-grade class would expect. The transition from one activity to another did not always go as smoothly as the teacher wanted; nonetheless, many things were happening in this classroom that supported the notion of comprehension as construction of knowledge. One important way was by the range and depth of reading materials available to students. Not only was there quality literature for these second graders, but reference books and simple content area textbooks, as well. Even the writing of their peers served as text as they eagerly read each other's writing. By using these resources continually in this way, students' knowledge of the world will constantly expand. The more they read in a wide variety of areas, the more they will be ready to engage with subsequent texts because of the storehouse of meanings they have constructed.

Comprehension was supported in another way because reading was an integral and natural part of everything else that happened; reading was not relegated to a certain time slot during the day. Students in this class read to construct landforms, read to write, read to question, and read to enjoy. They had real purposes for reading, and as a result comprehension was facilitated. If students want to know, they are sensitive to a loss of meaning when it occurs. They will reread, read more slowly, or perhaps simply ask for help. Giving students purposes for reading encourages them to monitor their own understanding, and prepares the way for the reading of increasingly more difficult texts.

The students I observed were constantly in the process of constructing meaning as they interacted with their peers. The conversations I overheard let me know that these students did not allow each other to get away with mistaken ideas, especially if the misconceptions had a bearing on a group project. Social interaction, then, was another way in which reading for meaning occurred. Students clarified what they knew by testing their ideas against those of others. Understanding of text was refined when they had the opportunity to discuss in depth the stories and books they had read. Through dialogue, they found that sometimes the meaning they had constructed was totally different from that of others. By talking out each other's meanings, their thinking was altered and new constructions arose.

Another factor supporting comprehension was that the reasoning abilities necessary for comprehension were interrelated and reinforced throughout the day. The students I saw were engaged in a variety of activities involving reading and were active processors of print. They did not use "identifying main ideas" for one activity and "recognizing cause and effect" for another. There was an overlap in the many kinds of thinking needed for making meaning. Students had multiple opportunities for inferencing, sequencing, drawing conclusions, predicting, and using other reasoning abilities as they solved real problems. As they worked to create their landforms or descriptions of their favorite books, they used their reasoning abilities to interpret information from the text in terms of their own understanding.

The amount of print, the opportunity to participate in a wide variety of activities related to reading, and social interaction were all important factors in helping the students construct meaning from text. The most important factor of all, of course, was the teacher. Through careful observation, she knew when meaning had broken down and stepped in to offer another book or a helpful hint. Often with just a skillful question, she led students to find the relationships between the text and their own background knowledge. And, by always gently probing their thinking about what they had read, she helped them learn how to become their own searchers after meaning. Through the many ways in which she guided their interactions with print, she set them on the path to understanding.

I conclude this chapter on the same note on which I began. To learn to make music, I was given cardboard keys. Students, likewise, have been given meaningless practice activities with the intention of helping them to improve their reading comprehension. Fortunately, however, reading programs are now changing as cardboard keys are being replaced with meaningful texts.

REFERENCES

Anderson, R. C., and Pearson, P. D. "A Schema-Theoretic View of Basic Processes in Reading Comprehension." In Handbook of Reading Research, edited by P. David Pearson. New York: Longman, 1984.
Mason, J., et al. "A Schematic-Theoretic View of the Reading Process as a Basis for Comprehension." In Comprehension Instruction: Perspectives and Suggestions, edited by G. G. Duffy, L. R. Roehler, and J. Mason. New York: Longman, 1984.
McNeil, J. D. Reading Comprehension: New Directions for Classroom Practice. Glenview, Ill.: Scott, Foresman, 1987.
Rosenshine, B. V. "Skill Hierarchies in Reading Comprehension." In Theoretical Issues in Reading Comprehension, edited by V. J. Spiro, B. C. Bruce, and W. C. Brewer. Hillsdale, N.J.: Lawrence Erlbaum Associates, 1980.
Rumelhart, E. E. "Understanding Understanding." In Understanding Reading Comprehension, edited by J. Flood. Glenview, Ill.: Scott, Foresman, 1987.

8. WHEN WAS 1864? READING COMPREHENSION—MAKING IT WORK

by Maryann Manning, Gary Manning, and Constance Kamii, University of Alabama at Birmingham

Maryann Manning, Gary Manning, and Constance Kamii present the results of an interview with a student after she read from the book, Caddie Woodlawn. *They analyze Roberta's responses, using a constructivist frame-work, which is congruent with the whole-language view. In fact, they see constructivism, Piaget's theory, as the underlying theory for whole language. According to Piaget, knowledge develops as an organized whole. Students' reading comprehension, then, depends on the knowledge they bring to a text. As they read and understand, students modify what they already know. In other words, comprehension is not just the accumulation of bits of information from the outside. Reading is an activity in which students construct meaning; consequently, the texts they read should be whole texts that are meaningful.*

This chapter is reprinted with permission of the publisher Early Years, Inc., Norwalk, CT 06854, from the May 1985 issue of Early Years/K–8.

There are several subtle facets to the fascinating subject of reading comprehension. If you analyze it, what is comprehension really all about? How can you, as a teacher, foster its development?

To answer these questions we will begin with an interview of a bright, middle-class seven-year-old we will call Roberta. She was given the book *Caddie Woodlawn*, and was asked to look at the cover of the book before being asked, "What do you think the book is about?" She responded by saying, "It must be about Indians on a farm and the girl must be Caddie Woodlawn since the name of the book is a girl's name."

She was then asked to read the following introductory paragraph of the book which is, by the way, recommended for middle-grade students:

In 1864 Caddie Woodlawn was eleven, and as wild a little tomboy as ever ran the wood of western Wisconsin. She was the despair of her mother and of her elder sister Clara. But her father watched her with a little shine of pride in his eyes and her brothers accepted her as one of themselves without a question. Indeed, Tom, who was two years older, and Warren, who was two years younger than Caddie, needed Caddie to link them together into an inseparable trio. Together they got in and out of more scrapes and adventures than any one of them could have imagined alone. And in those pioneer days Wisconsin offered plenty of opportunities for adventure to three wide-eyed, red-headed youngsters.

What did Roberta comprehend when she read this paragraph? To find out, she was asked the following questions while being allowed to reread the text as many times as she wanted—

Q: What was the paragraph about?
A: It was about Caddie Woodlawn.

Q: What kind of girl was she?
A: She was a tomboy.

Q: What is a tomboy?
A: A girl who acts like a boy and plays like a boy.

Q: Do you know anything else about the kind of girl she was?
A: No, just that she was a wild one.

Q: Did her mother like her?
A: I don't think so because she must have wanted her to be a lady.

Q: Did her father like her?
A: Yes, because it said he had a twinkle in his eye when he watched her.

Q: Did her sister like her?
A: Yes, sort of.

Q: Did her brothers like her?
A: Yes, they really liked her and must have thought she was like them.

Q: What did she look like?
A: I think she had two braids because it is on the cover and her hair was red.

The answers given by Roberta indicate her understanding of the text to be at a surprisingly high level for a seven-year-old; she brought enough knowledge to the text to assimilate it. She classified the kind of girl Caddie was—a tomboy—and how specific family members related to her. The only difficulty she had was the following: She said her mother did not like her, but her sister sort of liked her. She did not know the word "despair" and was unable to infer what it meant from the paragraph. Distortion of the meaning of the sentence took place at this point because she could not guess what "despair" meant. When children cannot modify their knowledge to infer the meaning of a new word, they often assimilate it to know the knowledge they already have, such as the general knowledge that mothers usually want their daughters to be ladies.

PIAGET

Jean Piaget's theory of knowledge is helpful in understanding comprehension; it states that we organize everything we know with two frameworks: a logico-arithmetical framework (that permits classification of what we know) and a spatio-temporal framework. All events take place in space and time, and adults can situate Caddie Woodlawn in Wisconsin and in 1864. Children, however, have not constructed a spatial framework or a temporal one, and it takes years for them to build these organizations. Likewise, it takes years for them to construct a logical framework such as classification systems of men and women, father and mothers, brothers and sisters, boys, girls, tomboys, etc. An understanding of numbers such as 10, 100, 800, 1000, and 1864 also belongs to the logico-arithmetical framework, and these numbers cannot be understood before nine or ten years of age.

SPATIAL FRAMEWORK

Because the interview up to this point did not reveal Roberta's understanding of where Caddie Woodlawn lived, we continued as follows—

Q: Where did she live?
A: In Wisconsin.

Q: Is that in another country or is it in America?
A: In America—is that right?

Q: Why do you think it is in America?
A: I know Wisconsin is a place in America.

Q: Is it a country?
A: Yes—is it?

Q: Is it a town?
A: No, it's like where we live in Alabama but different.

Q: Is it like where you live?
A: Yes, sort of but not all countries are alike—they have some thing different. If you are born in Wisconsin, you aren't an Alabamian.

Q: Is Wisconsin in the city or in the country?
A: It is in the country because there is a farm in the picture and Caddie must live there.

The above answers reveal that Roberta more or less knew "Wisconsin is in America" and "it is not a town." Although she did not know the word "state," she did know that Wisconsin and Alabama were alike.

86

When she used the word "country" to mean "state," we could see that the problem was a superficial one of merely not knowing the right label for the idea she had.

To explore her knowledge of spatial organization more explicitly, we asked her to show it in a drawing. We drew a circle on a blank sheet of paper to represent Birmingham and asked her to draw Alabama. As can be seen in Figure 1, she drew a circle around Birmingham and labeled it "AL." We then asked her to draw the United States and she drew an even larger circle and labeled it "US." On request, she drew a small circle for Wisconsin in the United States and marked it "WC." Following this, she was asked to think of another place to put on her map, and she selected New Jersey. She drew a little circle in Alabama outside Birmingham to show where New Jersey was located. She continued placing California, Texas, and New York—drawing little circles inside Alabama. When she was asked if New York was a city or state, she said it was city. Interestingly, whenever she drew a circle, she used initials to identify what it represented.

In her map, the part-whole relationships are very accurate as far as Birmingham, Alabama, United States, and Wisconsin are concerned. However, Alabama includes the other states as well as New York City. Classification of states and cities and spatial relationships develop together.

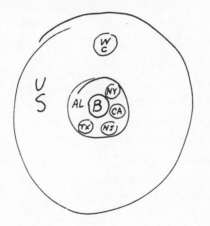

Figure 1

UNDERSTANDING A TIME LINE

To focus on Roberta's understanding of when the story of Caddie Woodlawn took place, we went on with the interview.

Q: How old was she?

87

A: Eleven.

Q: When did she live?
A: In pioneer days.

Q: When was that?
A: When settlers were here.

Q: What were settlers?
A: They were people who decided to settle down and stay.

Q: Where did settlers come from?
A: The north I think because cowboys were there too.

Q: What else do you know about pioneers?
A: Nothing.

Q: What did they ride in?
A: They had carts pulled by horses.

Q: Were there pioneers at the time of the pilgrims?
A: Not all of them but some of them were. Pioneers went on for a long time. Pilgrims and settlers did the same things. Pilgrims went in boats when they came but pioneers went in carts when they settled.

Q: Did pioneers live at the same time as the American Revolution?
A: Yes, there were pioneers then but some of them had to fight.

Q: Did pioneers live at the same time as the Civil War?
A: Yes, but they all wanted a free country.

Q: Do you think this book was at the same time as the Civil War?
A: I don't know if it was in that war or the First or Second World War. I do think that Caddie Woodlawn is dead.

Q: Was it about a hundred years ago?
A: Yes, because maybe she would be a hundred years old now.

Q: Was it 500 years ago?
A: Yes, because it was 1864.

When Roberta answered the question about when Caddie Woodlawn lived, she referred to the pioneer days and not to 1864. She did this because 1864 was meaningless both from the numerical point of view and from the viewpoint of her temporal organization. She was assimilating her new information into her old knowledge as revealed by her statements about pioneers, cowboys, and settlers riding in horse-drawn carts.

For Roberta, the pioneer days and historical events are one big whole that is not differentiated or sequenced in time. Interestingly, she organized history more through classification (the logico-arithmetical framework) than through a temporal framework. For example, she clearly stated that some of the pioneers were settlers who came in horse-drawn carts and some of them were pilgrims who came in boats. She also said that some settlers had to fight wars, but others did not. She thus knew something about the American Revolution, the Civil War, and the two World Wars but organized them in a category without any temporal structure (organization). Whether 1864 was a hundred years ago or 500 years ago could, of course, not be known by her either because seven-year-olds cannot understand place value (Kamii, 1985). Roberta nevertheless revealed her temporal understanding when she said, "I do think Caddie Woodlawn is dead."

In summary, what did Roberta understand about the paragraph? First, her understanding of family relationships was clear. In addition, her spatial organization was quite good in that she knew Alabama and Wisconsin were comparable and were in the United States. However, as revealed by her map, she thought other states such as New Jersey were in Alabama. Locating the time of the story was her weakest area. Nevertheless, she seemed to know it was a long time ago because she was quite sure the young girl, Caddie Woodlawn, had grown old and died.

IMPLICATIONS FOR TEACHING

Teaching reading comprehension is a subject of great debate today. Some reading authorities believe that comprehension consists of a group of segmental skills that can be sequentially taught through classroom games and worksheets and then tested by having students "'bubble'" in spots on answer sheets. In contrast, the psycholinguistic view of reading to which we subscribe suggests that a reader puts meaning into the text, and therefore reading comprehension depends not only on the text but also on the knowledge that the reader brings to it. Piaget's theory helps us understand that this knowledge develops as an organized whole, and that children's knowledge can be assessed by the teacher.

If comprehension depends on the knowledge children bring to a text, it follows that our objective in improving comprehension must be to extend children's knowledge. This is not done by having children accumulate bits of information from the outside, but by allowing them to modify what they already know.

Children who read books they have selected for themselves are more likely to comprehend well because they are interested in the subject, and already have some knowledge about what they are reading. Those who enjoy a particular subject will often read several books on the same or related subjects. For instance, children who enjoy insects will often go from one insect book to another, extending their knowledge of insects. Roberta, the girl we interviewed, was fascinated with nurses. She would probably enjoy books about Florence Nightingale and Clara Barton and these books would also help her put historical events into better relationships.

HELPING STUDENTS IMPROVE

There are many ways in which teachers can help students improve their reading comprehension. The three we will discuss below are: asking good questions, encouraging social interaction, and reading aloud to children—

Asking Good Questions: What is a good question? One answer is that a good question stimulates children to make new relationships and thus construct more knowledge. In the interview with Roberta we started with a general probe. By asking more and more specific questions we found that she did not understand the word "despair." To help her infer its meaning, we might have asked her to guess the meaning of "despair" by focusing on the word "But" in the sentence that follows the statement that Caddie was the despair of her mother ("But her father watched her with a little shine of pride in his eyes, and her brothers accepted her as one of themselves without a question."). We would of course let Roberta keep the text in front of her so she could refer to it when answering.

Questions should be based on an understanding of cognitive development. Asking a seven-year-old if the story of Caddie Woodlawn took place 500 years ago may have been good for our edification, but not for Roberta's education, because she could not even make sense out of the question. However, by fourth grade, children generally can be expected to understand place value better and would probably know that 1485 was before 1620. Temporal relationships are particularly difficult for children to make, as we learned from *The Child's Conception of Time* by Piaget (1946). Therefore, we would not try to teach the meaning of time, 1864, to Roberta.

Explanations are another kind of relationship. Following the reading of the paragraph from *Caddie Woodlawn*, when Roberta said that Caddie's father liked her, we could have asked her why he liked Caddie, the tomboy. We might then have asked her what she thought would happen in the story that would explain the attitudes of Caddie's parents. Focusing in this way should make Roberta more active mentally and prepare her to put her anticipation into relationship with what she will find later in the story. The desirability of predicting what will flow has been advocated by many people. Piaget's theory helps us think more precisely about predictions in terms of a variety of relationships children might make.

Encouraging Social Interaction: An important point we have learned from Piaget is that we cannot make relationships for children; they have to make their own. For example, we might tell a group of seven-year-olds that Roberta thinks Caddie is dead, and ask them if they agree or disagree with that. They may not all agree that Caddie is dead, but they will grapple with different points of view and this exchange of viewpoints will often lead them to think critically and to construct new knowledge by trying to resolve differences of opinion.

Younger children would probably not use other dates to support their arguments, but fourth graders might, as they have a better idea about time. Also, by this age they might have read historical books about the Wright brothers, Robert E. Lee, Abraham Lincoln, Booker T. Washington, Florence Nightingale, and Clara Barton; the books would have added to their general knowledge and would have helped them establish more differentiated and coordinated ideas about time.

We would also help Roberta and her classmates to construct spatial relationships when we ask questions that would stimulate interaction among the members of the class. However, we must be careful not to expect seven-year-olds to think like ten-year-olds. A question we might ask would be, "Is Alabama like Wisconsin?" Some of the students would probably say yes and others no. The teacher should encourage students to argue about and defend their views. A student might suggest going to the map to locate Wisconsin and Alabama. Another student might speak from her/his own experience on a trip. Piaget's (1951) article, "The Development in Children of the Ideas of the Homeland and of Relations with Other Countries," has been helpful to us in understanding how children construct relationships between a country and the towns in it.

Needless to say, helping children build knowledge is not the same thing as giving them "right answers." For instance, we would not try to teach Roberta that New Jersey is not in Alabama unless a natural context presented itself.

Good teachers have always encouraged children to discuss what they read. Piaget (1947) and his collaborators (Perret-Clermont, 1980) have shown that the exchange of viewpoints contributes significantly to children's construction of knowledge, because children think critically when they defend their own ideas while being motivated to resolve differences of opinions.

Reading Orally to Children to Help Them Build General Knowledge: Listening to a teacher read aloud helps children extend their knowledge through books that are of interest to them. Children's literature is rich with well-written books that intrigue children. Earlier we mentioned that children interested in insects might select books to read about insects. Also, we could read aloud other books about insects such as *The Grouchy Ladybug* by Eric Carle. Almost every issue of *Early Years* includes book reviews and interviews with authors, plus numerous columns by Carol Hurst and others that describe books which are very interesting to children and are also accurate in their contents.

When reading aloud to children, we should provide for discussion among the members of the class concerning the different meanings they are constructing as they listen. If Roberta's class were interested in pioneers, reading other books to them such as *Little House in the Big Woods* (Wilder, 1932) would help them build and modify their knowledge about pioneers.

Reading comprehension depends on the general knowledge a reader brings to the text. Knowledge of specific information, such as a historical figure like Florence Nightingale, depends on a logico-arithmetical framework and a spatio-temporal one. These frameworks are constructed by children as they assimilate new information. In other words, children cannot structure temporal sequence in history without any information about historical events to put into temporal relationships, and they cannot structure spatial relationships without information about places such as states, cities, and countries. This is why it's important for them to know about many different subjects because the more information they have, the better frameworks they are likely to develop. Further, the better their frameworks are structured, the better they will comprehend what they read.

The development of one framework depends on the development of another framework. For example, we saw in the temporal part of the interview that Roberta did not have much of an idea about the sequencing of time, but she had a surprisingly clear classification of "settlers," "pilgrims," and "pioneers." A child who has this classification scheme can use it to construct her temporal framework. Roberta also thought that Wisconsin definitely was not a town, and that New York was not a state. A child who has this classification scheme will be able to use it to perfect the spatial organization shown in Figure 1.

To extend reading comprehension, we must realize that children have to construct knowledge for themselves. So when was 1864? We cannot directly teach when 1864 was—only the child can construct it—and that's why it takes a very long time for a child to understand these four printed digits. Roberta—like other children—must construct number, historical events, and other knowledge through her own mental activity.

9. AUTHENTIC LANGUAGE ARTS ACTIVITIES AND THE CONSTRUCTION OF KNOWLEDGE

by Maryann Manning, Gary Manning, and Roberta Long, University of Alabama at Birmingham

In this chapter, Maryann Manning, Gary Manning, and Roberta Long describe a whole-language classroom with students engaged in a study of trees. The study began with an interest in the changing colors of leaves and extended to other areas. The authors describe students' construction of knowledge from a Piagetian perspective, using the study of trees to explain how new knowledge is constructed by exchanging points of view with others and by experiencing, listening, and reading. By engaging in expressive activities such as art, speaking, drama, and writing, the students elaborate and clarify their knowledge about trees.

Whole-language teachers try to make their classroom learning activities congruent with their beliefs about learning. Realizing that students bring prior knowledge and differing amounts of interest to any topic of study, they provide a variety of activities and allow learners to select those activities and topics that are of interest to them.

This chapter is based on the model, "Language Arts and the Construction of Knowledge," which appears in Reading and Writing in the Primary Grades, *by Maryann Murphy Manning, Gary L. Manning, Roberta Long, and Bernice J. Wolfson (Washington, D.C.: National Education Association, 1987).*

Not long ago, we walked into a whole-language fourth-grade classroom we often visit and observed two students enacting a short play they had written. One of the youngsters, playing the part of an oak tree, was arguing with another student who was playing a pine tree. The two were debating over which type of tree helped human beings most. The oak tree said, "Every fall of the year the roads are covered with cars that have come from cities so that people can see the beautiful colors of my relatives and me." The pine tree retorted. "Think about how many pine trees die just so people can have Christmas trees." And on the dialogue went.

The room was alive with the study of trees. During the lunch break, we discussed the tree dramatization with the teacher, Mrs. French, who told us about the events that led up to it. The leaves of a tree in her yard had turned a beautiful golden color, and she brought several of them to school to share with her students. The next day, some of the students brought in red and brown leaves. The different-colored leaves in the classroom sparked students' curiosity. Animatedly they discussed whether the leaves of all trees have the same colors and which colors appear first. Mrs. French encouraged the discussion because she knows that when children exchange points of view they construct new knowledge.

The teacher related some of the conversation as students expressed their ideas about leaves. Jessica said, "Most of the leaves on the ground are brown, so brown must come last." John disagreed. That leaves would change colors from green to yellow to red and finally to brown didn't make sense to him because he had observed a tree in his yard with leaves that turned from green to yellow and a tree next to it with leaves that turned from green to red.

When we returned to Mrs. French's classroom, walking around the room and interacting with students, we became increasingly aware of the depth and breadth of this unit of study on trees. Some students, for example, were compiling statistics about trees; others were engaged in reading about them. A variety of activities was going on, as the teacher had encouraged students to explore the study of trees in ways that were meaningful to them.

As we observed the students, we thought about how much more meaningful these activities were than those we see in some other classrooms. When students plod through a language textbook, write letters to fictitious people, or read an uninteresting story from a basal reader, little excitement about learning is evident. In such classrooms there is no link to the daily life experienced by students—hence, little relevance. To make classroom activities relevant is not easy. As Mrs. French confided to us: "There are so many students with different backgrounds, interests, and academic abilities that it is difficult to make all activities relevant all the time for all the students." Still, she never loses sight of her ultimate goal of making learning meaningful to specific students in a specific place at a specific time. She allows students to select their own topics for study and explore them in ways that are meaningful to them. For reading, students select their own books and confer with the teacher about the books read. They select ways—puppet plays, dioramas, and dramatizations—to share selected books with classmates. In writing, students select their own topics and write in different genres. As Mrs. French implements the writing program in her classroom, she uses the ideas of Donald Graves and Lucy Calkins (see Chapters 17 and 21). In short, she helps students construct knowledge. Let's look at how she does this in more detail.

According to Piagetian theory, students construct new knowledge by exchanging points of view with others, including peers and teachers; they also construct new knowledge through experiencing, listening, and reading. The students in Mrs. French's class were constructing new knowledge about leaves by debating their colors, reading books about trees, and examining real leaves and trees. Knowing how children construct knowledge, Mrs. French encourages her students to interact with one another and to engage in a variety of activities related to a specific topic.

In addition to having students interact with one another and exchange different points of view, Mrs. French also asks questions that help them think more clearly about certain topics. For instance, at one point she asked, "What happens when there is a huge forest fire such as the one that occurred in 1988 in Yellowstone National Park?" This question generated much discussion and caused students to think about a number of issues, such as animal life, the environment, and the loss of jobs. Following the discussion, several students explored the issue of forest fires by reading magazines and books. How different this question is from questions at the end of social studies chapters, for which students must find answers in the text. This question was not an arbitrary one, outside the context of the study and interest in trees. The teacher was the only adult who could make such a decision because she knew the interests of her students at that time, knew what they knew, and knew when and what kind of question to ask. A textbook publisher far removed from a classroom is not able to make such decisions.

On a later visit, Mrs. French told us that her class had recently taken a field trip to the city's botanical gardens. Students had a wonderful time looking at the name plates on the trees and comparing different varieties. They related this information to the knowledge they had gained about trees from their intensive study in the classroom. Thus the field trip became another source of information for them as they constructed more knowledge about trees.

At the beginning of the chapter we mentioned the two students engaging in a dramatization about trees. Through such activities as art, movement, music, speaking, drama, and writing, students elaborate and clarify their knowledge. Mrs. French realizes the importance of such expression and communication and ensures that these activities are available for her students. On a recent visit to her classroom, we saw the results of some of these forms of student expression—beautiful collages made from leaves of different colors, original poems about trees as well as a display of poems by famous poets, written reports about various facets of the tree study compiled by students. The room was rich with the results of students' activities.

Mrs. French does much more than theme and study units as she provides students with opportunities that aid in their construction of knowledge. The following pages describe some other ways she gives students meaningful learning experiences.

Solving Classroom Problems

Problems arise on a regular basis in most classrooms; Mrs. French capitalizes on these problems, involving students in the solutions. For example, when she was asked to submit a class book to the media center for open house, she asked students to help her comply with the request. Teacher and students noted that they had no class book and discussed ways they could comply with the request. Students worked out the solution and cooperated to complete a class book. As with adults, students who are involved in making a decision have a personal stake in its effective implementation. Personal involvement makes learning and doing authentic and meaningful.

Extensions of Classroom Activities of Interest

It is important for teachers to extend selected activities in which students are interested in order to add more depth and understanding to the areas of interest. For example, when Mrs. French's students saw a marionette company perform *Cinderella*, they became interested in the workings of marionettes and wanted to study about them. Consequently, the teacher read aloud to the class Katherine Paterson's *Master Puppeteer*. At the same time, she told students about the author's interest in puppeteers that led to her writing the book.

Of course, the interest in marionettes led to other activities. Students constructed marionettes, wrote and performed plays using them, and composed and sang songs using them. Once an interest is sparked, there is no limit to the number of extending activities with an imaginative teacher like Mrs. French. One idea leads to another and the teacher draws heavily upon an inexhaustible source of ideas—the students themselves.

Expressing Concern for Others

In any community problems are encountered by members of the group and their families and friends. On special occasions there is a need to express concern or support or appreciation. Teachers who want to make their activities authentic for students are constantly sensitive to these areas and make their classrooms more caring and human places. For example, Mrs. French's students wrote thank-you notes to the school custodian after he installed hooks on a classroom wall and stretched wire across the wall so that they could display their work. This provided an opportunity for students to engage in a meaningful writing activity that was important to them and appreciated by the custodian. In another instance, when a classmate's mother had surgery the members of the class decided to write get-well cards to her; some made gifts to send her. Such activities provide opportunities for students to elaborate and clarify knowledge in ways that have personal meaning for them. At the same time, as these two examples indicate, students show their concern and appreciation to others.

Studying Topics of Interest

Teachers can take advantage of an event that interests all students. As these topics emerge, effective teachers capitalize on those interests. When the Challenger disaster occurred, Mrs. French was sensitive to the concerns of her students regarding this tragedy. Teacher and students engaged in a study of the event that led to collecting pictures and articles from newspapers that described how the families coped with the loss of their loved ones. In addition to the personal issues that helped students cope with their own feelings, the class engaged in a study of NASA and America's space program. Teacher and students used several sources of information for their study and they expressed their ideas and feelings in a variety of ways. Through judicious questioning and interaction with her students, the teacher led a meaningful and helpful study of the tragedy.

CONCLUSION

In summary, it is important for teachers to be concerned about authentic learning activities. Informed teachers like Mrs. French know that students construct their own knowledge and that the language arts play a central role in this process. Students bring differing amounts of prior knowledge and interest to any topic of study. Thus, informed teachers know that they must provide a variety of classroom activities and allow students to select and explore topics of interest to them. Although it may not always be possible to do this with all students at all points during the day, wise teachers value the importance of such self-selection and subsequent exploration and provide for it as much as possible.

10. EARLY SPELLING DEVELOPMENT: WHAT WE KNOW AND WHAT WE DO

by Gary Manning and Maryann Manning

Gary Manning and Maryann Manning briefly review the developmental spelling research, pointing out the gap between what we know and what we do in spelling programs in the schools. Their conclusions—a number of efforts need to be made on several fronts in order to bring about positive improvements. The chapter includes two editorial comments about spelling: one written by a member of a newspaper editorial staff, the other a response by the authors. Both pieces deal with the recommendation made by an assistant superintendent in a large urban school system that first graders not be retained because of poor spelling test scores. The school official based her recommendation on recent developmental spelling research and shared some of those ideas in her presentation to the board of education. The editorial opposing the recommendation reveals a significant lack of understanding about the issue. The authors' letter supporting the assistant superintendent explains the need to base educational decisions about spelling instruction on sound scientific theory and research. The story has a positive ending—the board decided to stop using a spelling test as a criterion for promotion or retention of first graders.

A large amount of knowledge now exists concerning early spelling development. Many researchers—including Beers, Beers, and Grant (1977); Bissex (1980); Chomsky (1971, 1979); Gentry and Henderson (1978); Read (1971, 1975); and Zuttell (1978)—have shown how young students develop to successively higher levels of spelling. In addition to the work just cited, which has been conducted in English, studies by Ferreiro and Teberosky (1982) conducted in Spanish provided further insights into how young students develop as spellers. In their studies of young Spanish-speaking students' written language development, these researchers used a constructivist framework. After attending a seminar several years ago in which Ferreiro indicated that she was not aware of any constructivist studies of spelling conducted in the English language, we set out to study young students' spelling development using such a framework. With Roberta Long, we were guided in our efforts by two Piagetian scholars, Constance Kamii of the University of Alabama at Birmingham and Hermina Sinclair of the University of Geneva. The results of our study (Manning, Long, Manning, and Kamii, 1987) also show that spelling is a developmental process, with students going through one level after another of being "wrong."

A large gap exists, however, between what is known about young students' spelling development and how spelling is taught and assessed. Informed educators know the research, but are often in a minority or are not in a position to influence school spelling programs. Test manufacturers, on the other hand, are in a position to influence educational programs because many school systems are eager to modify instruction in order to achieve higher test scores. A recent experience was rather shocking to us. When we contacted a large testing company that publishes a subtest for assessing first graders' spelling ability, we were told by persons in charge of that section of the test that they were not aware of the developmental spelling research. When asked to send them material about these recent studies, we complied quickly but without much confidence that it would make any difference in the near future. Unfortunately, some teachers teach in ways that prepare students for tests. If correct spelling is the only response valued on a test, then many first grade teachers are going to focus on correct spelling in their instruction rather than on helping young students develop a coherent system of how English spelling works.

Educators sometimes find it difficult to change their instructional practices to reflect recent theory and to make use of recent research. Recently Ruth Strong, assistant superintendent of the Birmingham City Schools, asked the board of education to revise the promotion/retention guidelines so that first graders would no longer be retained for failing spelling as measured by an achievement test. She had noted that many first graders were being retained because they failed the spelling section of the test. Since Dr. Strong was aware of the developmental spelling research, she knew students were being retained inappropriately. Following the board meeting at which she made her recommendation, an editorial comment opposing the recommendation appeared in the local newspaper (*Birmingham News* 1987). (See Figure 1.) Certainly, the editor had a right to an opinion, but educational decisions must be based on more than opinion. A review of the remarks in the editorial shows a lack of understanding about how young students learn and develop as spellers, as well as a lack of knowledge about the scientific spelling research that has been conducted in the past two decades. The important question to ask is, Should we base our spelling practices and assessments on opinion only or on sound research?

In response to the editorial, we wrote a letter to the editor (Manning and Manning, 1987). This letter (see Figure 2) explains the need to base educational efforts on scientific theory rather than on personal opinion.

Figure 1
Spelling Should Stay*

The Birmingham Board of Education should take a hard look at recent proposals designed to take some of the pressure for promotion off first-graders. That's especially true of the idea that they shouldn't be required to pass spelling in order to move up.

Maybe requiring first-graders to pass the Birmingham Essential Skills Test (BEST) in addition to their classwork before being promoted is a little much. The board is right to consider letting first-graders be excused. The BEST exam, along with the Stanford Achievement Test, would still be given to help teachers evaluate students' progress.

The proposal to let kids who pass mathematics and reading but fail spelling be promoted is more questionable.

Dr. Ruth Strong, assistant superintendent for the Division of Curriculum and Instruction, explained it to the board by saying that first-graders are encouraged to "write what they think," so their ability to express themselves is not bothered by a concern to spell each word correctly.

It is not fair to require students to master the mechanics of spelling when they are being encouraged to spell creatively, she said, and such inventive spelling does not hurt their ability to learn to spell correctly later.

She also pointed out that of the 251 students in grades 1-8 who last year failed only because of spelling, 53 percent were first-graders.

We have some doubts about the logic of saying that because some students have difficulty passing a requirement, it ought not be required. We have no doubts at all about the value of learning the importance of correct spelling, even at the first-grade level. It gives one the attention to detail and concern for accuracy that will serve any student well throughout his school years.

Before someone can learn to write well creatively, he first has to learn to write correctly. You can't create fine music without first learning how to play the notes.

Given our choice, we'd just as soon see kids required to spell correctly, rather than encouraged to spell "inventively."

*The Birmingham News, July 27, 1987, p. 12A. Copyright © 1987, The Birmingham News. Reprinted with permission.

It compares oral language development and written language development, noting their similarity. Most parents, for example, realize intuitively that by accepting and encouraging early speaking attempts they enable their children to develop to higher levels of oral language. Accordingly, teachers and parents who accept and encourage students' early spelling attempts will enable them to develop to higher levels of spelling. The letter emphasizes the developmental nature of spelling and lists several levels: pictures and scribbles; letter strings; consonantal, alphabetic, and correct spelling.

If spelling programs for students are to be improved, educators must modify their practices to reflect the knowledge that is available as a result

Figure 2.
Let's Base Our Education Efforts on Science*

We commend the Birmingham Board of Education for considering a proposal to revise promotion regulations so that first-graders will no longer be retained for failing spelling as measured by an achievement test.

Dr. Ruth Strong, assistant superintendent for the Division of Curriculum and Instruction, wisely encouraged the board to revise the regulations, saying first-graders "invent" spelling. "Invented" spelling is a scientific fact known by informed educators throughout the world.

The board is not considering lower standards. For too long, policies such as the one to retain first-graders based on an ability to spell as measured by an achievement test have been formulated by well-meaning politicians, board members, news media and others who have not used scientific theory to make their decisions.

This sound policy change affords an opportunity for teachers to increase spelling ability in meaningful contexts.

Let's think about oral language development of young children for a moment. Parents accept and encourage the early speaking attempts of their young children. For instance, they respond to a young child's unclear utterances for a glass of water with a glass of water even though the sound uttered may not resemble the word water.

They don't reinforce poor speaking by accepting and encouraging these early attempts. On the contrary, their actions enable children to develop to higher and higher levels of oral language.

A comparison can be made between oral language development and spelling development. Just as parents accept young children's early speech, informed teachers and parents accept young children's early spelling. They know children will develop to higher levels in their spelling, if given written language opportunities.

Poor spelling is not reinforced. In fact, these parents and teachers realize frequent and meaningful practice with reading and writing, frequent and meaningful interaction with other readers and writers, and appropriate spelling instruction in the process of writing will enable children to develop rather quickly to higher levels of spelling competence.

The medical profession and many others base their practices in scientific theory. It's time for the education profession to do the same.

Spelling researchers have shown that spelling is a developmental process and have identified several levels. Initially, children draw pictures and scribble as they represent what they think. In later development, the letter string level, they write letters of the alphabet. They first make a string of letters with no sound-symbol correspondence which often varies in length depending on the word they attempt to write.

For example, in one of our research studies, a child wrote a string of 15 letters when he attempted to write the word "horse" because a horse is big. On the other hand, he wrote only two letters for the word "mouse" because a mouse is small.

At a higher level, young children continue to write letter strings, however, the strings have a minimum and maximum length. Children at this level usually think words must have at least three letters and no more than seven. At the next higher level of development, the consonantal level, children "'invent'' spelling or represent the consonant sounds of words with the appropriate consonant letters. The word cement might be written "smt" or "cmt" and vacation might be spelled "'vksn.''

As children continue to develop to a higher level, the alphabetic level, vowels appear and cement might be written "cemnt" or vacation spelled "vakashn." The highest level in spelling development is conventional or correct spelling which is the ultimate goal for spellers.

Insisting that first-graders spell conventionally when it makes no sense to them often causes confusion about written language. It may also undermine their confidence as writers and interfere with future language learning.

We are optimistic that Birmingham and other enlightened boards of education will form policies about spelling instruction and assessment based on sound research. Children's spelling should improve as a result of such policies.

Gary and Maryann Manning,
School of Education,
University of Alabama
at Birmingham.

of recent research and sound theory about literacy. Educators have a further responsibility to take a more active role in making necessary changes in assessment procedures and published spelling programs. Without question, the gap between what we know and what we do should be closed, or at least narrowed. Furthermore, as teachers and administrators attempt to make improvements in their spelling instructional programs, they must be encouraged and supported.

Spelling competence will not suffer because of the change in policy. In fact, as we stated in our response to the editorial, "frequent and meaningful practice with reading and writing, frequent and meaningful interaction with other readers and writers, and appropriate spelling instruction in the process of writing will enable children to develop . . . to higher levels of spelling competence." The debate is not whether or not to teach spelling; rather, it is how and when to teach spelling.

We conclude with good news. The Birmingham Board of Education acted positively on Dr. Strong's recommendation. First graders in the Birmingham City Schools are no longer retained because of the results of a spelling test. These students are the real beneficiaries of such a wise decision. Let us all continue to do everything we can to support such actions. Let's base our educational efforts on scientific theory.

REFERENCES

Beers, J. W.; Beers, C. S.; and Grant, K. "The Logic Behind Children's Spelling." *Elementary School Journal* 77 (1980): 238–42.
Birmingham News. "Spelling Should Stay." Editorial, July 27, 1987, p. 12A.

Bissex, G. *GYNS AT WRK: A Child Learns to Write and Read.* Cambridge, Mass.: Harvard University Press, 1980.

Chomsky, C. "Write First, Read Later." *Childhood Education* (1971): 292–99.

Chomsky, C. "Approaching Reading Through Invented Spelling." In *Theory and Practice of Early Reading*, edited by L. B. Resnick and P. A. Weaver, pp. 43–45. Hillsdale, N.J.: Erlbaum, 1979.

Ferreiro, E., and Teberosky, A. *Literacy Before Schooling.* Exeter, N.H.: Heinemann, 1982.

Gentry, J. R., and Henderson, E. H. "Three Steps to Teaching Beginning Readers to Spell." *Reading Teacher* 31 (1978): 632–37.

Manning, G., and Manning M. "Let's Base Our Education Efforts on Science." Letter to the editor, *Birmingham News*, July 29, 1987, p. 11A.

Manning, M.; Long, R.; Manning, G.; and Kamii, C. "Spelling in Kindergarten." Paper presented at the annual meeting of the American Educational Research Association, Washington, D.C., April 1987.

Read, C. "Preschool Children's Knowledge of English Phonology." *Harvard Educational Review* 41 (1971): 1–34.

Read, C. *Children's Categorization of Speech Sounds in English.* Research Report No. 14. Urbana, Ill.: National Council of Teachers of English, 1975.

Zuttell, J. "Some Psycholinguistic Perspectives on Children's Spelling." *Language Arts* 55 (1978): 844–50.

11. SOCIAL INTERACTION AND INVENTED SPELLING

by Constance Kamii, University of Alabama at Birmingham;
and Marie Randazzo, University of Illinois at Chicago

Constance Kamii and Marie Randazzo discuss the importance of social interaction in the construction of knowledge, specifically as it relates to spelling development. First, they explain how students learn through exchanging points of view with others. As the authors observe, "The construction of knowledge is facilitated when a child tries to put his knowledge into relationship with ideas that are at a similar level." Learning to spell involves social knowledge because the ways in which words are spelled are arbitrary conventions established and transmitted by people. According to Kamii and Randazzo, logical thinking is also necessary to acquire the skill as each person constructs knowledge about spelling from within "by putting things into relationships." The chapter also includes classroom observations of social interaction and invented spelling. Both teachers involved in the study foster student autonomy.

This chapter appeared in Language Arts, *vol. 62 (February 1985): 124-33. © 1985 by the National Council of Teachers of English. Reprinted with permission.*

The value of invented spelling has become widely recognized by psycholinguists in recent years (Read 1971, 1975; Chomsky 1971, 1979; Henderson and Beers 1980), and some teachers have been encouraging it daily in their classrooms (Giacobbe 1981; Hauser 1982; Milz 1980). These teachers understand the importance of not correcting invented spelling because errors are a necessary part of development, and corrections stifle children's confidence and desire to write.

Advocates of invented spelling unanimously agree that children's errors are part of their effort to build a coherent system of writing, and that these errors are progressively corrected by children themselves. But teachers feel the need to do more than encourage children to write. "What can I do next now that my children are writing?" they ask. Below is what one teacher did:

1. The children were expected to write at least three times per week.
2. A teacher-led group discussion (small or large group) on the writing topic almost always preceded independent writing.

3. The teacher circulated around the room *as the children were writing*, answering and asking questions, listening to children read, reading over their shoulders, and generally being involved with the students in the writing process.
4. The children's writing was shared in some way, whether it was put on the bulletin board, typed and made into a book, or read aloud to the class after lunch (Lancaster, Nelson, and Morris 1982, p. 911).

The procedures cited above were derived from the teacher's intuition about good teaching. We think teachers can go farther than the individual conferences and "sharing" reported in the above quote. Our reason for saying this is that Piaget's theory (1932, 1947, 1948) and recent research based on it (Perret-Clermont 1980; Doise and Mugny 1981) have demonstrated the importance of social interaction for the construction of knowledge. According to him, children construct knowledge by modifying their previous ideas, rather than by accumulating new bits transmitted from the outside, and the exchange of ideas among peers stimulates such modification.

WHY SOCIAL INTERACTION IS SO IMPORTANT

Piaget (1947) more specifically stated that knowledge is constructed through the differentiation and coordination of points of view, or relationships. "The level of water is higher in A, but A is narrower than B" is an example of a point of view, or relationship, that is more differentiated than "A has more than B." "The water that is now in B was initially in A" and "nothing was added or taken away in the process" are also relationships created by the child. A nonconserver can make each one of these relationships *successively*, but he cannot coordinate them into a *simultaneous* whole. When he becomes able to coordinate, or "group," them into a simultaneous whole, he becomes able to interpret the empirical information differently and conserves the quantity of liquid that is poured into B.

While the above "grouping" happens *within the individual*, this coordination can be stimulated when *different individuals* argue from different points of view and are motivated to resolve the conflict. By watching children argue, we become convinced that they are mentally very active in these situations, thinking hard to resolve the socio-cognitive conflict. The exchange of ideas among children is better than an exchange with an adult because children have points of view that are more or less at the same level. The construction of knowledge is facilitated when a child tries to put his knowledge into relationship with ideas that are at a similar level.

105

The pedagogical principles that can be drawn from the importance of social interaction are:

1. Encourage children to exchange points of view critically among themselves and
2. Reduce adult power and omniscience as much as possible, in order to encourage the exchange of viewpoints among children.

Reducing adult power and omniscience does not imply that the teacher must cease to give information. It means that the teacher must present ideas as one of the alternatives to be considered, just like any other idea offered by any other member of the class. When the teacher is neither omniscient or omnipotent, children are free to accept or reject her ideas. When they are thus free to accept the teacher's idea only if it makes sense to them, they can modify their own knowledge from within. When, on the other hand, they are not free to reject the teacher's suggestion, they can only submit to her authority and recite the "right" answer she wants.

Let us return to the last two of the four procedures cited at the beginning of this [chapter] from Lancaster, Nelson, and Morris (1982). We think that in this perspective of encouraging children to write with invented spelling, peer interaction is unfortunately missing. We think the exchange of ideas about invented spelling is desirable for two specific reasons: (1) it encourages children to *give* information in response to a request from a peer and (2) it encourages them to *evaluate* each other's ideas.

Giving information in response to another child's request is very different from giving information to a teacher. In the latter situation, the child knows that the teacher already knows the answer and that she asks questions to find out whether or not he knows the correct answer. This situation does not encourage the construction of higher-level relationships out of children's own autonomous thinking, since the "right" answer is predetermined. When no one claims to know all the answers, by contrast, children are motivated to contribute hypotheses by mobilizing the totality of their knowledge. Children thus have to think much harder and more honestly in this situation than when they answer a teacher's question.

When children have to evaluate each other's hypotheses to decide whether or not to accept them, they also have to think hard and critically and come to their own conclusions. By thus putting other ideas critically into relationship with everything they know, they have the possibility of constructing higher-level hypotheses of their own accord. In the traditional right-answer approach, by contrast, the responsibility of evaluating an answer belongs to the teacher.

SPELLING AND SOCIAL INTERACTION

Spelling belongs to social (conventional) knowledge, which is full of arbitrary bits of information. For example, there is no physical or logical reason why "cucumber" should not be spelled "kukmbr" or some other way if everybody agreed. Although social knowledge requires input from people, it, too, is *constructed* by each child from within by putting things into relationships, rather than by being absorbed or internalized directly from the environment (Furth 1980). As far as reading or writing is concerned, the constructive process was unearthed convincingly by Ferreiro and Teberosky (1982). Their research showed that, in spite of the specific arbitrary elements involved, writing is learned by the construction of a system through the children's quest for coherence.

Other classroom research conducted by Teberosky (1982) in Barcelona focused specifically on the spelling of kindergarten children writing in small groups. She found that, at an advanced level, children write with the knowledge that a conventionally accepted model exists, and that they must approximate this model. The results these children produce tend to conform not only the the child's intent but also to the social model that is intelligible to others. At this point, writing becomes a communicative act. At early stages, however, the writer's intention is all that matters. The function of early writing is related only to the point of view of the writer, and the need to write is not communicative in its intent or its result. In between the beginning level and the advanced level, children first try to achieve coherence between their intent and the results of their spelling and then to achieve interindividual agreement.

Teberosky analyzed the kindergarten children's interaction during writing activities and found three levels of interaction.

1. Independent writing, in which there are some interactions during the constructive process, but everyone essentially writes in his or her own way.
2. Collaboration, which includes (a) the children's possession of more information, (b) requests for information, (c) the volunteering of information not requested.
3. Confrontation about results, in which the characteristics of the previous level continue to exist, but in which conflicts about results appear in addition.

AN EXPERIMENT IN CHICAGO, ILLINOIS

Inspired by Teberosky's article, I (the second author) decided to encourage social interaction about invented spelling. Some of the children in my classroom of five and six year olds were already inventing spellings by themselves. "FAER STN" (Fire Station) and "PLC" (Police) were common signs that they had taped to their large block buildings to identify themselves in their play.

My coteacher and I began by trying an activity which formed the basis of Teberosky's activity involving names of animals or children they could see. The attempt failed completely because our children were not interested at all in this idea. We, therefore, decided that any writing activity we introduced should come out of the things the children were doing in the room. The first opportunity came when we made our Thanksgiving soup. Each child had brought a vegetable the day before Thanksgiving to put in the soup. (They were thrilled to do this.) At group time, I clipped a large piece of paper to an easel and suggested that we make a list of all the things we had put into the soup. Everyone agreed enthusiastically this time. I chose a child to start because she had been engaging in a great deal of invented spelling, often with the help of a playmate.

She began sounding out "cucumber," the ingredient she had brought. She said, "*cu-cu*, a 'Q.'" A few children began yelling, "No! Not 'Q,' 'K!'" She thought a moment and then wrote "KU." Her friend said, "'K' again." She began to sound out the word some more saying "*uh-uh-uh*." She wrote an "A" after "KUK." Finally, she said, "*ber-ber-ber*," and there was a chime of "B!" Some children yelled, "Now, 'R.'" Someone protested saying, "No, 'E.'" The result was "KUKABER."

The above process continued in similar fashion until everyone had written the vegetable he had added to the soup. Some children participated in the spelling of every word while others took part only when it was their turn to write. Some children ignored the information others gave and wrote their own version. The final results included some duplicate items and varied considerably in their degree of resemblance to conventional spelling: "SRE" and "SUDEHEFBI" (celery), "KARAT" and "KAREGH" (carrot), "BENES" (beans), "KORN" (corn), "TAMTNO" (tomato), "KELBAOOT" (cauliflower), "MOIEFOE" (parsnip), "PTAVO"(potato), and "NLLYLNE" (onion). The two children who had duplicate vegetables (celery and carrot) were not at all concerned about the consistency of their spelling and ignored the protests of those who argued that they should be the same.

I created the next opportunity by bringing pictures of animals for five children who said they would like to write the names of the animals. Each child used a pencil and sheet of paper, and the outcome was disappointing because one child emerged as the authority. He started sounding out the words and spelling them aloud. The other four copied from his paper or wrote the letters as he said them. When he decided to indicate the end of a word by drawing a vertical line at the end (|), all the other children did the same on their papers. I was very surprised by this, as I had felt that all the children were at an equal or higher level of writing than he. They did not argue with him at all—not even about a single letter!

A third example is from group time on another day. My coteacher and I suggested that the children might want to make the house corner into a place other than a house and invited them to make a list of their ideas. We used the easel again and, to prevent the activity from going on too long, we asked the children to write only the ideas that had not been written. Two of the suggestions made were a store and a laundromat.

Store. EL wrote "S" immediately and asked AL what came next. AL began sounding out, "*st-st-st*" and said, "T." EL wrote "ST." ID complained, "But that's not a 'T,' that's an 'X.'" TS said, "Yes, it's a 'T,' see? (pointing to the 'T' in the alphabet on the wall)." JA then yelled out, "Now, 'O' and then 'R!'" EL accepted this suggestion and wrote "STOR." When I asked, "Then what?" JA replied, "That's all!" EL agreed and said, "That's it, it says 'store.'" AN, who knew how to read, said "E," but JA retorted, "No, there's no 'E' in it." EL looked puzzled and then very slowly added an "E" at the end. Reading the result, JR announced, "Now, it says 'story.'"

Laundromat. NA asked, "How does it start?" as she got up to write. JA began sounding it out saying, "*la-la-la*. . . 'L.'" AL said, "And then 'O.'" JA disagreed: "*ah-ah-ah*, 'A,' not 'O!'" NA wrote "LAOD." AL exclaimed, "I have an idea! Let's get the book about the bear in the laundromat and see how to spell it!" Everyone, however, continued sounding out "laundromat" and ignored her suggestion. NA asked DA what came next, and the reply was: "I think 'E.'" NA wrote "LAODRE," but went on to declare, "This 'E' is wrong, I have to start over." She rewrote "LAODRE"(!) and announced, "I'm up to the 'E!'" Everyone started yelling different letters, so she said, "I want just EL to tell me!" EL offered "G." NA wrote it and went on to ask, "Then what?" JR obliged with "'H,' and that's it!" The final result was LAODREGH."

In both of the above examples the writers repeatedly asked what letter came next. EL was very thoughtful about the information she received concerning "store" and evaluated it before writing. NA, on the other hand, wrote down all the suggested letters and put in her own whenever she thought it belonged. Though "store" turned out to be the conventional form, it is obvious that most of the children felt this was not the right way to spell it. Most of them would have agreed that "STOR" was correct, but since they knew AN could read, they did not want to contradict him, EL reluctantly added the "E," but JR did not hesitate to say that he remained unconvinced.

AN EXPERIMENT IN SELMA, ALABAMA

A first grade teacher in Selma, Alabama, had been encouraging children to write with invented spelling for about a month. One day, after reading a translation of Teberosky's article, she decided to add social interaction to invented spelling. She stated that the result was "fantastic." She did not know that the children were capable of the kinds of responses they gave. They evaluated not only each other's spelling but also their punctuation, capitalization, and grammar, and even suggested the use of a dictionary for the first time.

Since George Washington's birthday was approaching, the class had been discussing [his] life, including the chopping down of his father's cherry tree. Initially the teacher asked the children to help her spell the word "honesty." After much discussion and a vote of agreement, the children came up with "ounesty." The teacher said she would leave this word on the board and that she wanted the children to think about what they thought the word meant, since they would all be talking about honesty during the week. Below are examples of children's remarks. In each case, one of five children went to the board to write with the help of the other members of the group. When the small group was finished writing, the teacher involved the entire class and asked for their reactions.

The first example illustrates a discussion about spelling. Three suggestions were made to change "always" in the following sentence:

George Washington all
wast told the trueth

The three ideas offered were: "waes," "waest," and "waestd." By majority vote, the group decided on "waes."

The second group had written:

Ounesty—
tell the truof
dno't tell a stoy
if you do sothing tell
your MoM.

Someone said that a period was necessary after "stoy," and someone else added that "if" then had to be written with "a big 'I.'"

The following example led to a discussion about grammar:

George Washington
tell the trueth when
He cheppt down his
fothers chre tree

One person pointed out that "tell" had to be changed to "told," and the others agreed.

110

When the group could not decide on how to write "trabl" in the following sentence, someone suggested getting a dictionary and looking it up:

If you tell a lie
youll get in trabl.

The teacher asked how the children were going to find the word they wanted to look up in the dictionary, and they figured this out, too, by exchanging ideas among themselves.

On Friday, the teacher decided to leave the last group's product on the board for further discussion on Monday. On Monday, the class found the following on the board: (The numbers are to assist the reader with the order of the discussion.)

when
(13)
you tell the truth

it mis you are onesty.
  (3)   (4)
You shood nevr tell a story
     (6)   (12)
Uf you Do Tell a Story
(2)   (9)(10)(11)(7)
somethig will hoppen to you
   (8)   (5)   (1)

The teacher asked the class "to read this aloud to see if there is anything we want to change in it."

The first idea offered was to put a period at the end (shown by the number "1").

The second suggestion was to change "Uf" to "If."

The third dissatisfaction expressed concerned "mis" (means). Someone said, "We should vote," and someone else retorted, "No, we should look it up in the dictionary." When they finally found "mean" in the dictionary, they decided that this was the wrong word because the first example given was "The boy was *mean* to his dog." To make a long story short, the final alternatives were "meen's" and "means," and the vote was ten to three in favor of the second choice.

The teacher then suggested reading it again. At the end of the first sentence, one child stated that the "y" in "onesty" (4) should be omitted. Someone then declared that the way to spell "honest" was "ounest" and got more votes than "onest."

The teacher led the class to finish reading "the whole thing." When the class got to the end, one child said "hoppen" should be written with an "a."

111

The class again reread the whole thing at the teacher's suggestion, and someone pointed out that "shood" should be changed to "shud." This idea was voted down when somebody else insisted that "oo" said $\overline{oo}$.

The teacher asked, "Do we have capitals and periods at the right places?" and someone replied, "We need a period after 'Story' (7) and a big 'S' for 'something.'" Most of the others disagreed, and the teacher asked what a period meant. "It stops a sentence," one child answered, and only two children thought "If you Do Tell a Story" required stopping.

The next idea (8) was to add an "n" in "somethig."

The three suggestions that followed (9,10, and 11) concerned the capitalization of "Do," "Tell," and "Story."

When someone said "nevr" did not look right, the solution agreed upon was to look it up in the dictionary.

The thirteenth and final suggestion was to capitalize the first word, "when." The children were all satisfied at the end of this discussion, which lasted twenty-seven minutes. To be sure, the final product was superior to the children's individual work, but the product was not the important thing. What mattered was the critical thinking that took place as the children generated new ideas, explained their reasons, argued, and evaluated each other's ideas.

CONCLUSIONS

All children know something about writing when they come to school at age four, five, or six (Ferreiro and Teberosky 1982). They must be allowed to continue to construct their knowledge from a dual source: (1) specific information provided by the environment and (2) each individual's possibilities of assimilating this information into the organization he has already constructed. Social interaction allows children to learn actively from this dual source. They *receive* information and *give* it with critical, immediate reactions from their peers. In this natural way, they are free to accept or reject their peers' ideas.

When readers and workbooks are used, all the initiative and information come from sources external to the child. The child is assumed to learn the system by internalizing the bits of information in ready-made form. Many children are developmentally advanced enough to *con*struct the system in spite of this *in*struction, but this kind of learning is undesirable for their development of autonomy. (Piaget's concept of autonomy means "being able to think for oneself and make decisions independently by taking relevant factors into account (such as other people's viewpoints).")

In dictating sentences to the teacher, the child learns to read and write with his own language and thought rather than those that come out of books. However, in dictations, the child receives information from the teacher, without the possibility of evaluating it critically. Since the teacher gives the correct model, the child can only assume that whatever the teacher writes is correct. In dictations, furthermore, children never provide information to others and do not have a chance to test their ideas against other people's evaluation. Dictations are good for certain purposes, especially at an earlier level, before invented spelling becomes possible. For the construction of spelling, however, they are not conducive to the most active systematization.

To the educator worried that children are bad sources of information, we say that they are bad sources if we assume that learning takes place through the transmission and internalization of information. Since children construct their knowledge, they learn not *from* each other but *with* each other by going from one level after another of being "wrong." The traditional method of teaching spelling was to present it all from the outside, with repetition and reinforcement or corrective feedback. Invented spelling went to the other extreme of encouraging the child to figure out the system essentially alone. While both approaches "work" in many cases, the one suggested in this [chapter] seems better for children's social and general intellectual development, as well as for their re-inventing our system of writing.

Two remarks seem necessary in conclusion. One is that the preceding activities took place in the context of fostering children's autonomy in the Piagetian sense (Kamii 1984, 1985). When every subject is taught in the context of autonomy as the broad aim, there is a great deal of argument and negotiation about everything all the time. Communication, persuasion, and rethinking then become important rather than "right" answers or "correct" behaviors. Spelling is only a small part of a total program that emphasizes thinking and the exchange of the ideas both in speech and in writing. The reader interested in further details about a total program based on Piaget's theory of moral and intellectual development is referred to Kamii and DeVries (1977, 1980).

The second remark concerns the contrast between children's writing this year and in previous years. The five and six year olds in Chicago wrote very little in previous years and often asked how to spell the words they wanted to write. This year, we decided not to give the information they requested and, instead, encouraged them to depend on their own resources as described in this [chapter]. As a result of this change and liberation from correct spelling, many children are writing entire paragraphs and pages with frequency and concentration.

REFERENCES

Chomsky, C. "Write First, Read Later." *Childhood Education* 47 (1971): 296–299.

————. "Approaching Reading Through Invented Spelling." In Lauren B. Resnick and Phyllis A. Weaver (Eds.), *Theory and Practice of Early Reading*. Hillsdale, N.J.: Erlbaum, 1979.

Doise, W., and Mugny, G. *Le Developpement Social de l'Intelligence*. Paris: InterEditions, 1981.

Ferreiro, E., and Teberosky, A. *Literacy Before Schooling*. Exeter, N. H.: Heinemann, 1982.

Furth, H. G. *The World of Grown-ups*. N.Y.: Elsevier, 1980.

Giacobbe, M.E. "Kids Can Write the First Week of School." *Learning* 10 (1981): 132–135.

Hauser, C. M. "Encouraging Beginning Writers." *Language Arts* 59 (1982): 681–686.

Henderson, E. H., and Beers, J. W. (Eds.) *Developmental and Cognitive Aspects of Learning to Spell*. Newark, Delaware: International Reading Association, 1980.

Kamii, C. "Autonomy: The Aim of Education Envisioned by Piaget." *Phi Delta Kappan 65 (1984):* 410–415.

Kamii, C., and DeVries, R. "Piaget for Early Education." In M. C. Day and R. K. Parker (Eds.), *The Preschool in Action (*2nd ed.). Boston: Allyn and Bacon, 1977.

————. *Young Children Reinvent Arithmetic*. NY: Teachers' College Press, 1985.

————. *Group Games in Early Education*. Washington, D.C.: National Association for the Education of Young Children, 1980.

Lancaster, W., Nelson, L., and Morris, D. "Invented Spellings in Room 112: A Writing Program for Low-reading Second Graders." *The Reading Teacher 35* (1982): 906–911.

Milz, V. E. "First Graders Can Write: Focus on Communication." *Theory into Practice 19* (1980): 179–185.

Perret-Clermont, A. N. *Social Interaction and Cognitive Development in Children*. London: Academic Press, 1980.

Piaget, J. *The Moral Judgment of the Child*. N.Y.: Free Press, 1965 (first published in 1932).

————. *The Psychology of Intelligence*. Paterson, N. J.: Littlefield, Adams and Co., 1963 (first published in 1947).

————. *To Understand Is to Invent*. N.Y.: Viking, 1973 (first published in 1948).

Read, C. "Pre-school Children's Knowledge of English Phonology." *Harvard Educational Review* 41 (1971):1–34.

————. *Children's Categorization of Speech Sounds in English*. Urbana, Ill.: National Council of Teachers of English, 1975.

Teberosky, A. "Construcción de Escrituras a través de la Interacción Grupal." In Emilia Ferreiro y Margarita Gómez Palacio (Eds.), *Nuevas Perspectivas Sobre los Procesos de Lectura y Escritura*. Mexico City: Siglo XXI, 1982.

12. KID WATCHING: AN ALTERNATIVE TO TESTING

by Yetta M. Goodman, University of Arizona, Tucson

Although Yetta Goodman wrote this chapter over ten years ago, she decries the heavy reliance on standardized testing to judge whether students are good or poor readers, noting that teachers are focusing more and more on isolated skills like those found on tests, drilling students on skills in order to increase test scores. Because more time is spent on drill, less time is spent on actual reading for information and enjoyment. Unfortunately, the situation is as bad today, if not worse, as it was a decade ago, despite mounting evidence about how students learn to read and write.

The standardized testing movement continues to contradict what we know about how language is learned. And Goodman's realistic alternatives for testing continue to be relevant. For example, "The best alternatives to testing come from direct, and, in most cases, informal observation of the child in various situations by the teacher." To observe students effectively, teachers must (a) possess current knowledge about language development, (b) understand that errors are a natural part of language learning, (c) observe the student interacting with peers and adults in many different settings on a variety of subjects, (d) keep records of the observations, and (e) collect samples of the student's use of written and oral language over a period of time. Goodman concludes with a call for teachers to continue to grow as kid watchers to better support their language learning.

For additional coverage of this topic, see Reading Miscue Inventory: Alternative Procedures, *by Yetta Goodman, Carolyn L. Burke, and Dorothy J. Watson (New York: Richard C. Owen, 1978) and* Reading Strategies: Focus on Comprehension, *by Yetta Goodman and Carolyn L. Burke (New York: Richard C. Owen, 1980).*

This chapter appeared in National Elementary Principal, *vol. 57 (June 1978): 41-45. Copyright © 1978 by the National Association of Elementary School Principals. Reprinted with permission.*

Since 1960, our knowledge of how children learn language and how people use language has exploded. While many questions remain unanswered, we do know that children are actively involved in their own language learning. Indeed, the evidence shows that children initiate and create language years before they come to school.[1] Through interaction with the society into which they have been born, children discover rules about language, and they use their language to make sense out of the world and to share their meanings with others.[2]

In the last few years, it has been discovered that even preschool children are learning to read the print in their environment, responding to signs in the streets and commercials on television.[3] In addition, children invent their own spellings to match their generalizations about the sound system of English.[4]

At the same time that scholars are discovering significant knowledge about how children develop language, we have heard a growing cry to test children's language in schools. But the credence that has been given to language tests in the last few years is misleading, to say the least. It suggests that we know enough about language and testing to rely on test results to make claims about literacy and language development in all populations in our society. The fact is, the items in tests and the way tests are carried out are often at odds with the knowledge we get from the psychologists, psycholinguists, and sociolinguists studying language development. These two directions in education—testing language in standardized tests and learning how language develops in human beings—provide contradictory evidence for educators about children. Clearly, if educators are to make decisions that will support children's language development, they will need a firm knowledge of both testing and language development theory.

The misuses and abuses of tests have been well documented in the pages of this journal and others, through resolutions by national groups, and in speeches all over the country. I do not intend to repeat that data. Instead, I hope to support the growing national concern about the negative effects of our reliance on tests and to provide some suggestions for alternative ways to observe the development of language in the classroom.

Children are language learners by virtue of being born into human society. The role of the school can never be to teach language since children learn language naturally through their interaction with others. The role of the school must be to provide an environment in which children will expand their use of language in a variety of settings and situations and for a variety of purposes.

In a supportive, rich environment where language is encouraged and there are plenty of opportunities to read, write, speak, and listen, children will make many discoveries about language. They will not always be right in their discoveries, but they will be in good company. Scientists have always made mistakes and learned a great deal from them; in fact, in the scientific world, mistake making is expected. Scientists generally hypothesize something and expect that, when they test their own hypotheses, they may often go astray. If scientists were sure that their hy-

116

potheses were always right, they would not even bother experimenting in the first place. Why work on problems when you already know the answers?

Learning language is similar to scientific method. Children hypothesize about certain features of language and test out a variety of options. Depending on the responses of the community to their hypothesis testing, children add to their knowledge about language. In the preschool years, most children are rewarded for trying out their options. Parents, grandparents, neighbors, peers, and siblings are often excited by young children's attempts to communicate and seldom correct their language in the home setting, since communication is the purpose of the language.

In some settings, however, certain aspects of language learning are frowned on and actually discouraged. Children can learn very early that it is better to use language as little as possible in certain settings—notably, and regrettably, in the classroom. Their language will continue to grow with their peers, and in the community, but they do not find it comfortable to share what they know in the classroom—especially if their exploration of language is viewed as a deficiency.

The stifling of language development is supported and enhanced by the way standardized tests are used. If tests were used simply as one tool among many in the evaluation of children, the results would not be so damaging. But that is not the case. It is assumed that tests of reading measure the reading process; that tests of writing measure writing achievement; that tests of language measure language ability; that tests of intelligence measure thinking—even though such assumptions have been challenged by the knowledge that is emerging from the study of language development.

The way tests are used today leads teachers to believe that they need to focus on the most meaningless parts of language. The names of letters and sounds, the rules for spelling, syllabication, and punctuation, and the definition of words are aspects of language that children eventually may learn through a lot of experience with reading, writing, speaking, and listening. But teaching these specifics out of the context of real language experiences does not help children become effective and flexible users of language, and it surely does not make them aware of its power.

If language specifics are central to the tests, however, many teachers believe it is their duty to focus on them in the classroom. The curriculum narrows and becomes a matter of teaching to the test. People begin to call for mastery learning, and publishers begin to push programs designed to help students pass tests. Isolated skills in reading, writing, and math are stressed in response to these concerns, leaving no time for reading, writing, or the humanities; no time for taking field trips, for discussing controversial issues, for exploring the world. The learning environment becomes sterile as teachers put away the woodworking materials, store the easels and paints, and move away from block play and the care of animals and plants. Even excellent teachers often have to divert their energies from the exciting activities through which children can expand their language effectiveness and spend time instead on narrow prescriptions to help the kids get ready to pass the test. New teachers, or teachers who are somewhat insecure about trying new ideas with students, find the risks too great. They retreat into using textbooks exclusively or teaching in ways that diminish the use of oral language in the classroom and focus on single correct answers and fill-in-the-blank worksheets.

Students' responses to testing have a great impact on their view of themselves as learners. All children are learners. Yet when children are told repeatedly that they are not working as well as they should, and when they see that half of the children who take standardized tests are, by definition, below the mean, they begin to lose belief in themselves. Children do not try as hard or work as hard when they believe that they can't do it anyway.

Those children who do well on tests sometimes do get opportunities for expanding language activities. They may be encouraged to write stories and read to younger children. They may work in the library and go to plays. These richer experiences help them expand their language learning.

In many cases, however, the kids who don't do as well are drilled even more on the specifics. Sometimes they are not permitted recess until they've filled in all the blanks. They may be kept from Rodeo Day or International Activities Week because they haven't been checked off for a particular blend or vowel digraph. Their learning experiences are narrowed, and their opportunities for expanding their language in the school setting are poor. Bluntly put, the rich get richer and the poor get poorer. There is little time for talking and even less time for actually writing a story or reading a good book.

Moreover, the one right answer required by standardized tests encourages students to believe that there are single answers to complex personal and social problems. Experimenting and exploring issues becomes a frill, as even good students begin to believe that finding the one right answer is what learning is all about. Children begin to do what they must in order to please teachers, and the notion that the essence of learning is for the self is lost.

If we truly want to find out about the development of children and, through that knowledge, to develop educational experiences for them, then standardized testing is not the most efficient means to that end. Many evaluative activities that teachers can use in the classroom are less expensive than standardized tests and provide a lot more information about the child.

The best alternatives to testing come from direct and, in most cases, informal observation of the child in various situations by the classroom teacher. Since the process itself is somewhat informal, perhaps the term "kid watching" is preferable to the more formal "observation." Either way, the process is the same.

The basic assumption in kid watching is that development of language is a natural process in all human beings. Two important questions explored through kid watching are: (1) What evidence is there that language development is taking place? and (2) When a child produces something unexpected, what does it tell the teacher about the child's knowledge of language?

When Susie says to Mr. Farrel, her first-grade teacher, "That's the goodest story I've ever heard," she is providing evidence that she is developing rules about how comparatives are generated. Mr. Farrel can now observe Susie in many different situations. Susie seems to use *best* and *very good* as well as *goodest*. If Mr. Farrel keeps a record, he may discover four months later that Susie never says goodest any more, although her friend Mary may not eliminate the use of goodest from her language until some time later.

When Fred reads *headlights* for *headlamps* in a story, he is providing evidence that he understands what he is reading well enough to interpret the written language into the oral system he uses and understands best.

When Tony has written his teacher's name correctly for six months as *Miss Willis* and then in January begins to spell it *Mes Welles,* he is providing evidence of growth because he is moving away from simply copying from the board to generating his own phoneme-grapheme rules. This evidence is supported by a sentence in a letter he writes to his grandmother: "It is wentr and stel cold."

The first step in observation is having up-to-date knowledge about language. Many myths and misunderstandings are reflected in test items. For example, simple dialect differences or speech immaturities are often marked as errors on tests, rather than viewed as normal parts of language development and use. To help correct such misunderstandings, administrators would do well to provide inservice programs on language development for teachers. In addition, schools of education should provide courses in this area for both preservice and inservice teachers.

The kid watcher must also understand the role of errors in language learning. Research in all areas of language—speaking, listening, reading, and writing—suggests that errors are not random and in most cases can be explained by understanding how people learn language.

Mistakes can reveal a great deal about children's language develop-

119

ment. Errors often indicate that children are involved in organizing all of their knowledge and searching for additional information. What did these two fifth graders understand when they wrote down the pledge of allegiance? One student wrote, "to the republic of Richard's stand," while a second wrote, "to the republic of richest stand." The teacher has some information now about what the children are learning about their own nation. They are bringing knowledge together and trying to organize it into something meaningful. When teachers have insight into such responses, they can plan curriculum experiences to help youngsters rethink their understandings and expand their views of the United States.

Mistakes, errors, and miscues provide a great deal of knowledge about a child's language responses, but children are not permitted errors on tests. An error is defined as something that is wrong and must be corrected or righted immediately. Only the test author has the correct answer. Such significance is attached to a test author's correct answers that even teachers of very young children feel inadequate to correct tests, workbooks, or questions at the end of chapters without using answer books. Yet, when children are asked for explanations of their answers to test questions, they often give reasoned responses to wrong answers, while right answers are sometimes reasoned through in an inappropriate fashion.

Of course, what a teacher thinks of as a mistake may simply be a different view of the world based on the child's personal experiences or cultural background. In a "what goes with what" question, for example, an orthodox Jewish child may have trouble grouping eggs with meat and other proteins or with milk items found in the dairy case. Eggs are often classed with either meats or dairy products in many health or science units, but to an orthodox child, eggs are in a separate category, according to dietary laws.

The kid watcher observes the child in a variety of social and cultural settings, reacting to print on the playground, in the hallway, or on the school bus. Ms. Roberts becomes aware that Bobby can respond to *McDonald's* and *stop* signs, although he is still opening books upside down. She knows that he is aware of print and using written language to create meaning but that he needs a lot of experience with books. Maria is observed as she speaks with her mother, grandmother, siblings, and teacher. She talks to her grandmother in Spanish, speaks a mixture of English and Spanish to her mother and siblings, but speaks English only to her Spanish-speaking teacher. She is showing that she believes only English should be spoken in school and that she knows to which people which language forms are most appropriate.

The environment in which learning takes place must provide opportunities for the teacher to observe children using language in a variety of settings, on a variety of topics, and through interaction with a variety of people. Reading must include much more than workbooks, worksheets, or texts. Signs, instructions, magazines, personal letters, tickets, newspapers, clocks, and maps must be available for children's interactions. Writing must go beyond filling in blanks or completing sentences. It must take place continually in response to science experiments, writing stories or notes to classmates, typing up invitations, and printing class newspapers.

Records should be kept of kid watching. The teacher should keep notes on the degree to which children talk, write, listen, and read. Observations need to be made in one-to-one interactions, small-group discussions, question-and-answer sessions, and large-class settings. A chart can be kept on each child, indicating the various settings and responding to such questions as: Does the child use language to a greater extent in one situation than another? Does the child appear to be more comfortable in one setting than another? Is the child attentive during discussions even if someone else is speaking? With which classmate does a less talkative child communicate the most?

When watching children read, it is important to note if they read on their own or only at the teacher's request. Does the child come up to the teacher and share something read at home? How much reading does the child do? What different kinds of things does the child read? Does the child go eagerly to the library? When reading aloud, do the miscues the child produces suggest that the child is understanding the content of the reading selection? Such miscues tend to change the meaning of the text minimally, even though the miscues may not look much like the text.

In addition, tapes can be kept of a child's oral reading and retelling of a story or article at different times during the year. At the end of the year, the tapes can be compared to see if the child is reading material of increasing conceptual difficulty and if the miscues show that the child is really interpreting what is being read. Together, the child and the teacher (and the parents if possible) can examine the development that has taken place during the year and select areas that need more work. Some growth will almost always be obvious, and the child will be excited and encouraged by it.

To observe writing development, samples of writing should be kept in a folder for each child. At the end of a week of work, the child might select the piece of writing he or she thinks is best to place in the folder. The others can be taken home. At the end of the month, the child and the teacher can discuss the growth that has taken place and choose the best selection of the month to leave in the folder until the end of the year. Together, the teacher and the child (and, again, the parents, if possible) can examine development in handwriting, spacing, punctuation, spelling, and, most important, the content of the material.

As kid watching goes on, the teacher will find that the various questions used as the basis for observation will change as children mature and change. The questions should be rethought regularly, according to the teacher's knowledge of the class and his or her developing knowledge about language. A group of teachers in a school can often work out a list of questions and keep reevaluating them and changing them as the need arises. In fact, it is through kid watching that the best questions can be formulated.

These kinds of observation techniques have often been criticized because of the time they take. A considerable amount of the teacher's time is already being spent nonproductively, however, in giving children pre-tests and post-tests. Then even more time is spent checking off the items children need to know in order to pass the tests. Kid watching takes place as the teacher interacts with the child in the many language experiences available for children in every part of the school day. The times the child is actually reading, writing, speaking, and listening are the best times for observation. Kid watching is not something apart from on-going learning experiences.

These ideas have come from my own teaching, as well as from the many talented teachers I have had the privilege of working with over the last twenty-five years. Good teachers have always been kid watchers. They have always observed the language learning of the children in their classes. That kind of teaching should be encouraged and rewarded. Teachers and administrators who need a test score that compares their children with others in the nation in order to gauge their effectiveness as educators are not tuned in to the language development of their children.

School people who are concerned with how young children learn language cannot allow inadequate measures like standardized tests to get in the way of the best kinds of learning experience for every child. Whether children expand their language effectiveness in the classroom or narrow their vistas to minimum competencies depends on the teacher. The school environment must support teachers to advance their own professionalism by developing the ability to observe children and understand their language strengths.

NOTES

1. R. Brown, *First Language: The Early Stages* (Cambridge, Mass.: Harvard University Press, 1973).

2. M. A. K. Halliday, "Learning How to Mean," in *Foundations of Language Development*, ed. Lennenberg and Lennenberg (New York: Academic Press, 1975), pp. 239-65.
3. See Y. Goodman and K. S. Goodman, "Learning to Read is Natural," in *Theory and Practice of Early Reading*, vol. 1, ed. Resnick and Weaver (Hillsdale, N.J.: Erlbaum Associates, 1977); A. D. Forrester, "What Teachers Can Learn from Natural Readers," *Reading Teacher* 31 (November 1977): 160-66; and I. Ylisto, "Early Reading Responses of Young Finnish Children," *Reading Teacher* 31 (November 1977): 167-72.
4. C. Read, *Children's Categorization of Speech Sounds in English*, National Council of Teachers of English Research Report No. 17 (Urbana, Ill.: the Council, 1975).

13. LITERATURE AS THE CONTENT OF READING

by Charlotte S. Huck, The Ohio State University

When Charlotte Huck says, "Imaginative literature must be the content of the reading program," she is delivering a significant message to the skills-dominated U.S. educational system. In a literature-based reading program, she writes, a reason for learning to read is to read your own stories and the stories of other authors. If students enjoy what they are reading, they work hard to grow as readers. Huck suggests several practices that are important for a literature-based reading program: (a) the teacher reads aloud to students daily, (b) students have time each day to read self-selected books, (c) students talk about books they are reading in ways that are meaningful and enjoyable to them, (d) biographies, stories, and reference books are used in all areas of the curriculum, and (e) students have time for expressively representing their ideas and understandings in response to the books they have read.

Huck believes that good literature entertains and educates, helps students make order out of their lives, develops compassion, and stretches students' imaginations. In classrooms where teachers' practices are congruent with Huck's suggestions, students take delight in learning and reading; both teachers and students experience the joys of good literature.

This chapter appeared in Theory Into Practice, *vol. 16, no. 5 (December 1977): 363-71. Copyright © 1977 by the College of Education, The Ohio State University. Reprinted with permission.*

One group of primary children rearranged the books in their classroom library into two groups which they labeled "Real Books" and "'Readers." Evidently even very young children know the difference between those books which sustain and excite their imaginations by telling real stories and those basic texts which are primarily designed for instruction in reading. And yet what is there to prevent a child from learning to read from a real story, or a teacher from using that story to teach reading? I believe that the motivation for learning to read comes from the desire to read "real books" and that imaginative literature must be the content of the reading program.

THE CONTRIBUTION OF LITERATURE TO THE READING PROCESS

Stories are one of the best ways into literacy at the earliest stages of a

124

child's development. Barbara Hardy, from the University of London, suggests that all human beings' constructs of reality are in fact stories that we tell ourselves about how the world works. She maintains that the narrative is the most common and effective form of ordering our world today:

> We dream in narrative, day-dream in narrative, remember, anticipate, hope, despair, believe, doubt, plan, revise, criticize, construct, gossip, learn, hate, love by narrative (Hardy, 1968).

What is true of adults is even more characteristic of children. Watch young children and all the stories that they are playing out in their lives. They are naughty and sent to their rooms and they immediately begin to tell themselves a story of how mean their parents are and how they will run away from home and make everyone sorry. An eight year old was told that she couldn't go to the corner ice-cream shop with her friends because she had to stay home while her baby brother took his nap. Her response was that she felt just like Cinderella! This is the reason for the tremendous appeal of the folk tales and such modern classics as Sendak's *Where the Wild Things Are;* they tap the well-springs of the very stories children have been telling themselves for years.

Teachers who know the power of these self-told stories will make them the content of children's beginning reading. After children have read their own stories, they will want to move to the familiar and well-loved folk tales and the modern picture books that echo the dreams and wishes of the very young.

Children will want to learn to read because they want to read stories—their own and other persons', real stories where something happens to believable characters; not non-stories of collective persons carefully selected to represent a proper sampling of race, sex, and creed. Imaginative literature cannot be written to order. Today's sociological and politically conscious basal readers with their cast of United Nations characters are no more authentic literature than the earlier readers which attempted to create the life story of the great American WASP family. Fortunately, trade book publishers have produced a wide range of good stories and books which are well-written and illustrated and do represent the pluralistic nature of our society—but not all in one book! The basal reader is an anachronism reminiscent of earlier times when we had few books, no school libraries and thought all children had to have the identical material to learn to read. Today over 40,000 trade books are in print and this does not include the increasing number of children's paperbacks which are available. Teachers and children may choose from a vast array of books including picture books for all ages, folktales, modern fantasy, realistic stories, mysteries, science fiction, historical fiction, biography and non-fiction on almost every topic. The books are here and we need to learn to use them not as supplementary to basal readers, but as the very heart of the reading program.

Children do not have to be motivated to learn how to ride a skate board or a bike, or to swim or ski. They will work long and hard pushing themselves to achieve these skills that they know will bring them much pleasure. Youngsters will work equally hard to master the ability to read their own stories or stories which give them as much enjoyment as *Frog and Toad Are Friends* by Lobel, *Chicken Soup with Rice* by Sendak or the Frances stories by Russell Hoban. I remember visiting a primary classroom in London and reading with Gareth, a tall serious boy of about six and one half. Gareth was teaching himself how to read from the stories about Frances, a mischievous and loveable badger. He told me he could read two of the stories and that he was working on the third. I offered to read one to him if he would read one to me. He chose *Bread and Jam for Frances* and when he came to the part where Frances skips rope and sings her Jam Song, he unabashedly sang it. There was no doubt in my mind that he was taking delight in books in the process of learning to read. His joy was not delayed until after he had learned all the skills of reading, it was the intrinsic reward for being able to read a favorite book which he had chosen. For motivation is also enhanced when children have the opportunity to select their own reading materials. Gareth's favorite books were the Frances stories; other children might select *The Gingerbread Boy* as illustrated by Galdone, while still others might delight in the Monster books by Blance and Cook. A child's first reading book should be one that she or he wants to read and can read with reasonable ease and success.

We know that children learn best when what is learned has personal meaning for them. Kenneth Goodman (1970) describes the reading process as a constant search for meaning. In reading programs which emphasize meaning and comprehension, decoding skills are taught in the context of reading the story, not pulled out for separate isolated drill. Frank Smith (1971, p. 222) maintains that children learn to read by experience in reading. It is almost too simple for teachers, who are used to manuals and elaborate charts of sequential skills which are supposed to be taught at a particular time and place in the reading program to understand. Reading like learning to swim takes hours of practice, but the practice must be in a real book that gives back as much personal satisfaction as plunging in the cool water of a lake gives to the swimmer.

Through reading books themselves and hearing them read aloud, children become familiar with "book language" and slowly develop a sense of story. They begin to build a frame of reference about how stories are written and what to anticipate in the pattern and language of the book.

They easily recognize such conventional beginnings and endings of folk tales as "Once upon a time" or "... they lived happily ever after." They learn that action occurs in threes, and if Little Billy Goat Gruff is going to go trip-trapping over the bridge, they can predict that Middle-Sized Billy Goat Gruff will also trip-trap over the bridge and that she will be followed by Great Billy Goat Gruff! And so book language becomes internalized and the context of the sentence and the story provides verification of the child's ability to predict. The more reading exposure which the child has, the greater will become this predicting ability.

In discussing the role of fiction in the reading program, Margaret Spencer observes that:

> One of the recurrent handicaps of illiterate adults is their inability to anticipate what may happen in a story they are learning to read because they have never learned how the rules of the story are transferred to the print on a page. Most of them were never read to as children (Spencer, p. 2).

THE VALUES OF LITERATURE FOR THE CHILD

Probably the greatest value of using literature in the reading program is that children experience joy in reading and become "hooked on books." Instead of reading "bits and a pieces" of a story, they have a chance to become engrossed in an entire book. They may reread favorite books if they so desire, or favorite parts of well-loved books. Students who experience this kind of pleasure in reading are well on their way to becoming lifetime readers. It should be the goal of every reading program to produce children who not only know how to read but who do read. There is little value in just having the ability to read if one never uses it. Suppose we evaluated a school's reading program on the basis of how many books children actually read and enjoyed? We aim too low when we measure a child's performance by scores on the reading vocabulary tests or the comprehension tests of isolated sentences and paragraphs. We should evaluate the child's lifetime use of books!

Literature also has the power to influence children's lives. Much of what a child learns in school is concerned with *knowing*; literature is concerned with feeling. It can educate the heart as well as the head. As children learn to identify with such characters as Chibi, the little shy boy in the story of *Crow Boy*, they can empathize with his feelings of loneliness and isolation. Or perhaps like fat Harold in Byar's *After the Goat Man*, they can have a moment of sudden awareness of feeling what it would be like to be someone else, to be old and as alone as the goat man. Chukovsky, the Russian poet tells us that the goal of the story-teller:

> Consists of fostering in the child, at whatever cost, compassion and human-

127

ness—this miraculous ability of man to be disturbed by another being's misfortunes, to feel joy about another being's happiness, to experience another's fate as your own (Chukovsky, p. 138).

Besides developing compassion, literature can stretch children's imagination and help them to see their world in a new way, or entertain the possibilities of new worlds. Tana Hoban's exciting photographic puzzle *Look Again!* gives children a rich visual experience and helps them to see a dandelion, or a snail, or a pear from a new perspective. The poem "To Look at Anything" by John Moffitt suggests that just looking at something will not do; you have to "Be the thing you see . . . the dark snakes of stems, the ferny plumes of leaves . . . you must enter into the small silences between the leaves." James Higgins speaks of the books of childhood as mystical fancy which "lead forth," "leading [the child] to share experiences beyond his immediate tangible horizons." And so the reader can journey to the Land of Oz, or sail to the outermost reaches of Earthsea *(The Wizard of Earthsea* by LeGuin) or battle the evil echthro within the ecosystem of Charles Wallace's body *(Wind in the Door* by L'Engle). Each trip should bring the reader back from this journey a little nearer to understanding the true nature of reality.

Good literature not only entertains, it educates. The folk tales with their many cultural differences yet common motifs show the universality of humankind. Every culture has its tricksters, its witches and wolves, its stepmothers and fairy godmothers. Bruno Bettelheim in his book *The Uses of Enchantment* maintains that though set in never-never land and dealing with fantastic events, fairy tales conduct a "moral education" subtler and richer than any other type of story within a child's comprehension. He emphasizes that what children read should be worthy of the effort they put into the learning. "The acquisition of skills, including the ability to read, becomes devalued when what one has learned to read adds nothing of importance to one's life" (p. 4). Today we have a literature of childhood that will add to the value of children's living and reading.

USING LITERATURE IN THE READING PROGRAM

If literature is to become the central focus of the reading program, it cannot be relegated to something you do "after all your other work is finished," a phrase frequently heard in schools. Many primary teachers spend over one half their day teaching the skills of reading, yet never provide a time for children to actually read and enjoy a book! Teachers who plan to use literature in the reading program will want to provide a variety of ways in which it can be utilized in helping children become fluent satisfied readers.

128

1. The Read-Aloud Program

Ideally, the process of learning to read begins at home the very first time a loving adult shares a book with a child. In fact, the best preparation for school that parents can give their children is to read aloud to them from the time they can first sit up and enjoy looking at pictures. Children then begin to associate books and reading with a warm pleasant relationship where someone holds them and reads them a story. As the child points to the characters in the stories, asks questions, or simply says "Read it again!" he or she is actively participating in the story period. This involvement with the book is very important for the child's language development and growing sense of story.

Realistically, we know that many children come from homes which do not even own a book, let alone provide a bedtime story each night. This means that some children will not have heard a story or touched a book until they come to school. Pre-school and kindergarten teachers will want to share books three and four times a day with small groups and/or the whole class in order to provide the language stimulation and enjoyment derived from hearing stories and nursery rhymes.

The research of Dorothy Cohen (1968) showed the positive effects of reading aloud to some twenty classes of seven-year-olds in New York City. Teachers were asked to read aloud everyday from a selected list of trade books and then have the children respond to the story in some way (i.e., through discussion, retelling, drama interpretation; through art or music)—to make the story memorable. At the end of the year the classes which had had the daily story hour were significantly ahead of the control group in reading vocabulary and comprehension. Evidently, reading to children had improved the children's ability to read.

In a study of language development of children between six and ten years old, Carol Chomsky (1972) found a high correlation between their linguistic stages of development and their previous exposure to literature. Courtney Cazden (1972) also advocates reading aloud to the young child as a potent form of language stimulation. She found that reading aloud provoked much discussion about the pictures and the story at the same time it provided children with the experience of book language, patterns of stories and types of literature.

Older children also need a well-planned Read-Aloud Program to stimulate interest in books and to introduce them to quality literature which might be beyond their reading ability but not their comprehension levels. Children in the middle-grades will go on "reading jags," reading all the Judy Blume books or all the Paddington Stories. Such reading of series books provides much practice on easy reading materials for this age level and should not be discouraged. It should be balanced, however, by the teacher's reading of such well-written books as *Tuck Everlasting* by Natalie Babbitt or *Abel's Island* by William Steig, both stories which will stretch children's minds and capture their imaginations. After a teacher has read a well-loved book, children will clamor to read it themselves. In this way the teacher may indirectly influence choice and develop appreciation for the well-written book.

2. Provision for Wide Reading

In order to develop children who read fluently and happily, we need to provide a daily time for them to practice their reading skills by reading books of their own choosing and at their own pace and for their own purpose. Television viewing has made increasing inroads on the amount of time that children spend on recreational reading at home. Children also prefer viewing TV to reading books; it is easier and requires less concentration. Marie Winn (1977) reports a survey of over 500 fourth and fifth-graders in which all subjects showed a preference for watching TV over reading contents of *any* kind. If teachers want their students to have the opportunity to practice their reading skills through wide reading, they must reorder their priorities and provide school time for children to enjoy reading. Ironically, we frequently give this kind of time to the better readers (who then become even better readers), while we drill remedial readers on more isolated decoding skills, thereby denying them the opportunity to develop fluency or enjoyment of reading.

One way to see that all children have an opportunity to read widely is to provide a certain time for recreational or free reading. Some teachers prefer to call this period SSR or Sustained Silent Reading (MacCracken, 1972), in which everyone must read a book of his or her own choosing, including the teacher. Starting with only 8 or 10 minutes, the time is gradually increased until children can sustain their reading at least 30 to 45 minutes each day. During this period children will see their peers and an adult quietly reading and enjoying books. Some teachers take a few moments at the end of this period to ask for volunteers who want to tell something about what they have read. Some teachers have agreed that during this time they will read only children's books thereby becoming acquainted with new books to share with their students.

3. In-Depth Discussion Groups

Wide reading needs to be balanced with in-depth discussion of certain books by groups of five or eight children. Teachers frequently buy sets of six to eight paperbacks of the same title which they then use for such discussions. During this time children may share general impressions of the book and reactions to it. Teachers should usually invite children's comments on the content or story first. Later, the teacher may ask questions related to the literary strengths of the book. For example, in discussing *Tuck Everlasting* by Natalie Babbitt, children would want to raise the central issue of that fantasy, namely, Winnie Foster's decision as to whether to drink the magic water which would allow her to live forever. Some children may agree with her choice, others may disagree. Only after they had had a chance to state their positions and give their reasons should their teachers then raise the question of how the author had made the story so believable as to create that kind of controversy. Middle graders who were capable of reading *Tuck Everlasting*, would also want to look at the character development of Winnie Foster; of how an overprotected child grew and "became" a person in her own right by her experiences with the Tuck family. And finally I would hope that a question concerning Babbitt's frequent reference to wheels and toads would lead to their discovery of the value of motifs and symbols in intensifying the meaning of that remarkable story. Teachers must know literature and the needs and capabilities of their children, however, in leading such group discussion. It is important to help children discover the ways authors create meaning, rather than to superimpose an adult concept of literary analysis. An in-depth discussion should increase children's delight in stories, not be a lesson in literary criticism.

4. The Use of Literature Across the Curriculum

Teachers need to be alert to the ways literature can enrich all subjects across the curriculum. Children may be helped to see various points of view in social studies by reading well written literature. Recently, the Newbery Award winning book, *The Matchlock Gun* by Walter Edmonds, was criticized for presenting a "stereotyped" picture of an Indian attack on the Colonists. Yet *The Matchlock Gun* is written from the Colonist point of view and is based upon a true historical incident. Rather than criticize a story for its point of view, we need to balance it by sharing a book which presents some reasons for the provocation of the Indian raids. Hickman's *Valley of the Shadow* is an exciting authentic story of the massacre of some 92 Christianized Indians by the Virginia Militia in 1781. Recognized as a notable book of the year by the National Council of Social Studies, this book could be compared with the Newbery Award winning *Matchlock Gun* with both points of view discussed.

Children fortunate enough to have seen the New York Metropolitan Museum's exhibit of The Treasures of Tutankhamun would enjoy looking at and reading Macaulay's remarkable book simply titled *Pyramid* which describes in text and illustrations the step by step process of building the great pyramids in Egypt. *How Djadja-em-ankh Saved the Day* is a literal translation of an ancient Egyptian story written in hieroglyphics. One side of the mural-like pages presents the story, while the other side describes the finding of the Rosetta Stone and the eventual breaking of the code for decyphering Egyptian writing. The catalogue for the exhibit itself simply titled *The Treasures of Tutankhamun* helps to create the same awe and wonder in the reader as the actual exhibit. The introduction details the opening of the tomb and the hushed moment when Lord Carnarvon asks Carter if he can see anything by his flickering candle, and Carter answers "Yes, beautiful things!"

No textbook in social studies or science can begin to present the wonder, the excitement, the tragedy of man's discoveries and mistakes as the biographies, stories and informational books that are available for children today. Not to use them is to deny children their right to participate in the drama of the making of our civilization.

5. Providing for Varied Response to Books

Finally, if we want children to think about what they have read, teachers need to provide time for children to respond to them in various ways which will make them more memorable and interest others in reading the stories. Piaget (1970) maintains that "to know an object is to act upon it and transform it." This is not to suggest that a child has to give a deadly dull book report or "do something" with every book which he or she finishes, but it does imply that children should have an opportunity to interpret books in ways which will take them more deeply into the meaning of the story. For example, one group of primary children identified all the stories that they could think of that had surprise endings. Their list included *Rosie's Walk* by Pat Hutchins, *Mr. Gumpy's Outing* by Burningham, *The Camel Who Took a Walk* by Tworkov, *Owliver* by Kraus and many others. Several children then created their own surprise stories, while another group gave a surprise party, and a third group dramatized *Albert's Toothache*, by Williams, a funny tale about a turtle without teeth who had a toothache. These children were comparing endings of stories, dramatizing and creating their own stories all based upon one element in story making.

Another class of eight, nine and ten-year-olds studied folk tales. Different groups reviewed the folk tales from different countries identifying the food, characters, animals and topographical features mentioned in each tale. They looked at the beginnings and endings of tales. Some children wrote further adventures of Anansi the African spider who plays the traditional role of a trickster. Another group made a wall hanging of scenes from favorite fairy tales which have first been determined by a

132

classroom survey. A third group created a fairy tale museum in which they collected and labeled such displays as "The pea which the princess slept on." "The poisoned apple from Snow White." "Cinderella's glass slipper" and "the needle which pricked Sleeping Beauty."

All these activities synthesized children's knowledge of literature and created a deeper interest and appreciation for it. Other activities might include making puppets of favorite stories, creating a game based upon one story or a group of stories, making books for younger readers, or developing a diorama of a particular scene from a book.

SELECTING BOOKS FOR A LITERATURE-BASED READING PROGRAM

Obviously, such a program as has been described would require many many books. Increasingly, elementary schools have obtained school library media centers and trained librarians. Most teachers have established classroom reading centers which include both a permanent collection of two or three hundred books (frequently paperback) and a changing collection borrowed from the school or public library. A minimum of some ten books per child is required for the classroom library, while the American Library Association Standards (1975) recommend some 16 to 24 volumes per student for the Library Media Center. If children are to have a real choice of books, there needs to be a large variety of genres representing a wide range of interests and reading ability. These books should be constantly and freely accessible both in the classroom and the library.

Books should be selected on the basis of their interest for children, their literary quality and their intended use in the classroom. Many high-interest books by popular authors or well-liked series books should be provided to foster children's fluency of reading and their delight in books. Such books as The Encyclopedia Brown stories by Sobol, The Henry Huggins series by Cleary, The Paddington books or The Little House books by Laura Wilder are all popular titles for the middle grades. Books by Judy Blume and Roald Dahl are favorites, as are such single titles as *How to Eat Fried Worms* by Rockwell, *Freaky Friday* by Rodgers and *Wrinkle in Time* by L'Engle and the *Guinness Book of World Records*. These are the books which capture children's interest and help them to develop a love of books.

Books which might lend themselves to in-depth discussions by small groups of children could be ordered in sets of multiple copies. Possibilities for the middle grades might include *The Island of the Blue Dolphins* by O'Dell, *Friedrich* by Richter, *Edge of Two Worlds* by Jones, *My Dad Lives in a Downtown Hotel* by Mann, *Luke Was There* by Clymer, *A*

Wrinkle in Time by L'Engle. The books used for these study groups would depend upon the children's background of experience as well as their previous exposure to literature. There is no list of books that every child must read. It is just as easy to discern a universal theme in *Stevie* by Steptoe as it is to discover it in *Call it Courage* by Sperry. The point is to select books which will stretch children's thinking, their feelings and their imaginations.

Books which teachers select to read aloud should be too good for children to miss both in the quality of the theme and the quality of the language. These books should provide a balance to what children are reading on their own. If, for example, students are engrossed in reading contemporary fiction, the teacher might want to select a compelling book of fantasy such as Hunter's *The Stranger Came Ashore*. One excellent teacher of middle-grade children regularly shares a picture book, some poetry and a continued story each day. She hates to have her students miss the beautifully illustrated picture books such as *Dawn* by Shulevitz or the *Snow White* edition illustrated by Nancy Burkert. If the class is studying a particular unit in social studies, the teacher may want to share a story such as *The Door in the Wall* by De Angeli or *One is One* by Barbara Picard, both superior stories of medieval days. There is a real danger that children will hear only historical fiction or biography if such an approach is used constantly. Therefore teachers will want to keep a list of the books they have shared with their classes to be sure they are introducing a variety of genres.

Both public and school libraries can be very helpful in finding a title and/or media to use in studying subjects in science or social studies. As children prepare reports it is important that they use a variety of sources rather than rely completely upon the use of encyclopedias. If children are to become critical readers they need to compare sources and evaluate the most reliable.

COMMITMENT TO LITERATURE

This is not an easy way to teach reading. It requires a thorough knowledge of children's literature, an internalization of the reading process, and a thorough understanding of children. But for teachers who are enthusiastic about books and who know the value of fine literature, it is the only way to teach reading. They know the pleasures and the knowledge that books can give and they will not be satisfied until each of their students becomes a real reader.

REFERENCES

American Library Association. *Media Programs: District and School*. Chicago, Illinois, 1975.

Bettelheim, Bruno. *The Uses of Enchantment*. New York: Alfred A. Knopf, 1976.

Cazden, Courtney B. *Child Language and Education*. New York: Holt, Rinehart and Winston, 1972.

Chomsky, Carol. "Stages in Language Development and Reading Exposure." *Harvard Educational Review*, Vol. 42 (February 1973), pp. 1–33.

Chukovsky, Kornei. *From Two to Five*. Translated by Miriam Morton. Berkeley: University of California Press, 1963.

Cohen, Dorothy. "The Effect of Literature on Vocabulary and Reading Achievement." *Elementary English*, Vol. 45, (February 1968), pp. 209–13, 217.

Goodman, Kenneth. "Behind the Eye: What Happens in Reading," in K. Goodman and O. Niles (eds.), Reading: Process and Program. Champaign, Ill.: National Council of Teachers of English, 1970.

Hardy, Barbara. *The Appropriate Form, An Essay on The Novel*. London: The Athlone Press, University of London, 1968.

Higgins, James E. *Beyond Words: Mystical Fancy in Children's Literature*. Columbia University: Teachers College Press, 1970, p.1.

McCracken, Robert A. and Marlene McCracken. *Reading Is Only the Tiger's Tail.* San Rafael, California: Leswing Press, 1972.

Piaget, Jean *Science of Education and the Psychology of the Child*. New York: Orion, 1970, pp.28-29.

Smith, Frank. *Understanding Reading: A Psycholinguisitic Analysis of Reading and Learning to Read*. New York: Holt, Rinehart and Winston, 1971.

Spencer, Margaret, "The Role of Fiction," *Language Matters*. London: The Centre for Langauge in Primary Education. Vol. I: 4 August, 1976, p.2.

Winn, Marie, *The Plug-In Drug: Television, Children, and the Family*. New York: The Viking Press, 1977.

CHILDREN'S BOOKS

Babbitt, Natalie. *Tuck Everlasting*. New York: Farrar, Straus and Giroux, 1975.

Blume, Judy. *Are You There, God? It's Me, Margaret*. New York: Bradbury, 1970.

Blume, Judy. *Blubber*. New York: Bradbury, 1974.

Blume, Judy. *It's Not the End of the World*. New York: Bradbury, 1972.

Blume, Judy. *Tales of a Fourth Grade Nothing*. New York: Dutton, 1972.

Blume, Judy. *Then Again, Maybe I Won't*. New York: Bradbury, 1971.

Bond, Michael. *A Bear Called Paddington*. New York: Houghton Mifflin, 1960.

Bond, Michael. *More About Paddington.* New York: Houghton Mifflin, 1962.

Bond, Michael. *Paddington at Large*. New York: Houghton Mifflin, 1963.

Bond, Michael. *Paddington Marches On*. New York: Houghton Mifflin, 1965.

Burningham, John. *Mr. Gumpy's Outing*. New York: Holt, Rinehart and Winston 1971.

Byars, Betsy. *After the Goat Man*. New York: Viking, 1974.

Clymer, Eleanor. *Luke Was There*. New York: Holt, Rinehart and Winston, 1973.

DeAngeli, Marguerite. *Door in the Wall*. New York: Doubleday, 1949.

Edmonds, Walter. *The Matchlock Gun*. New York: Dodd, 1941.

Galdone, Paul. *The Gingerbread Boy. New York: Seabury*, 1975.

Gilbert, Katherine, et al., Editors. *The Treasures of Tutankhamun*. New York: The Metropolitan Museum of Art, 1976.

Grimm Brothers. *Snow White and the Seven Dwarfs*. Translated by Randall Jarrell, illustrated by Nancy Ekholm Burkett. New York: Farrar, Straus and Giroux, 1972.

Hickman, Janet. *Valley of the Shadow*. New York: Macmillan, 1974.

Hoban, Russell. *Bread and Jame for Frances*. New York: Harper and Row, 1964.

Hoban, Tana. *Look Again!* New York:Macmillan, 1971.

Hunter, Molly. *The Stranger Came Ashore*. New York: Harper and Row, 1975.

Hutchins, Pat. *Rosie's Walk*. New York: Macmillan, 1968.

Kraus, Robert. *Owliver*. Illustrated by José Aruego and Ariane Dewey. New York: E.P. Dutton and Co., 1974.

L'Engle, Madeleine. *Wind in the Door.*New York: Farrar, Straus, 1973.

L'Engle, Madeleine. *Wrinkle in Time*. New York: Farrar, Straus, 1962.

LeGuin, Ursula. *The Wizard of Earthsea*. Berkeley, California: Parnassus Press. 1968.

Lobel, Arnold, *Frog and Toad Are Friends*. New York: Harper and Row, 1970.

Macaulay, David. *Pyramid,* New York: Houghton Mifflin, 1975.

McWhirter, N. and R. (Editors). *Guinness Book of World Records*. New York: Sterling, 1976.

Manniche, Lise (Translator). *How Djadja-em-ankh Saved the Day*. New York: Crowell, 1976.

Moffitt, John. ''To Look at Anything'' in *Reflections on A Gift of a Watermelon Pickle*. Edited by Stephen Dunning. et al. Glenview, Illinois: Scott, Foresman, 1966.

O'Dell, Scott. *The Island of the Blue Dolphins*. New York: Houghton Mifflin, 1960.

Picard, Barbara. *One Is One*. New York: Holt, Rinehart and Winston, 1966.

Richter, Hans Peter. *Friedrich*. Translated by Edite Kroll. New York: Holt, Rinehart and Winston, 1970.

Rockwell, Thomas. *How To Eat Fried Worms*. New York: Dell Publishing Company, 1973.

Rodgers, Mary. *Freaky Friday*. New York: Harper and Row, 1972.

Sendak, Maurice. *Chicken Soup with Rice*. New York: Harper and Row, 1962.

Sendak, Maurice. *Where the Wild Things Are*. New York: Harper and Row, 1963.

Shulevitz. Uri. *Dawn*. New York: Farrar, Straus, 1974.

Sobol, Donald. *Encyclopedia Brown and the Case of the Dead Eagles*. New York: Nelson, 1975.

Sobol, Donald. *Encyclopedia Brown Lends a Hand*. New York: Nelson, 1974.

Sobol, Donald. *Encyclopedia Brown Takes a Case*. New York: Nelson, 1973.

Sperry, Armstong. *Call It Courage*. New York: MacMillan, 1940.

Steig, William. *Abel's Island*. New York: Farrar, Straus and Giroux, 1976.

Steptoe, John. *Stevie*. New York: Harper and Row, 1969.

Tworkov, Jack. *The Camel Who Took a Walk*. Illustrated by Roger Duvoisin. New York: Dutton, 1951.

Wilder, Laura Ingalls. *Little House in the Big Woods*. New York: Harper, 1953.

Wilder, Laura Ingalls. *Little House on the Prairie*. New York; Harper, 1953.

Wilder, Laura Ingalls. *On the Banks of Plum Creek*. New York: Harper, 1953.

Wilder, Laura Ingalls. *The Long Winter*. New York: Harper, 1953.

Wilder, Laura Ingalls. *By the Shores of the Silver Lake*. New York: Harper, 1953.

Wilder, Laura Ingalls. *Little Town on the Prairie*. New York: Harper, 1953.

Wilder, Laura Ingalls. *Those Happy Golden Years*. New York: Harper, 1953.

Williams, Barbara, *Albert's Toothache*. Illustrated by Ray Chorao. New York: E.P. Dutton, 1974.

Yashima, Taro. *Crow Boy*. New York: Viking, 1955.

14. SHARED BOOK EXPERIENCE: TEACHING READING USING FAVORITE BOOKS

by Don Holdaway, International Educational Consultant

*Don Holdaway of New Zealand helps readers see the connections be-
tween oral and written language development in his discussion about the
use of shared book experiences. The novel idea of enlarging written text
grew from observing what happens in literate homes where children select
the books they want to read again and again and enjoy them in their parents' laps. Holdaway and his colleagues simply applied these ideas from
their observations to early literacy instruction in schools. They began by selecting books that were enjoyed by five-to seven-year-olds and enlarged
the texts. This work was soon followed by developing practices for teachers
to use with the enlarged texts.*

*Holdaway's shared book experience is an important aspect of literacy
programs for young children; it is encouraging that many teachers in the
United States now use this strategy. A number of companies, including
major basal reader publishers, produce "big books" or enlarged texts of
predictable children's literature. As "big books" and shared book experiences are incorporated into early literacy programs, it is important to ensure that quality children's literature is represented; that the strategies
used are developmentally appropriate; and that the major goal continues
to be children making sense of what they read.*

This chapter appeared in Theory Into Practice, *vol. 21 (Autumn 1982):
293-300. Copyright © 1982 by the College of Education, The Ohio State
University. Reprinted with permission.*

Most children would agree that listening to stories is a most enjoyable
activity, especially during the early years of schooling. Most teachers do
read to their children and they, too, enjoy the experience. By contrast,
the *instructional* reading program, however, does not seem to be characterized by anything like the same level of enjoyment for either children
or teacher—it is often a time of boredom or stress and the ritualistic performance of unmotivating activities. Story time and reading time have
different purposes, different content, and different rewards. They are so
different that one must ask, "which best embodies literacy?"

As teachers, we tend to take the differences between these two situations for granted: story time is for pleasure and nothing—least of all

word-solving—should be allowed to break the spell; reading time is for learning to read and is a necessarily difficult and painful activity for many children, requiring hard work and application—no spellbinding here. For the work of learning to read we attempt to motivate the children artificially and reward them extrinsically, neglecting the deep satisfactions which spring naturally from a proper engagement with books of high quality. We accept the structured materials provided for instruction without questioning their lack of intrinsic interest or worth.

Most surprisingly for an intellectually oriented institution like the school, we assume that problem solving—represented in reading by such "skills" as word-attack and in written language by such skills as spelling and calligraphy—cannot possibly be a rich source of pleasure. In contrast, we know by simple observation that the stumbling approximations of infants as they attempt to solve the problems of walking or talking *do,* in fact, provide them with immense pleasure, but we are so myopic in our observation of reading behavior that we fail to register the intense joy which may be experienced by children in solving the most basic problems of literacy. Before long the reading program has so completely excluded such forms of joy that they are no longer there to observe. To turn a topical Australian phrase, literacy, inasmuch as it has anything do do with life, wasn't meant to be easy.

Children who are already reading and writing when they enter school at five, or who are so ready to learn that they take literacy in their stride, have had a rather different introduction to the real processes of literacy. Some of their deepest satisfactions for several years have centered around their fumbling but excited attempts to read, write, and spell. Almost invariably they are familiar with a wide range of favorite books which, to use one of Bill Martin's delightful phrases, they can "zoom through with joyous familiarity" (1972).

These are the books they loved so much that they pestered people to read to them again and again. These are the books which they played at reading to themselves, puzzled and pored over with aggressive curiosity about the devices of print. In this naturally joyful activity they learned rapidly about the mysterious relationships between fascinating language and pages of print. Their learning from these loved books was self-selected, intrinsically rewarded, and highly individualized.

Although story time in primary classes tends to be as enjoyable as it is in the book-loving home, it is not so effective in producing this "favorite book syndrome," and this is so for a number of reasons. There is not the same opportunity for personal selection. The teacher is not so free to respond to clamoring requests to "read-it-again." There is seldom the opportunity for all the children to handle the books independently as they become favorites. Because of visual and tactile distance from the text, there is not the same tendency for children to become curious about print at the crucial moments when they are reveling in the sounds of language, nor is there the opportunity for them to point with their little fingers to details in the text and ask pointed questions. However, despite these losses in providing some of the crucial conditions to turn enjoyed books into favorite books, story time is still a powerhouse of natural motivation. Sadly, its output is largely wasted as a reinforcement for healthy reading behavior.

THE ADVENT OF SHARED BOOK EXPERIENCE PROCEDURES

About 15 years ago a group of teachers and academics in Auckland, New Zealand, began to take this natural literacy-learning situation very seriously. They were stimulated by a new challenge presented by a rapidly growing migrant movement of Polynesian people from the Pacific islands and Maori people from rural districts into inner city schools. They were supported by a particularly lively climate of research and educational enthusiasm which was articulated throughout the system from department officers to practicing teachers, from university personnel to student teachers. They began cooperating and experimenting in new ways while maintaining healthy patterns of both criticism and support. The teaching procedures which began to develop and to be clarified in the ensuing years came to be known as "shared book experience." These procedures were integrated with already well-developed techniques in language experience approaches forming a complementary body of insights and techniques rather than a new methodology.

We were concerned to transform the educational context of the school in such a way as to achieve two goals.

a. To make available the most efficient learning environment possible in which to achieve literacy readiness for five year olds who did not come from literacy-oriented backgrounds, and without segregating them from those who did.

b. To make entry into literacy a more natural and successful process in which children of widely differing backgrounds could make optimum progress without developing a sense of failure in the first years of schooling.

The prevailing model for literacy-learning was failing to provide a satisfactory structure for a large proportion of children, especially those from cultural backgrounds widely different from the culture of the school. We wished to avoid those aspects of traditional approaches which highlighted invidious comparisons among children, such as lockstep

139

movement through a series of readers. We were looking for procedures to develop competence in written English, without forcing children to regard their own spoken dialects as wrong or inferior. We were, as well, looking for procedures which teachers could readily use and understand.

Our studies indicated that under suitable motivation and in a favorable learning environment children would master literacy skills in a way very similar to that in which they master other developmental tasks, especially those of spoken language. The adults involved in providing the conditions for such natural learning do so without expert, academic knowledge, with justifiable optimism and with evident personal reward, It might, after all, be possible to approach these ambitious goals we set for ourselves.

A DEVELOPMENT EXPEDITION

The magnificently successful process of learning spoken language in infancy provided the central model for the project and in an important sense provided justification for many thinly researched conclusions. What follows should be understood as implying that the spoken language learning model has been taken very seriously, and we know of no evidence that it is improperly applied to literacy learning.

One of the features of early research and development in this project was a determined attempt to study and understand the learning background which produces children who become high-progress readers in their first year at school. As with the spoken language model, this study leads us into a fascinating field of natural, developmental, pre-school learning. It is remarkable how little was really known 10 years ago about the conditions which produced our literacy-oriented children. Everyone agreed that it was a "good thing" to read to young children, and joked tolerantly about their tiresome demands to hear their favorite stories read again and again, but that's about as far as it went. Everyone talked about pre-reading skills and programs without reference to the learning situations which actually produced the most literacy-ready children at school entry. A more systematic study of pre-school literacy activities soon highlighted some surprising features.

First, book-handling activities began at a very early stage, expanding the child's exposure to special forms of language and special types of language process long before the tasks of spoken language were mastered. These children began experimenting with book language in its primary, oral form while they were still using baby grammar and struggling with the phonology of speech. Yet it seemed an ideal time for this exposure and experiment. The sooner book-oriented activities began, the more likely it was that book-handling and experimental writing would become

140

an important part of the daily preoccupations of the infant. Literacy orientation does not wait upon accomplished spoken language.

Second, the literature made available by ordinary, sensible parents to their children, even before the age of two years, was remarkably rich in comparison to "readers" used in the first year of school. They often included highly structured or patterned language of a repetitive, cumulative, or cyclic kind. Although the adults always seemed willing to attempt to explain new vocabulary, meanings, and idioms, the stories usually carried growing understanding from their central human concerns, and the adults were seldom worried about making certain their children understood every last word, or that they had had direct sensory experience of every new concept. Just as speech develops in an environment which is immensely more rich than the immediate needs of the learner, so the orientation to book language develops in an environment of rich exposure beyond the immediate needs of the learner. In both situations, the learner selects appropriate items from the range.

Third, by determining *which* books they will have repeated experience of, children are involved in selection of those book experiences which will deeply preoccupy them from the earliest stages. The request to "read it again" arises as a natural developmental demand of high significance and an integral part of book exposure. Furthermore, in the behavior described in ensuing paragraphs, children quickly avail themselves of the opportunity to practice and experiment with a selection from the material made available to them. As in the mastery of other developmental tasks, self-selection rather than adult direction characterizes the specific and intensive preoccupations of early literacy orientation.

ROLE PLAYING AS READER—A NEGLECTED FEATURE OF LITERACY LEARNING

By far the most interesting and surprising aspect of pre-school book experience is the independent activity of these very young children with their favorite books. Almost as soon as the child begins to be familiarized with particular books by repetitive experience, self-motivated, reading-like behavior begins. Attracted by the familiar object, the child picks it up, opens it, and begins attempting to retrieve for himself some of the language and its intonations. Quite early this reading-like play becomes story-complete, page-matched, and picture-stimulated. The story tends to be reexperienced as complete semantic units transcending sentence limits.

The time spent each day in these spontaneous attempts to retrieve the pleasurable experiences of favorite books is often greatly in excess of the time spent in listening to books being read by the adult(s) being emulated. The child attends for surprisingly long periods of time until the experience has achieved a semantic completeness, and the process may be repeated immediately with the same or another book.

A superficial assumption about this reading-like behavior would be that it was a form of rote learning based on repetitive patterning without deep comprehension or emotional response; that it would produce attempts at mere surface verbal recall. However, detailed study of this behavior through the analysis of tape recordings did not bear this out. On the contrary, what was displayed was a deep understanding of and response to central story meanings. The younger the child, and the less verbally competent, the greater was likely to be the distance from the surface verbal features of the text. The responses often involved what could only be called translation into forms of the language more typical of the child's current stage of linguistic development.

Here are two brief examples of this behavior at different levels of development:

Damion, age 2.0 years, retrieving *Are You My Mother* by P.D. Eastman:

Text	Responses
4 The egg jumped."Oh, oh!" said the mother bird. "My baby will be here! He will want to eat."	Ow ow! A mummy bird baby here. Someping a eat ("a" used throughout to replace "to" and "for").
6 "I must get something for my baby to eat!" she said. "I will be back." So away she went.	Must baby bird a (i.e. "to") eated Dat way went. Fly a gye.
8 The egg jumped. It jumped and jumped! Out came the baby bird.	Ig jumped and jumped! Out baby bird!
10 "Where is my mother?" he said. He looked for her.	Whis my mudder? She look a her and look her.
12 He looked up. He did not see her. He looked down. He did not see her.	Her look up, look down. See her. (Damion cannot yet form a negative so he uses the affirmative in all such cases, adding a special intonation and a shake of the head!)

Far from producing the text in parrot-like fashion, Damion is guided by deep meanings to perform brilliant translations of meaning into baby grammar, displaying what have come to be known as "pivot structures."

Lisa-Jane, 4.0 years, from the same book:

142

| 34 | The kitten and the hen were not his mother. The dog and the cow were not his mother. Did he have a mother? | So the pussy wasn't his mother. The hen wasn't his mother. The dog wasn't his mother. The cow wasn't his mother. And the baby bird said, "Did I have a mother?" and he DID! |
| 36 | "I did have a mother," said the baby bird. "I know I did. I have to find her. I will. I WILL!" | What a sad face. That one says: Did he have a mother? Did he have a mother? HE DID! |

Note how on page 34 reported speech is transposed into direct speech and the converse is carried out on page 36. Note also that the side comment, "That one says," is an indication that Lisa-Jane knows the story comes from the print. She also has perfect control of the registers of both conversation and book language, and can change readily from one to the other.

The remarkable thing about the developmental difference between the two and the four year old is not that it is different in kind, but that it is different in the degree of syntactic sophistication—an expression of the level of syntactic control available in deep processing. Both children start from whole-story understanding and retrieve in sentence units encoded into an appropriate syntax at the level of their spoken language development. Neither has memorized the vocabulary or the grammar word for word—they have memorized the meaning.

Approximation is a ruling principle, just as it is in learning spoken language. It should not come as a surprise—but to many it does—that these two learning situations in developmental behavior display classical reinforcement theory more clearly than any but highly contrived situations in school. Here is perfect exemplification of immediate reinforcement for every approximation in the right direction which learning theory recommends to us so strongly. Far from it being the case that developmental or "play" learning is something inferior to organized learning which sets up rigorous and efficient contingencies, developmental learning, in its almost flawless control of learning contingencies, puts the classroom to shame. We should not be saying that developmental learning is a hit-and-miss affair, lacking the efficient guidance and control provided in the school environment. It is *so* efficient and delicately controlled that we should, as teachers, be approximating towards that right learning structure. Yet we allow almost no place for approximation in learning to read, write, or spell.

Another noteworthy feature of this reading-like behavior is that it lacks an audience and is therefore self-regulated, self-corrected, and self-sustained. The child engages in this behavior without being directed to do so, at just those times when the loved adult is *not* available to do the reading. The child is not self-conscious or over-awed by the need to please an adult, nor is the child dependent on the adult for help or correction. Clay (1972) has shown how important the self-corrective strategy is to success in the early stages of reading.

To summarize, the bedtime story situation should not be separated from the independent output behavior which it generates. Such behavior normally engages the infant in extensive, self-monitored, linguistic behavior for longer periods of time than are spent in the input activity of listening. The input and the output activities are complementary aspects of the same language-learning cycle. In both aspects there is close visual and tactile contact with the book, becoming increasingly oriented to print detail. All of the most powerful strategies of mature reading are being established and practiced in the reading-like, output behavior. The complexity and sophistication of the processes being mastered make the normal corpus of pre-reading skills look quite ridiculous.

There is obviously a great deal of positive reinforcement provided by both the input and output activities. In the first is the pleasure and delight of listening to the familiar human voice, full of warm intonation and bringing meaning to the special language where it differs from conversational language. The situation is socially rewarding, giving pleasure to both the adult and the child. It is a secure situation associated with proximity to or bodily contact with the adult.

The output activity is equally rewarding. Success in recreating the story is rewarded in a continuous, cyclic fashion similar to the rewards of experimenting with speech, and therefore tends to be self-sustaining. It is a situation which recalls the secure, pleasurable presence of the loved adult, and provides recall of the explanatory comments and answers to questions in the input sessions. The experience builds confidence in the ability to control language without outside help and, by the absence of criticism or correction, encourages self-regulation of complex language tasks.

In this situation, we have a further model for literacy-learning consistent in every way with the model derived from learning spoken language. Furthermore, it is the actual model demonstrated in the learning of those children who become our high progress readers or who teach themselves to read before entering school. In the model, the adult does not give instructions which the learner then attempts to carry out: rather, the adult provides real experience of the skill in joyful use. The skill then becomes a central feature of the learner's natural play and natural striving.

The early stage in the development of any complex human skill is activity which is *like* that skill and approximates progressively toward an activity which incorporates real processes and operations in mature use of the skill. Appropriate processes and strategies provide the foundation for successful practice and refinement—practice and refinement do *not* lead to the mature processes and strategies.

For literacy these strategies include:

- A deep, meaning-centered drive.
- Predictive alertness which harnesses background abilities such as syntactic responsiveness, semantic purposefulness, and experiential meaningfulness.
- Confirmatory and corrective self-monitoring by which output is constantly compared with sound models in prior experiences.
- Self-regulating and self-corrective operations leading to reinforcement patterns which are largely intrinsic and maintain high levels of task attention without extrinsic intervention.
- Risk-taking by approximation and trial backed by these sound strategies of self-monitoring.

(More detailed examples and implications are given in Holdaway, 1979.)

APPLICATION TO CLASSROOM TEACHING

This model of natural, developmental learning in language could provide a powerful framework for a literacy program if the application to classroom conditions could be worked through. Such a program would be meaning-centered and process-centered rather than word-centered. It would be based on books from a wide literature which had become favorites for the children through enjoyable aural-oral experience. It would promote readiness in powerful ways associated with books and print, and would allow for a gradual transition from reading-like behavior. Approximation would be rewarded, thus supporting the early development of predictive and self-corrective strategies governed by meaning, which are crucial to healthy language use.

All of these factors seemed to be pointing in quite different directions from current methods, although they shared many features with language-experience approaches. We decided to take the model seriously and, at least for the purposes of exploration, see if it were possible to build a literacy program in which these principles were given genuine priority.

A growing body of psycholinguistic and developmental research seemed to be pointing in similar directions but a classroom methodology had not been worked out (e.g. Goodman, 1968). Early work in individualized reading, led by Jeanette Veatch (1959), had broken much of the ground and provided valuable practical pointers, but teachers had been wary of this movement. In our own country, the work of Sylvia Ashton-Warner (1963) among rural Maori children had provided a useful debate and a persuasively documented account of classroom procedures consistent with many of the principles we were seeking to embody. In the United States, Bill Martin had begun to publish the materials which led

145

to the Holt Rinehart *Sounds of Language* series, and we were certainly on the same wavelength. We gained much from a study of all of these movements.

What was missing from this rich body of knowledge about developmental teaching was some set of procedures whereby all the important aspects of the bedtime story cycle could be replicated in the classroom. How was it possible to provide the same impact, the same level of participation, the same security and joy, the same prominence of print when there were 30 children rather than one? As so often happens, however, once the priorities had been set up, practical applications fell into place quite simply.

Three requirements needed to be met in order to achieve comparable or stronger impact than is achieved in the ideal pre-school, home setting. First, the books to be used in the reading program needed to be those that had proved themselves as loved by children. In this respect we, as teachers, had many advantages over parents both in determining which books children enjoy most and in obtaining them. We soon had some 200 titles, largely from the open literature rather than from reading schemes, known to be loved by five to seven year olds.

Second, the books needed to have comparable visual impact from 20 feet as a normal book would have on the knee of a child. This requirement was met by using enlarged texts. We made "blown-up" books about 30 inches by 24 inches—mainly from heavy brown paper. Every child in a class group could see the print very clearly without needing to strain and press foward. Other devices such as charts, overhead transparencies, and projected slides were also used. Here again we found advantages over the home situation in that pointing and identifying details in an enlarged text suited the undeveloped muscular coordination of beginners.

Third, the teacher needed to present new material with wholehearted enjoyment, rather more as a performance than would be the case with most parents. The professional training of teachers normally ensures that this is a task they can carry out with skill and conviction.

Achieving the same level of participation as may occur in the one-to-one setting proved more difficult because only one question or comment could be fielded at a time. However, there were social compensations which far outweighed this limitation. Provided the children could engage in unison responses where it was natural and appropriate, we found that all the ancient satisfactions of chant and song were made available to sustain the feeling of involvement. Indeed, by using favorite poems, jingles, chants, and songs as basic reading material—that is, in the enlarged print format—another naturally satisfying part of normal school experience could be turned directly to literacy learning.

Security and joy developed naturally for both children and teacher. Favorite books soon carried with them all the secure associations of an old friend; children began going to books to achieve security. Because of the high impact of the books, and the teacher's pleasure-sharing role, joy was a common experience for all the children.

As for the teachers themselves, because they were doing something at the center of their competence rather than attempting to follow a half-understood methodology, they, too, experienced security and joy. They were able to develop their skill in using the natural opportunities for teaching gradually from a confident base—if attention were lost or a teaching point fell flat, they simply stepped back into the story, got it moving again, and recaptured the interest of the children.

Furthermore, they were able to engage in the input, reading activity with the whole class or a large group without a sense of guilt. (Try reading a captivating story to one group while the others carry out group tasks within earshot!) The problem of matching children to appropriate materials, or of keeping a group going at the same pace so as not to end up with nine or ten groups, almost disappeared. It was now the responsibility of each learner to select the materials he or she would "work on." Even though the teachers were using a new methodology with unusual priorities, their sense of relief from the pressures of structured programs and their enjoyment of the language period grew rapidly.

Once the decision had been made to put other priorities aside in an attempt to establish this model as the central framework of the reading program, the practical application proved a remarkably simple matter. The task now was to refine the procedures in the light of professional knowledge from many sources in order to get optimal educational returns from the simple learning structure which had been set up.

A typical teaching-learning sequence of shared book experience in many classrooms developed along the following lines:

Opening warm-up	Favorite poems, jingles, songs, with enlarged text. Teaching of new poem or song.
Old favorite	Enjoyment of a favorite story in enlarged format. Teaching of skills in context. Deepening understanding. Unison participation. Role playing, dramatization.
Language games, especially alphabet	Alphabet games, rhymes, and songs, using letter names. Fun with words and sounds, meaningful situations. (Not isolated phonic drills.)
New story	Highlight of session. Long story may be broken naturally into two or more parts. Inducing word-solving strategies in context, participation in prediction and confirmation of new vocabulary.

147

Output activities	Independent reading from wide selection of favorites. Related arts activities stemming from new story. Creative writing often using structures from new story. Playing teacher—several children enjoy favorite together—one acting as teacher.

Development of shared book experience techniques went on for several years in key schools. Because the procedures tended to be communicated through demonstration and discussion, documentation was regrettably limited during this time. As a result of local and national in-service courses, and observation by hundreds of teachers and students in these key schools, the ideas spread rapidly. They tended to be used to supplement current procedures, and many mixed styles of teaching arose.

In 1973, convinced that the ideas deserved careful trial, the Department of Education nominated a large experimental school in a new housing area for the trial of these and other approaches. It was important to determine that shared book experience procedures could lead to effective literacy without the support of other programs or materials, and so one class of 35 beginners was taught for two years by these procedures alone. No graded or structured materials were used and all word-solving skills were taught in context during real reading. This experimental group proved equal or superior to other experimental and control groups on a variety of measures including Marie Clay's *Diagnostic Survey* (1980). Of greatest significance was the highly positive attitudes toward reading displayed by the slow-developing children after two years in the natural, shared book experience environment.

Following this study, the Department of Education embarked on an ambitious, national in-service program for primary teachers which was known as the "Early Reading In-service Course," and a complementary program for parents in both radio and print media (Horton, 1978). The radical movement of early schooling toward developmental models has been accomplished on a national scale, albeit the scale of a small nation.

Much has been done internationally since then, and more remains to be done. From our own symposium Yetta Goodman (1980), Margaret Meek (1982), and Dorothy Butler (1979 and 1980) have contributed to that growing movement in literacy toward plain, human, good sense. The pioneering figures, Goodman (e.g. 1968, 1979), Frank Smith (e.g., 1978), and Marie Clay (e.g., 1980), have continued to inform the movement. Recent work in writing, such as is brought together in Temple et al. (1982), extends insights over the full corpus of literacy. Practical professionals, such as Robert and Marlene McCracken (1979), Bill Martin Jr. and Peggy Brogan (1972), Mark Aulls (1982), Anne Pulvertaft (1978), and F. L. Barrett (1982) in their diverse ways support teachers in the daily enterprise of application. Researchers too numerous to list, among

148

them David Doake, Judith Newman, Elizabeth Sulzby, and Robert Teale, push back the frontiers.

Space does not permit a discussion of the written language and related arts aspects of shared book experience programs. When children are motivated to express themselves under the influence of a rich and highly familiar literature, and when such facilitating conditions for expression are provided, the outcomes are extremely satisfying. The whole set of ideas, sometimes referred to now as "holistic," is complex, rich, and compelling. Certainly it promises us a clarity beyond eclecticism and an opportunity to use our own deep responses to what is memorable in print toward the mastery of literacy within the environment of early schooling.

CONCLUDING REMARKS

This [chapter] has attempted to describe a complex movement of research and development spread over some 15 years and involving professional contributions too numerous and too subtle to be fully analyzed. There is an obvious need for specific research of many kinds within this framework. The purpose of this [chapter] has been to bring together a set of ideas which both challenges some of our most sacred instructional assumptions and points to alternative models as appropriate and eminently workable.

The acquisition of spoken language in infancy is a highly complex process, but there are a number of very simple and natural insights at the center of our success in providing favorable conditions for the process to be learned. Experience and research suggest that a very similar set of simple and natural insights facilitate the mastery of literacy skills. Among these is that we may provide favorable conditions for learning literacy tasks in developmental ways such as using children's favorite books, and the powerful strategies they induce, at the very center of the literacy program.

REFERENCES

Ashton-Warner, Sylvia. *Teacher*. New York: Simon and Schuster, 1963.
Aulls, Mark, W. *Developing readers in today's elementary school*. Boston: Allyn and Bacon, 1982.
Barrett, F. L. *A teacher's guide to shared reading*. Toronto: Scholastic, 1982.
Bennett, Jill. *Learning to read with picture books*. Gloucester, Ont.: Thimble Press, 1979.
Butler, Dorothy. *Cushla and her books*. Auckland: Hodder and Stoughton, 1979.
Butler, Dorothy. *Babies need books*. Toronto: Bodley Head, 1980.

Butler, Dorothy, and Clay, Marie. *Reading begins at home*. Auckland: Heinemann, 1979.

Clay, Marie. *Reading: The patterning of complex behaviour*. Auckland: Heinemann, 1972.

Clay, Marie. *The early detection of reading difficulties: A diagnostic survey with recovery procedures*. Auckland: Heinemann, 1980.

Eastman, P. D. *Are you my mother?* New York: Beginner Books, 1960.

Goodman, Kenneth S. (Ed.). *The psycholinguistic nature of the reading process*. Detroit: Wayne State University Press, 1968.

Goodman, Kenneth, and Goodman, Yetta M. Learning to read is natural. In L. B. Resnik and P. B. Weaver (Eds.), *Theory and practice of early reading*, Vol. 1, pp. 137–154. Hillsdale, N.J.: Lawrence Erlbaum Associates, 1979.

Goodman, Yetta M. and Burke, Carolyn. *Reading strategies: Focus on comprehension*. New York: Holt Rinehart, 1980.

Holdaway, Don. *The foundations of literacy*. Sydney: Ashton Scholastic, 1979.

Horton, Jo. *On the way to reading*. Wellington: Department of Education, 1978.

McCracken, Marlene J., and Robert A. *Reading, writing and language*. Winnipeg: Peguis Publishers, 1979.

Martin Jr., Bill, and Brogan, Peggy. *Teacher's guide to the instant readers*. New York: Holt, Rinehart and Winston, 1972.

Meek, Margaret. *Learning to read*. London: Bodley Head, 1982.

Pulvertaft, Anne. *Carry on reading*. Sydney: Ashton Scholastic, 1978.

Smith, Frank. *Understanding reading*, 2nd ed. New York: Holt, Rinehart and Winston, 1978.

Temple, Charles A., Nathan, Ruth G., and Burris, Nancy. *The beginnings of writing*. Boston: Allyn and Bacon, 1982.

Veatch, Jeanette. *Individualizing your reading program*. New York: Putnam, 1959.

15. ONE-ON-ONE ON READING

by Roberta Long, Maryann Manning, and Gary Manning,
University of Alabama at Birmingham

In this chapter, Roberta Long, Maryann Manning, and Gary Manning present ideas for individual reading conferences as a part of a literature-based reading program. Reading conferences on books that students have selected are important in a whole-language program. The need for teachers to be "sensitive listeners and skillful questioners" as they confer with students on a regular basis is also emphasized. Students benefit because reading conferences (a) support their personal selection of books, (b) help them read at appropriate levels, (c) assist them in making relationships and improving thinking, and (d) make reading fun. The teacher benefits because the conference provides an opportunity to foster a closer working relationship with students. In this personalized approach to reading instruction the teacher is able to assure that reading is pleasurable, helping to make it a lifelong activity for the student. ·

This chapter is reprinted with permission of the publisher Early Years, Inc., Norwalk, CT 06854, from the February 1987 issue of Teaching/K–8.

Most American teachers assume that they should teach their students to think for themselves. Such an assumption, however, is alien to many teachers throughout the world. For example, one of the authors of this article lived and taught in the Soviet Union; while there, she had many opportunities to visit Russian schools and to talk with Russian teachers. She observed that children are taught, from the very beginning of their formal schooling, to think in the same way and to give the right answers. Children in Russia learn to sacrifice their individual thoughts, interests and needs to those of the group, and the needs of the group are always determined by the leaders of the State. Drill, memorization and correct response epitomize Soviet classrooms.

Unlike Soviet teachers, American teachers are educated to believe that one of their responsibilities is to teach children to think critically and independently. Encouraging children to think, of course, takes time, forethought, empathy and sensitivity on the part of the teacher. If you are trying to accomplish this goal, individualizing your reading program and having conferences with your students will help you to do so. (For more information on a total individualized reading program, we suggest you read *Reading in the Elementary School* by Jeannette Veatch. The latest edition was published by Richard Owens, New York, 1985.)

By individualizing your reading program, we mean organizing reading so that children select their own reading materials, pace themselves through the materials and have individual conferences with the teacher. We believe conferences are the key to the success of an individualized program.

During reading conferences the child may read to the teacher, retell a story, or respond to questions asked by the teacher. The teacher can talk with the child about his or her reading selection, learn what prior knowledge the child brings to the selection, or assess how the child interacts with print. It may also be a time for teaching the child a reading strategy that will improve his or her reading.

We believe teacher-student conferences are an important component of the reading program at all grade levels. Before children are formally reading, they can have conferences with the teacher about picture books, wordless books or simple, highly predictable books such as *Brown Bear, Brown Bear, What Do You See?* by Bill Martin, Jr. (Holt, Rinehart and Winston, 1967). After children are reading independently, their conferences will continue to be about books or stories they have selected to read.

Ideally, there should be a time during the school day when just the teacher and one child spend a few minutes together focusing on the child's reading. The length of the conference can be as short as three minutes or as long as ten minutes, depending on the purpose of the conference and the needs of the child at that particular time. The teacher does not have to listen to every child read every day, but should try to have at least two conferences a week with each child.

For the conference to have maximum benefit for the child, the teacher must be a sensitive listener and a skillful questioner. In short, the teacher must be a good "kid watcher." Being a kid watcher is simply being sensitive to all aspects of a child's development. When you begin a reading conference, for example, spend a few moments in general conversation. Ask questions about the child's family, pets, or some special event. You might note that the child is wearing something new or has a different hair style. Elaine volunteered that her mama had to go to work because her daddy lost his job. Another child said he couldn't sleep at night because his mother and daddy were always fighting and he was afraid his daddy was going to move. In addition to problems at home, you'll learn about children's peer group relationships and about the things that make them happy or sad. The conference provides a special opportunity to foster a close relationship with your children.

You'll also learn much about a child's reading behavior when just the two of you sit together and talk about the child's book selection, and as you listen to a favorite passage read aloud. You can learn how the child is processing print by the type of miscues that are made. For example, substituting *gorgeous* for *pretty* and *enormous* for *big* reveals a rich vocabulary, a minimum attention to print and a focus on meaning rather than individual words. The enthusiasm expressed for a particular book or book character will let you know how the child feels about the selected book and will provide a basis for guiding future reading.

The retelling of a story and the response to your questions tell you what meaning the child has created from the text. Relationships the child has made between prior experiences and the content of the story will also be evident.

In the remainder of this [chapter], we describe more specifically the benefits of individualized reading and teacher-student conferences. For each benefit discussed, we include excerpts from actual classroom conferences.

BENEFITS OF READING CONFERENCES

1. Self-selection capitalizes on interest.

Traditionally, teachers have said, "When you finish your work, you can choose a book to read." We suggest, however, that children's choices should be the heart of the reading program, not just something to do if there's free time. There's nothing that fires up the internal combustion system of a reader like being able to read self-selected materials.

When children select their own material for reading, they'll choose a story which appeals to them. They're likely to choose something for which they have a prior knowledge, an essential element for constructing meaning in reading.

Children may not select the book you would have selected for them; nor will they always share the information you expect. David, grade 1, selected Ethel and Leonard Kessler's, *Do Baby Bears Sit in Chairs?* (Doubleday) to use for a conference with the teacher. He couldn't wait to tell Ms. Hughes that chair rhymed with underwear. He also thought that the bear being kissed by his mother was special. When asked why the bear was kissed, David said, "Well, he deserved it because he did all those good things." When the teacher asked if the bears did anything that he, too, liked to do, David said, "Yeah, I like to float red tug boats and I write a bunch of stories and I do lots of good things. My mama kisses me, too."

In this conference, David expressed his knowledge of rhyming words and of tug boats. The teacher learned more about David and what he brought to the reading selection. It was evident that he was interested in the story and could relate the content to his own experiences.

When children are allowed to select their own reading materials, they, like David, will select something that makes sense to them and which will, in turn, lead to the understanding that reading is constructing meaning from print.

2. Students read at an appropriate level.

Not only are prior knowledge and interest essential for the construction of meaning in reading, but children must also read material at a level appropriate for their stage of reading development. In an individualized reading program based on teacher-student conferences, we know when children are reading at a level appropriate for them. In fact, children themselves usually know when a book is at an appropriate level. For example, in a reading conference we heard Anthony, a fourth grader, tell his teacher, "I ain't got all that much time to read a big book. Some big books say read me all in a week, and even smart kids take a week and a half to read it."

After much pondering, Anthony selected a picture book to read. His retelling of the story indicated he had selected a book for which he could create some meaning. Anthony had been considered a non-reader by his previous teachers, not an uncommon situation when all children in the same room are expected to read at the same level.

Anthony's classmate, Diane, had just completed reading *Johnny Tremain* by Esther Forbes (Houghton Mifflin, 1960). We listened in on her conference with the teacher and were amazed at her retelling of this advanced book. She was excited about the book and could obviously comprehend text much above her grade level.

Anthony and Diane, two children in the same classroom who were worlds apart in their reading ability, were each reading at a level appropriate for their stage of reading development.

3. Students make relationships and improve thinking.

Through skillful questioning, the teacher can help students relate what the author is saying to their own experiences. The following excerpt from a conference with Mary Jean about Laura Ingalls Wilder's *The Long Winter* (Harper and Row) reveals this process.

The teacher asked, "How do you think Laura felt about living on a farm?"

"She like some things, but she didn't like it because just to go to church was hard," Mary Jean replied. "In the book, *The Long Winter*, they couldn't go to church even for Christmas because it was snowy, and the children and grown-ups would catch pneumonia.''

The teacher reminded Mary Jean of the good time Laura's family had on Christmas Eve when Ma, Laura and Carrie had finished the Christmas cooking and decided to have a loaf of light bread and some cranberry sauce for supper. They were excited about Christmas and Laura thought, ''It seemed too bad to lose any of that happy time in sleep.'' The teacher then asked Mary Jean if she had ever felt the same as Laura.

Mary Jean gave several examples about times in her life when she lost ''happy time'' because she had to go to sleep. She recalled the time at her slumber party when everyone was laughing and talking, and her mother said they all had to go to sleep. She also told about one time when they were at the beach and she wanted to look at her shells and watch television, but her parents insisted, ''You must go to bed *now!*''

As evidenced from this conference, Mary Jean was able to relate Laura's experiences in the 1800's to her own 1980's experiences. The teacher knew the kinds of questions to ask that helped Mary Jean make relationships. Had the teacher stopped at the point of asking only about Laura's experiences, little might have been learned about Mary Jean's thinking and the strengths and knowledge she brought to Wilder's books.

4. Reading is fun for both teachers and children.

What could be more enjoyable than sitting beside a child and talking about a book the child has read, sharing a funny incident or laughing about a character's antics?

Let's join Stacy as she tells her teacher about Peggy Parrish's *Amelia Bedelia and the Baby* (Greenwillow, 1981).

Stacy: You see, Amelia Bedelia is a babysitter for Missy and she does everything wrong. Missy's mother said to have a bath and a playtime and a nap. Well, Amelia Bedelia did what Mrs. Lane told her to do. She took a bath and she had her playtime. She even took a nap. See, Missy was supposed to do these things but Amelia Bedelia did them.

Teacher: Was there a part of the story that you liked best or made you laugh the most?

Stacy: (giggling): Yes. When Mr. and Mrs. Lane came in and Mrs. Lane screamed, 'What did you do to my baby?' Missy had red stuff all over her because Amelia Bedelia had let her eat catsup and strawberries.

Teacher: What do you think about Amelia Bedelia's abilities as a babysitter?

Stacy: She was good 'cause the baby loved her and the whole family loved Amelia Bedelia's strawberry tarts.

There was no question that Stacy enjoyed reading about funny Amelia Bedelia. The teacher laughed with Stacy as she told about Amelia Bedelia's literal interpretation of the Lanes' messages. We, too, enjoyed sitting in on this conference. Conferences are relaxing, pleasurable and fun for all involved.

The following remarks were made by Ann, a teacher who recently changed her traditional basal reading program to the kind of program recommended in this [chapter]. We think that what Ann has to say clearly illustrates the benefits of conferences to both children and teacher.

"When I began using reading conferences," she says, "I witnessed the difference that self-selection of reading materials can make in a reading program. Enthusiasm for reading increased one hundred percent when my students were allowed to choose their own books for reading. Their attitudes towards reading have changed. They're excited about reading and they're reading for meaning.

"But perhaps the most overwhelming thing that has happened since I started reading conferences has been in my own thinking about reading. It began with changing my working definition of reading. I knew reading had to include meaning when I insisted on one hundred percent accuracy in oral reading and taught isolated skills."

Ann has some positive things to say about reading conferences, too.

"I'm now able to literally witness children's thinking about language, and to understand how they're really interacting with print. No standardized test, no skills worksheet and no reading group could tell me as quickly or as thoroughly what a child is thinking as can a few minutes spent with a child in a reading conference. Aren't thinking, growing and loving what teaching is all about? It's exciting to think that a good reading conference can encompass it all."

16. FIFTH GRADERS RESPOND TO A CHANGED READING PROGRAM

by Cora Lee Five, Scarsdale Public Schools, New York

Cora Lee Five describes the influence of the work of Atwell, Giacobbe, and Harste on her teaching of reading. The result, as depicted by Five, is a classroom alive with interested readers. The alert faces of students are one expression of the effects of a meaningful language program. Written conversations between a teacher and students about books they have read are an example of the kind of work that enhances Five's reading process classroom. Five's account of some of her students—Danny, Josh, John, Etay, and David—gives the reader insight into how a sensitive teacher can inspire students to grow as literate members of society. If a classroom is to be a place where students can develop as readers, the environment itself must be a literate one.

Other teachers, too, have been inspired by the work of Atwell, Giacobbe, and Harste, and have made their reading programs more meaningful as a result. Middle-level teachers interested in additional ideas for improving their language programs will enjoy Nancie Atwell's In the Middle, *(Portsmouth, N.H.: Boynton/Cook, 1987).*

This chapter appeared in The Harvard Educational Review, *vol. 56 (November 1986): 395–405. Copyright © 1986, Harvard Educational Review. Reprinted with permission.*

How can teachers continue to learn about teaching? This question receives much attention in the current discussion about improving schools. Throughout my teaching career I have attended many university courses and inservice workshops. Usually these are opportunities for teachers to learn about new curricula and teaching approaches. Although these sessions have introduced me to many ideas I would not have come across on my own, I have had to find my own ways to make new ideas work in my classroom.

My own classroom research has helped me understand the impact new approaches have in my own classroom. As a teacher-researcher I welcome the opportunity to test hypotheses and pay attention to what my experiences teach me. Observing, listening, and questioning keep me alert to my students' needs and help me find ways to improve my instruction. Often this means involving the students in the research. I do this by telling them that I, too, want to learn, and by explaining what it is I want to learn. As my students become an active part of my research, we become a community of learners, rather than a teacher-centered classroom. The result is reciprocity in our learning: I learn from my students as they learn from me.

Classroom research helped me improve the way I teach reading. What follows is an account of my efforts to adapt and try out a new reading program with my fifth graders. I will acknowledge the ideas I received from other people who inspired the various changes I attempted. But I will concentrate on what I learned as I made these program changes and how my research enabled me to figure some things out for myself.

Over the past few years, the work of three people—Nancie Atwell, Mary Ellen Giacobbe, and Jerome Harste—has profoundly influenced my teaching of reading. Atwell's (1984, 1985) description of how her eighth graders responded to their reading by writing letters to her in dialogue journals stimulated my own thinking. She became involved in students' reactions to books by writing letters back to them. Giacobbe (1985) made me realize that teachers must be responsive to children and their reading. She described ways to hold a quick reading conference with each child every day. Harste (1984, 1985) interested me in viewing children as informants and learning from them. His ideas helped me recognize the benefits of encouraging children to use many strategies to make meaning and of allowing time for collaborative learning—time for students to talk, time for them to think and respond.

Inspired by the insight of these three people, I embarked on a new venture two years ago—the creation of a reading program that would give children time to read and time to make meaning through writing and talking about books. The twenty-five students in my self-contained classroom had a wide range of abilities. The class included children who had learning disabilities and children who spoke English as a second language. I hoped all of these students would turn into readers who loved reading, and I hoped research would help me recognize how that happened.

The first thing I did was the most difficult: With much trepidation, I gave up the reading workbooks. As an alternative, I set up a reading program based primarily on Atwell's approach using dialogue journals. It had worked with her eighth graders; would it work with my ten-year-olds? The answer turned out to be, "Yes." My students became immersed in books—they began to talk books, authors, reading, and writing. And so did I.

As I considered how I wanted to use the ideas of Atwell, Giacobbe, and Harste, I noticed that three crucial elements—time, ownership, and response—made my new approach to teaching reading similar to the process approach to teaching writing. It was essential to increase the amount of school time children had for reading. Each forty-five minute reading period began with a mini-lesson during which the class and I discussed character development, setting, titles, different genres, or various aspects of the reading process. Following this lesson students read books of their own choosing. During this reading time I spoke briefly with each child about his or her book, and then I spent the remainder of the period reading a book of my own choice. We ended the period with either a group sharing-time, often related to the mini-lesson, or discussions among two or three students who talked about some aspect of their books.

The children maintained ownership in this process because they decided what to read. Books from home, from the public and school libraries, and from the classroom all became texts for our reading period. Children read the books they selected, not those assigned by me.

The third element, response, became the focus of my research. Discussions during the reading period were not the only way the students communicated about what they read; they also responded to their reading in a variety of ways in their literature journals. The primary way of responding was a letter to me when they finished a book. I read their journals and wrote letters back to them. They also wrote several letters each month about their books to a friend or partner in the classroom. This written communication following the completion of a book or the arrival of a partner's letter was completed during the reading period.

One of my first observations was of the difference between the oral and written responses. When the students talked to each other, they usually retold the literal details of the story. When they wrote, they apparently used time to reflect, to think. The letters, in particular, fascinated me because I could return to them and read them again. As each child's work accumulated, I could more easily follow the changes and development in their thinking about literature. At the beginning of the year the journal responses resembled the book reports which the students had prepared in their earlier grades. The children summarized plots and offered recommendations about their books. Gradually, the topics addressed in the mini-lessons and in our discussions of the books I read aloud began to appear in the children's journal entries. Their letters to me and to each other eventually included discussions of the following:

- the characters, often making personal connections to them
- the main idea or focus of the book
- the tone or mood
- characteristics of a particular author or techniques used by the author that they wished to apply to their own writing
- the way a certain lead, ending, image or a particular voice or feeling contributed to a story

159

- their predictions, inferences, and questions based on the books
- their own interpretations of their reading
- their own reading process, and of how they learned to read.

As I collected and compared students' responses and asked myself new questions about how students handled this task and became more involved in their reading, I learned much from Danny. Danny, who did not like reading at the beginning of the year, used one of his journal entries to describe his experience of learning to read.

Dear Miss Five

when I was 4 years old my mom ust to read to me. some times she would let me try. I was pretty pitifull. then in kindergarden I always acted like I was reading and never raised my hand to read out loud. then in first grade we had a reading period and I sat and turned the pages. by this time I was a pro at turning the pages. when the teacher came over I don't know how she noticed but she did and she knew I didnt know how to read and she taugt me how to read. Also the new kid on the block was danish and he didnt know any english so as I taught him I taught myself in a way. . . .

After two months of the school year there were signs of Danny's increasing involvement with books. Here is how he responded at the time to Okimoto's (1982) *Norman Schnurman, Average Person.*

November 27

Dear Miss Five,

This letter is about Norman Schurnman—"Average Person". The things I liked best about this book were, feeling and comedy. Especialy feeling. Because when I read the part when he told his Dad he didn't want to play football. I think he desvered "Ten Medals"! Because if I had a Dad like that I would have probably played the whole season even if I was that bad and got hurt alot. Because I wouldnt have the heart to watch him put his head down in dissapointment. And if he did put his head down, I would have felt so guilty I would have came back ten minutes later and said Dad I'll play, No matter how bad it felt. But I guess me and norman are different people. And I thought the author had a good ending because it made you in a way forget about the incident with his Dad.

Truly Yours,
Danny

In my letter back to Danny I commented on the personal connections he was beginning to make with the characters.

November 27

Dear Danny,

I could tell you were really involved with the characters in this book. I agree with you that Norman had a difficult decision to make. It must have been very hard for him to tell his dad, but I imagine it was also very hard for Norman to

160

keep playing on the team. I guess Norman felt he did the best he could do and had to make his own decision.

You made a good point about the ending. Perhaps the author wanted a happy ending, and the ending in the book does make you forget about the situation with his father.

Sincerely,
Miss Five

Four months later Danny loved to read and write and developed an interest in the authors of the books he was reading. He discovered the writer Byars through *Good-bye, Chicken Little* (1979) and began to wonder about the basis for her story.

> . . . I thought that this book was so true and this may have happened to a kid. I think I might send a letter to Betsy Byars to see if this book was based on experience. I thought his biggest mistake was fighting with conrad. this book was so good I wish I could read it forever.

That discovery was important to Danny in several ways. He wrote to Byars and treasured the letter he received in return, stapling it into his literature journal. He read all the rest of her books. He also decided to write in his personal journal every night because, as he explained it, "In case I really do become an author, I want to remember all my experiences so I can put them in books for kids my age."

As the year progressed, many students began to experiment, struggling to interpret the ideas in the books they read. Josh described the character Jess in Patterson's (1977) *Bridge to Terabithia.*

Dear Miss Five,

> Jess has so many feelings its hard to discribe him. Let's say he had three stages. First, a normal, hardworking stage at the beginning, and feelings, if he had any, would never be shared with anyone else. The second stage, when Leslie came into his life, tured into a kind of magical stage in a way for him. The third stage, when Leslie died, he began to relate to adults. These three stages make him real.

Sincirly,
Josh

John, a less able reader, responded to the same book.

Dear Miss Five,

> I think that Jess is changing on the inside because of lesslys death. He is starting to undersand not only his father but all gronups and I think that he likes his sister better.

Etay began to interpret and extend his ideas after only a few weeks. His response to Byar's (1974) *After the Goatman* and his other letters showed his developing ability to look beyond the story line.

Dear Miss Five,

On Thursday I finished *After the Goat Man*. I thought it was better than all the other books I read by Betsy Byars. I think she got the idea of the goat from as goats are supposed to be stubborn and the character is stubborn. I think thats her symbol for the character. I also like the way she puts Harold as a kid still in his fantasys and still dreaming about himself. I like the way she put her characters. There is also something that I liked about an anology about life. Figgy puts life as a spider-web and everybody's all tied up except for him, and he's only tied up by one string which is his grandfather (the Goat Man.)

Etay

Etay found a connection between *The Night Swimmers*, also by Byars (1982), and Patterson's (1977) *Bridge to Terabithia*.

. . . In the end of the book Roy asked his olderst sister "is the Bowlwater plant really a big gigantic plant with bedspreads for flowers" and he went on explaining his fantasy. His oldest sister answered "no." At that moment I thought about the book. I thought maybe that was Roy's bridge (like Bridge to Terabithia) from his fantasy world to reallity world.

Etay

The development of the comments in the letters suggested to me that students become better readers when their early, and perhaps less successful, attempts to search for greater depth in their books are not treated as comprehension problems. Just as experimenting and risk-taking are important in learning to write, they are also important in learning to read. I began to pay more attention to how students found ways to express what certain books meant to them.

In the winter Etay discovered Alexander's (1981) *Westmark* trilogy. When he finished the last of the three books, he wrote a long letter relating the ideas throughout the trilogy. The conclusion of the letter summarized his thoughts.

. . . In the end it wasn't the monarchy that won the war but the people. And the people are the ones who took over everything. I think in this triology Lloyd Alexander shows what happened in England. In the start England's monarchy had power over everything, like in the first book (Westmark). Slowly the power of the monarchy lessened, until now the monarchy has probably no power at all. In the *Beggar Queen*, in the end, the monarchy was overthrown by the people.

Etay

Many students, including David, used their letters to express the joy of finding a wonderful book.

Dear Miss Five,

 Yesterday I finished the best book, called, *The Green Futures of Tycho.* As soon as I read the back of it at the book fair I knew it was the book for me. And I was right, it felt as though it was made especially for me. . . . Ever since I was a little kid, I loved the thought of going into the past & the future, & telling my future, & thinking about all of it.

But David's response was not limited to this personal interest in the book's topic. He also commented on the author's craft.

. . . I like how the author kept changing & making the future & past more exciting. Like in the future he invented things, but didn't tell what they did, he let you figure it out. You should definitely read it to the class.

From
David

 The letters to partners raised some new questions about children as responders to literature. Three or four times a month each child would write about his or her book to another child in the class. The understanding was that if they received a letter, they were required to write back. Their letters to each other often differed from the ones they wrote to me; they struck me as having a more casual tone, and the writers seemed less concerned with what they thought I expected them to say in their response. Early in the school year David and Etay started to write to each other.

OCT. 8

Dear Etay,

I just finished *A Wrinkle in Time.* It is great book. I think you should read it again. Some parts of the book are pretty confusing though.

From,
David

Dear David,

I hate science fiction!!!
Etay

By November more of an exchange of ideas appeared.

November 14

Dear Etay,

 I am reading a book called *Alice's Adventures in Wonderland.* I don't like it very much. I think it is to boring! It seems that it takes forever. I have always liked *Alice in Wonderland,* but I don't like this one. Even though it is by the original author, Lewis Carrol. I am up to the The Mock turtle's story. My favorite parts so far is when she was playing croquet & when she kept growing & shrinking when she ate the mushroom, even though those parts are not so good. I am not going to read, *Trough the Looking Glass.*

David

Dear David,

I can see that you didn't like this book. I didn't like it either. I thought it was just an adventure after an adventure and then all it lead to was a dream. It was written the best way it could but I don't think it was made for our age. I think it was made for smaller kids (who see it as a cute little fantasy) or for grownups (who see it with some meaning). We're in the middle because we're too big to see it as a cute fantasy and we're too small to see it with some meaning.

Etay

The letters my students wrote to me and to each other also made me think about the classroom context needed to support their reading. I realized that they read with greater depth when they selected their own books, ones that appealed to them rather than those that I thought they "should" read. I also realized that they probably took risks to find ways to express themselves because I did not label their comments as "correct" or "incorrect." A classroom environment that accepted and respected what children said about books was necessary for these journal entries and their increased interest in reading. Furthermore, the example of the peer correspondence shows that the acceptance from other students can be as important as the teacher's.

Writing letters was not the only way my students responded to literature. "Mapping" is another strategy. Krim (1985, 1986) uses mapping with her senior high school students. Intrigued with her concept, I decided to try it with my fifth graders. I asked some students to map Patterson's (1977) *Bridge to Terabithia*. Some of their drawings appear on pages 165–67.

Bridge to Terabithia is a story about a fifth-grade boy, Jess, who has difficulty relating to other people. He has no friends until Leslie moves near his home. Together they create Terabithia, a kingdom where Jess is king and Leslie queen. Jess loses his friend when Leslie has a fatal accident in Terabithia. As he tries to adjust to her death, Jess grows and begins to build a closer relationship with his father and others. In the end, Jess is able to give the magic of Terabithia to his younger sister Maybelle.

In his map Josh used lines and numbers to connect his drawings of important events. Although most of the events appear in comparatively small drawings, Josh represented two key points of the story with larger drawings. In one he made a bridge between Jess and his father; in the other he showed Jess rebuilding the magic of Terabithia for his sister Maybelle.

Amy mapped the story in a different way. She saw the book in terms of feelings and made a flow chart with the characters Jess and Leslie at the top. They come together at school, where Jess is at first "anxious" and Leslie feels "different and out of place." "Proud but mad" are Jess's feelings after a specific school experience that made Leslie feel

164

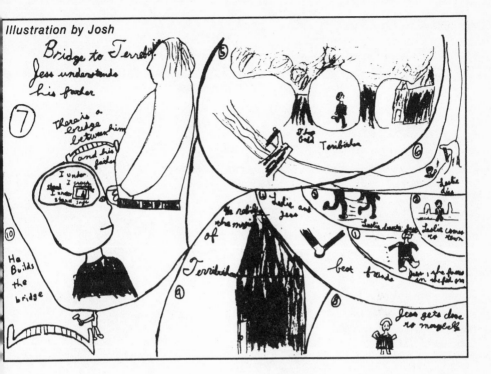

Illustration by Josh

"happy." As their friendship progresses, they are both happy but, as Amy notes, in different ways. Amy follows with other feelings that describe the characters until Leslie's death. Then she continues with the range of emotions Jess experiences as he tries to deal with and accept the loss of his best friend.

Another strategy I used is one suggested by Harste (1985) called Sketch to Stretch. In this approach, as in mapping, the students pick out the most important ideas in their books and combine them in a sketch. This turned out to be a good way to develop sequencing skills as students connected events in a logical order to make a meaningful whole.

David has sketched the important parts of *Good-bye, Chicken Little* and has numbered his sketches to show the order in which they occur: the uncle drowns, Jimmy feels guilty and responsible, he fights with Conrad, they become friends again, and in the last picture David wrote that Jimmy "almost" forgets, and "everything turns out almost perfect."

The effect this kind of reading program had on both my students and me continues to amaze and excite me. By the fourth month of the program I could see children listening to each other and seeking

165

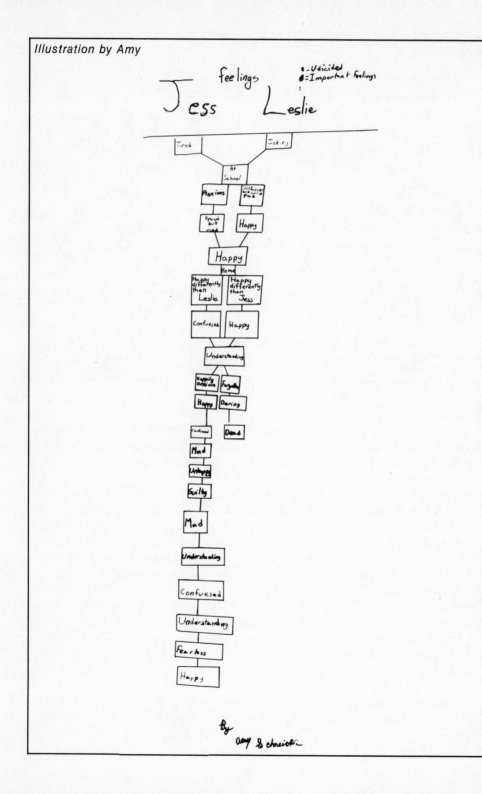

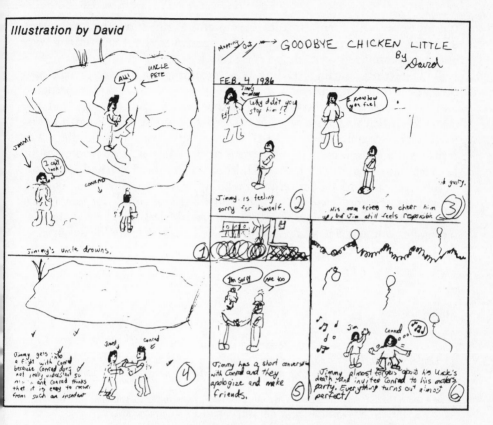

Illustration by David

recommendations for their next selections. They wondered about authors and tried to imitate authors' techniques in their own writing. They looked for feelings, for believable characters, and for interesting words, and they were delighted with effective dialogue.

Another indication of students' interest and joy in reading was the number of books they read during the year. The less able readers, including students with learning disabilities and those for whom English is a second language, read between 25 and 42 books each; the average readers read about 47; and the top readers between 47 and 144 books.

And the new approach had an effect on me. My students and I began to talk books before school, at recess, and at lunchtime; their reading period never seemed to end at twelve, even though the bell had rung. Their enthusiasm was infectious. I was constantly drawn into their discussions and especially their thinking, as I became more and more involved in their reading and their responses. This approach and my researcher's role helped me continue to learn more about these students, their read-

167

ing processes, and their attitudes. Again and again, I saw the importance of giving them freedom to read and opportunities to experiment with and to explore their own ideas.

By collecting, sorting, reading and rereading their letters, maps and sketches, I found for myself a much closer view of how children struggle and then succeed to find meaning in books. The process also kept me engaged in learning because it led me to new questions. What do children learn from my mini-lessons? In what situations will children take more risks with interpreting what they read? These new questions might be ones that help me reach more children in the way I reached John.

John, a real hold-out in terms of reading and loving books, a boy who completed reading few books in the fourth grade, could not have given me a greater gift. One day, I found him at his desk when everyone else had gone to lunch. He was reading. When I walked in he looked up and smiled, saying, "I love this book. I just have to finish this chapter before I go out."

REFERENCES

Alexander, L. (1981). *Westmark*. New York: Dutton.
Alexander, L. (1982). *The kestrel*. New York: Dutton.
Alexander, L. (1984). *The beggar queen*. New York: Dutton.
Atwell, N. (1984). Writing and reading literature from the inside out. *Language Arts, 61,* 240–252.
Atwell, N. (July, 1985). *Reading, writing, thinking, learning* [course]. Institute on Writing, sponsored by Northeastern University. Martha's Vineyard, MA.
Byars, B. (1974). *After the goatman*. New York: Viking.
Byars, B. (1979). *Goodbye, Chicken Little*. New York: Harper and Row.
Byars, B. (1980). *The night swimmers*. New York: Delacorte.
Giacobbe, M. E. (July, 1985). *Reading, writing, thinking, learning* [course]. Institute on Writing, sponsored by Northeastern University. Martha's Vineyard, MA.
Harste, J.C., Woodward, V.A., and Burke, C.L. (1984). *Language stories and literacy lessons*. Portsmouth, NH: Heinemann Educational Books.
Harste, J.C. (July, 1985). *Creativity and intentionality* [course]. Institute on Writing, sponsored by Northeastern University. Martha's Vineyard, MA.
Krim, N. (1986). Where do we go from here? Try mapping. Unpublished manuscript.
Krim, N. (March, 1985). *Integrating reading, writing and critical thinking skills in the teaching of literature: Focus, mapping, and sequencing strategies*. Presentation at the annual spring conference of the National Council of Teachers of English.
Okimoto, J.D. (1982). *Norman Schnurman, average person*. New York: Putnam.
Patterson, K. (1977). *Bridge to Terabithia*. New York: Crowell.
Sleator, W. (1981). *The green futures of Tycho*. New York: Dutton.

17. ALL CHILDREN CAN WRITE

by Donald H. Graves, University of New Hampshire, Durham

Donald Graves is the leader of the writing process movement, which is congruent with whole language. In this chapter, he describes how Billy, a learning-disabled student, grew as a writer. He points out that all students can write and that they develop as writers in similar ways. The ideas he discusses here are relevant for teachers of typical and atypical students.

Graves emphasizes several essentials for a successful writing program: time, topic choice, response, and sense of community. He recommends that students write at least four days a week if they are to develop as writers and enjoy writing. At the heart of the writing process, Graves believes, is letting students choose their own topics. If teachers want to nurture writers, they must help them become aware of what they already know and how to use these experiences and interests as they write. Another important element of the writing process is the need for writers to have audiences who respond to their writing. Graves recommends that each writing period end with students sharing their work with one another. At intervals teachers may also share their writing with students. Finally, he points out, "Writing is a social act. If social actions are to work, the establishment of a community is essential." As students write regularly, take responsibility for their writing, share what they write, and help one another with their writing, they become a community of writers.

Graves also adds a reminder about the importance of teachers working on their own writing in order to teach writing effectively. Many teachers have found Graves' book Writing: Teachers and Children at Work *(Portsmouth, N.H.: Heinemann, 1987) to be especially helpful in implementing a writing workshop in their classrooms.*

This chapter appeared in Learning Disabilities Focus, *1985, 1, 36–43. Copyright 1985 by the Division for Learning Disabilities. Used with permission.*

I stood at the side of Ms. Richards' third grade classroom watching the children write. We were at the beginning of our two–year National Institute of Education study of children's composing processes. The school had diagnosed two of the children in Ms. Richards' room as having severe visual-motor problems. They were not hard to find.

Both leaned over their papers, their elbows crooked at right angles to their bodies to protect the appearance of their papers. I walked over to take a closer look at one of the two children's papers. Billy's paper was smudged, wrinkled, letters blackened; in several instances, his paper was thinned and blackened still more where he had gone through several spelling trials on the same work. The more serious aspect of Billy's writing profile was not his visual-motor difficulty, the appearance of his paper, or his numerous misspellings. Billy was a self-diagnosed poor writer. He connected his writing problems with a lack of worthwhile ideas and experiences. In addition, he was well-versed in what he couldn't do.

Billy had been in a separate program emphasizing visual-motor skills, letter formation, and various fine-motor tasks. No question, using a pencil was painful and arduous for him. Teachers complained that Billy rarely completed his work and was constantly behind the others, though he seemed to be articulate. Billy's program was skill-based, disconnected from meaning, and filled with positive reinforcement about his ability to form letters on good days. There was no attempt to connect his writing with the communication of ideas.

Children with learning disabilities often work on skills in isolation, disconnected from learning itself, and therefore disconnected from themselves as persons. Therefore, like Billy, though their skills may improve slightly in isolation, the children do not perceive the function of the skill. Worse, they do not see the skill as a means to show what they know. Skills work merely supplies additional evidence for the misconception that they are less intelligent than other children.

Billy was in a classroom that stressed writing as a process. This meant the children received help from the time they chose a topic to the time they completed their final work. Ms. Richards played the believing game, starting with what Billy knew, particularly his experiences. In fact, Billy's breakthrough as a writer came when his teacher discovered his interest in and knowledge of gardening. As Ms. Richards helped him to teach her about this subject, she learned how to plant, cultivate, water, fertilize, and provide special care for certain varieties of tomatoes. Although Billy wrote more slowly than the other children, he became lost in his subject, forgot about his poor spelling and handwriting, ceased to cover his paper, and wrote a piece filled with solid information about gardening. Once Billy connected writing with knowing—his knowing—it was then possible to work with his visual-motor and spelling problems, but as incidental to communicating information.

Ms. Richards is now one of the thousands of teachers who teach writing as a process in the United States and the English-speaking world. New research and publications, university courses, and numerous summer institutes, are now helping teachers and administrators to find out for themselves what students can do when they focus on the meaning of writing. Much of the focus of these institutes and courses is on the teachers' own writings: most of us had to rediscover the power of writing for ourselves before we could learn to hear what these young writers had to teach us.

Although writing-process work helps all writers, it seems to be particularly successful with people who see themselves as disenfranchised from literacy. I place in this group learners like Billy who have diagnosed learning disabilities and the accompanying 'I-don't-know-anything'' syndrome.

The writing-process approach to teaching focuses on children's ideas and helps children teach the teacher or other children in the class what they know, with emphasis first given to ideas and clarifying. This is the first experience many children have with other humans who work hard to point to what they know, instead of what is lacking in the message. Small wonder then that the writing process works best with the disenfranchised, who become a bit giddy at the prospect of seeing their words on paper affecting the thinking of others.

Understanding writing as communication is the heart of teaching the writing process. This [chapter] will first focus on the nature of writing, look in greater detail at research on the writing process itself, examine two principles in teaching writing, and then describe four basics in establishing a writing program. It also has a brief section on further reading and recommendations for summer programs for people interested in continuing their study of the writing process.

WHAT IS WRITING?

Writing is a medium with which people communicate with themselves and with others at other places and times. When I write, I write to learn what I know because I don't know fully what I mean until I order the words on paper. Then I see...and know. Writers' first attempts to make sense are crude, rough approximations of what they mean. Writing makes sense of things for oneself, then for others.

Children can share their writing with others by reading aloud, by chatting with friends while writing, or (in more permanent form) by publishing. Billy found that writing carried a different authority from spoken words. When he took the gardening piece out in December, he found that words written in September could be savored three months later. Furthermore, when he read the published books of other children in his room, he began to realize that his book on gardening was read by others when he wasn't present.

Written language is different from oral language. When Billy speaks, he reinforces his meaning by repeating words and phrases. Unlike when he writes, an audience is present; when the audience wanders or indicates disagreement, he changes his message with words, hand signals, facial expressions, and body posture. This is the luxury of oral discourse.

171

"Error," adjustment and experimentation are an expected part of oral discourse.

There is a different tradition surrounding most teaching of writing. Only one attempt, one draft is allowed to communicate full meaning (without an audience response). Red–lined first drafts are the norm; we blanche at any misspellings or crudely formed letters.

Still worse, writing has been used as a form of punishment: "Write your misspelled word 25 times." (This is called reinforcement of visual-memory systems.); "Write one hundred times, 'I will not chew gum in school'"; "Write a 300–word composition on how you will improve your attitude toward school." Most teachers teaching in 1985 were bathed in the punishment syndrome when they were learning to write. Small wonder that most of us subtly communicate writing as a form of punishment. We have known no other model of teaching.

THE WRITING PROCESS

When children use a meaning–centered approach to writing, they compose in idiosyncratic ways. Each child's approach to composing is different from the next. Some draw first, write two words, and in 10 minutes or less announce, "I'm done." Others draw after writing or do not write at all; instead, they speak with a neighbor about what they will write. Some stare out the window or at the blank page and write slowly after 20 minutes of reflection. At some point in their development, writers believe one picture and two words beneath the drawing contain an entire story. In the writer's mind, the story is complete; members of the audience shake their heads and try to work from drawing to text and back to understand the author's intent.

Such idiosyncratic approaches by children seem capricious to outsiders, confusing to children, and bewildering to us as teachers. We intervene with story starters to "get them going," produce pictures as stimuli for writing, and consult language arts texts for language activities. The texts provide "systematic" approaches, often through the teaching of the sentence, advance to two sentences, and finally development of the paragraph. Our detailed observation of young children writing shows they simply don't learn that way. Rather, they write three sentences in one in their first year, not understanding where one sentence ends and the other begins. Studies of children's understanding and use of sentences show they don't acquire full sentence sense until much later (about fifth grade).

The most pernicious aspect of teacher interventions is that children begin to learn early on that others need to supply topics because they come to the page with nothing in their heads. A focus on skills and form

172

to the exclusion of child–initiated meaning further confirms their lack of fit with the writing process.

Prepared materials seek to reduce the stress and the uncertainty that writers face when they encounter the blank page. But the attempt to produce certainty through standardization bypasses the opportunity for child growth. There is good reason to expect tension when a child first writes.

When writers write, they face themselves on the blank page. That clean white piece of paper is like a mirror. When I put words on the page, I construct an image of myself on that whiteness. I may not like my spelling, handwriting, choice of words, aesthetics, or general cleanliness of the page. Until I can begin to capture what I want to say, I have to be willing to accept imperfection and ambiguity. If I arrive at the blank page with a writing history filled with problems, I am already predisposed to run from what I see. I try to hide my paper, throw it away, or mumble to myself, "This is stupid." But with every dangerous, demanding situation, there is an opportunity to learn. Teachers who follow and accompany children as they compose help them to deal with what they see on the page. The reason writing helps children with learning disabilities is that they do far more than learn to write: They learn to come to terms with a new image of themselves as thinkers—with a message to convey to the world.

TEACHING WRITING—TWO BASIC PRINCIPLES

After 12 years of working with writing research and the teaching of writing, I have found two principles essential for effective teaching of writing: (1) The teacher teaches most by showing how he/she learns, and (2) the teacher provides a highly structured classroom.

The best demonstration of how teachers learn is through their gathering of information from the children. They place the children in the position of teaching them what they know, usually through conferences. "Now you say that you have to be careful how deep you plant lettuce, Billy. Can you tell me more about that? And do you think the precise depth should be in your piece for the other children? Will they want to know that?" Billy's teacher has shown him how she learns and how he should learn to listen to questions he soon will be able to ask himself.

Ms. Richards, Billy's teacher, has a basic lifestyle of learning from everyone. Whether seated next to someone on a plane, in the teachers' room, or talking informally with children, she wants to be taught; in a lifetime she has learned how important it is to help others to teach her. People leave Ms. Richards' presence surprised they knew so much about their subjects.

173

Ms. Richards' classroom is a highly structured, predictable classroom. Children who learn to exercise choice and responsibility can function only in a structured room. Furthermore, the up–and–down nature of the writing process itself demands a carefully defined room. Predictability means that writing occurs daily, at set times, with the teacher moving in the midst of the children, listening to their intentions, worries, and concerns. They know she will be nearby attending to their work. She rarely addresses the entire class during writing time. She works hard to establish a studio atmosphere. Predictability also means she won't solve problems for them. Rather, she asks how they might approach the problem. She listens, clarifies their intentions and their problems, and moves on.

Children learn to take responsibility not only for their topics, content of their drafts, and final copy, but also for carrying out classroom decisions. A structured classroom requires an organized teacher who has set the room up to run itself. The teacher has already made a list of the things to be done to help the room function. From September through June, he/she gradually passes on those duties to the children. Attendance, caring for room plants and animals, room cleanliness, lunch lines, desk supervision, and cleaning are but a few examples of these delegations. When room structure and routine do not function well, the teacher and students plan together for the best way to make it function more smoothly. Ms. Richards' room is based on extensive preparation in room design and knowledge of materials, the children, and the process by which they learn to take responsibility.

Teachers who function well in teaching the writing process are interested in what children have to teach them. Writing-process teaching is responsive, demanding teaching that helps children solve problems in the writing process and in the classroom.

CARRYING OUT A WRITING–PROCESS PROGRAM

I am often asked, "What are the essentials to strong writing programs?" Although the list could be extensive, I think that if teachers understand the following four components, their writing programs will serve the children well. These components are adequate provision of time, child choice of topic, responsive teaching, and the establishment of a classroom community, a community that has learned to help itself.

Time

Our data show that children need to write a minimum of four days a week to see any appreciable change in the quality of their writing. It takes that amount of writing to contribute to their personal development as learners. Unless children write at least four days a week, they won't like it. Once–a–week writing (the national average is about one day in eight) merely reminds them they can't write; they never write often enough to listen to their writing. Worst, the teacher simply has no access to the children. He/she has to scurry madly around the room trying to reach each child. With little access to the children, the teacher can't help them take responsibility, solve problems for them, or listen to their responses and questions. The very important connection between speaking and writing is lost.

Although teaching writing four to five times a week helps the teacher, it helps the children even more. When children write on a daily basis, we find they write when they aren't writing. Children get into their subjects, thinking about their texts and topics when they are riding on buses, lying in bed, watching television, reading books, or taking trips. When they write regularly, papers accumulate. There is visible evidence they know and are growing. They gain experience in choosing topics and very soon have more topics to write about than class time can accommodate. Children with learning problems need even more time. They need to learn to listen to themselves with help from the teacher. In summary, regular writing helps:

1. Children choose topics,
2. Children listen to their pieces and revise,
3. Children help each other,
4. Teachers listen to child texts,
5. Skills develop in the context of child pieces,
6. Teachers to have greater access to children.

Topic Choice

The most important thing children can learn is what they know and how they know it. Topic choice, a subject the child is aware that he knows something about, is at the heart of success is writing. Billy struggled with handwriting and spelling and equated those problems with not knowing topics to write about. When his teacher helped him to discover his knowledge and interest in gardening, he began to write, first haltingly, then with greater flow. He was open to help with spelling and handwriting when he knew he had something to say. Skills are important; learning disabilities cannot be ignored, but neither can teachers or researchers forget that writing exists to communicate with self and others.

"How can I get the child to write? Do you have any good motivators?" are frequent questions asked of me in workshops. The word *get* embraces the problem. There are thousands of "motivators" on the market in the form of story starters, paragraph starters, computer software, animated figures, picture starters, and exciting "sure–fire" interest getters. We forget that children are very sophisticated consumers of motivators from Saturday morning television alone. Worse, motivators teach the child that the best stimulus comes from the outside. Writing actually demands dozens of motivators during the course of composing, but they are motivators that can only be supplied by the writer himself. All children have important experiences and interests they can learn to tap through writing. If children are to become independent learners, we have to help them know what they know; this process begins with helping children to choose their own topics.

Very young children, ages five through seven, have very little difficulty choosing topics especially if they write every day. As children grow older and experience the early effects of audience, even under favorable learning conditions, they begin to doubt what they know. From that point on, all writers go through a kind of doubting game about the texts they produce. They learn to read better and are more aware of the discrepancy between their texts and their actual intentions. If, however, overly severe, doubting teachers are added to the internal doubts of the child, writing becomes still more difficult.

If children write every day and share their writing, we find they use each other as the chief stimulus for topic selection. If teachers write with their children, demonstrating the origin of their topics, and surround the children with literature, topic selection is even easier.

Topic selection is helped through daily journal writing where children take 10 minutes to record their thoughts. Teachers may also give 5– to 10–minute writing assignments, such as: "Write about how you think our room could be improved" (just following a discussion about how the room could be improved with the entire class) or "That upsets you? Well, blast away on paper with the first thoughts that come to mind. But write it for you; if you feel like showing it to me, okay." The teacher finds many occasions where it is useful to record thoughts and opinions on paper. Each of these approaches demonstrates what writing is for, as well as helping the children to have access to what they know and think..

Response

People write to share, whether with themselves or others. Writers need audiences to respond to their messages. The response confirms for the writer that the text fits his/her intentions. First, the teacher provides an active audience for the writer by confirming what he/she understands in the text and then by asking a few clarifying questions. Second, the teacher helps the entire class to learn the same procedure during group share time. Each writing period ends with two or three children sharing their pieces with the group while the group follows the discipline of first pointing to what is in the text, then asking questions to learn more about the author's subject. All of these responses, whether by the teacher or the other children, are geared to help writers learn to listen to their own texts.

While the children are writing, Billy's teacher moves around the room, responding to their work in progress. Here is an interchange Ms. Richards had with Billy about his piece "My Garden." (The child's text is presented, followed by the conference with the teacher.)

MY GRDAN

I help my Dad with the grdan ferstyou have to dig it up an than you rake an get the racks out of it. The you make ros an you haveto be cerfull to make it deep enuff so the letis will come up.

Ms. Richards first receives the piece by saying what she understands about what Billy has written. She may also have him read the writing aloud to her:

Ms. Richards:	You've been working hard, Billy. I see that you work with your dad on your garden. You know just what you do; you dig it up, rake it to get the rocks out, and then you have to be careful how deep you plant things. Did I get that right?
Billy:	Yup.
Ms. Richards:	Well, I was wondering, Billy. You say that the lettuce has to be planted deep enough so the lettuce will come up. Could you tell me more about that? I haven't planted a garden for a long time.
Billy:	Well, if you plant it too deep, it won't come up. Lettuce is just near the top.
Ms. Richards:	Oh, I see, and did you plant some other things in your garden?
Billy:	Yup, carrots, beans, turnips (I hate 'em), spinach (that, too), beets, and tomatoes; I like tomatoes.
Ms. Richards:	That's quite a garden, Billy. And what will you be writing here next?
Billy:	You have to water it once you plant it.
Ms. Richards:	Then you already know what you'll be doing, don't you.

There are many problems with Billy's text: misspelled words, run-on sentences, missing capitalizations, and incomplete information. But Billy has just started writing his piece. Therefore Ms. Richards works on word flow, helping Billy to know that he knows something about his subject and that he has a clear understanding of what he will do next. Later, when his piece is finished, she will choose one skill to teach within the

177

context of his topic. Above all, she works hard to help Billy teach her about his subject, to keep control of the topic in his hands, no matter how uncertain Billy might feel about his subject.

Notice that Ms. Richards has spent no more than a minute and a half in response. She then moves to other children while responding in the same manner, receiving a text and asking questions. As she moves to different children in other parts of the room (she does not move in rotation or down rows; the movement appears to be random), the other children can hear that the teacher expects them to help her with what they know. Lengthy responses tend to take the writing away from the child. For example, if Ms. Richards were to say, "I had a garden once, Billy. I planted all kinds of things too: I planted cabbages, those same turnips, yellow beans, pole beans, and corn. Yes it's hard work," she'd be identifying with Billy's garden and the hard work that goes into it, but *she* is now the informant. Such sharing should come only when his piece is completed and his authorship of this piece established.

Ms. Richards' statement is specific. When she receives Billy's text, she uses the actual words he has composed on the page. All writers need to know their words (the actual words on the page) affect other people. Notice that very little praise is given to Billy in this type of response. Instead, the listener, Ms. Richards, points with interest to the words; they are strong enough for her to understand and to remember them. The use of specifics, rather than the exclusive use of praise, is a fundamental issue in helping Billy to maintain control of his piece, as well as to take more responsibility for his text.

Establish a Community of Learners

Writing is a social act. If social actions are to work, then the establishment of a community is essential. A highly predictable classroom is required if children are to learn to take responsibility and become a community of learners who help each other. Writing is an unpredictable act requiring predictable classrooms both in structure and response.

Children with learning disabilities often have histories of emotional problems. Many have become isolated and feel very little sense of community. They thenselves may produce unpredictable classrooms. Their histories in taking responsibility are equally strewn with failure. Notions of choice and responsibility are threatening and require careful work on a broad front. The following ingredients help to build a structured, predictable community of more independent writers.

1. Write daily, at the same time if possible, for a minimum of 30 minutes.

2. Work to establish each child's topical turf, an area of expertise for each writer.

3. Collect writing in folders so that writers can see the accumulation of what they know. Papers do not go home; rather, the collected work is present in class for student, teacher, parent, and administrator to examine. Some writing is published in hardcover or some more durable form.

4. Provide a predictable pattern of teacher participation by sharing your own writing, moving in the midst of students during writing time, and responding in predictable structure to your students' writing.

5. End each writing time with children responding to each other's writing in a predictable format: receiving, questioning.

6. Set up classroom routines in which you examine the entire day to see which responsibilities can be delegated to the children. Solve room problems in discussion. The group learns to negotiate, whether in working with a draft or solving a classroom problem.

7. Continually point to the responsibilities assumed by the group, as well as the specifics of what they know.

The writing classroom is a structured, predictable room in which children learn to make decisions. The external structure is geared to produce a confident, internal thinking framework within which children learn what they know and develop their own initiative.

CONTINUING EDUCATION
OF PROFESSIONALS

Most teachers have been drawn into process work because they have seen significant personal growth by their students with learning problems. Students who lacked confidence and initiative and were disenfranchised from literacy learn to write, share their writing with others, and take charge of their own learning. Although some teachers may wish to start work on the writing process based on this [chapter], I suggest additional reading and work with their own writing.

The single most important help to teachers who work with young writers is work with the teacher's own writing. Both the National Writing Project and our work here at the University of New Hampshire stress work with the teacher's own writing. Thus teachers become acquainted with writing from the inside by actually doing it themselves. It would be unheard of for a piano teacher, a ceramicist, or an artist working with water colors to teach someone their craft without practicing it themselves. Most of us have had little instruction in learning the craft of writing. We've written term papers, letters, and proposals, but we haven't worked with someone who has helped us to know what we know, then

179

showed us how that knowledge is increased through the writing process.

I strongly encourage teachers to become involved in summer programs or consult their own universities to see if writing–process programs or courses are available. The following intensive summer programs concentrate on the teacher's own writing and the teaching of writing:

- Dean Timothy Perkins, Northeastern University, 360 Huntington Avenue, Boston, MA 02115
- Prof. Thomas Newkirk, English Department, Hamilton Smith Hall, University of New Hampshire, Durham, NH 03824
- Prof. Lucy Calkins, Teacher's College, Columbia University, New York, NY 10027.

The National Writing Project has programs in almost all of the 50 states offering three– to four–week summer programs. Information about the National Writing Project is available from Dr. James Gray, National Writing Project, University of California at Berkeley, CA 94720.

For Further Reading

The following books will be helpful in acquiring more detail on teaching writing and organizing classrooms, as well as general background on learning and language theory.

Calkins, L.M. (1983). *Lessons from a child.* Portsmouth, NH: Heinemann.

Graves, D. (1982). *Writing: Teachers and children at work.* Portsmouth, NH: Heinemann.

Hansen, J., Newkirk, T., and Graves, D. (Eds.). (1985). *Breaking ground: Teachers relate reading and writing in the elementary classroom.* Portsmouth, NH: Heinemann.

Harste, J., Burke, C., and Woodward, V. (1984). *Language stories and literacy lessons.* Portsmouth, NH: Heinemann.

Newkirk, T., and Atwell, N. (Eds.). (1982). *Understanding Writing.* Chelmsford, MA: The Northeast Regional Exchange.

For teachers who wish to work with their own writing, I suggest the following:

Murray, D.M. (1983). *Write to learn.* New York: Holt, Rinehart, Winston.

Zinsser, W. (1980). *On writing well.* New York: Harper and Row.

FINAL REFLECTION

Before children go to school, their urge to express is relentless. They learn to speak and to carry messages from one person to another. They burst into their homes to tell what just happened outside. They compose in blocks, play games, mark on sidewalks, and play with pencils or crayons. For most children, early audiences are receptive: adults struggle to make sense of the child's early attempts to communicate.

When children enter school, their urge to express is still present. A few enter already scarred from attempts to communicate with others. But the urge to be, to make a mark on the universe, has not left them. As children grow older and spend more time in school, many become still more disenchanted with writing. They can't keep up with the rest of the class and equate their struggles with handwriting, spelling and early conventions as evidence that their ideas are unacceptable and that they are less intelligent than others. Even for these children, the urge to express, to make worthwhile contributions, to express a meaning that affects others, does not go away.

The most critical factor for children with learning disabilities is the meaning–making question. Teachers need to first believe they know important information, then work overtime to confirm for the child the importance of that information. The children see their teachers write; they see and hear them struggle for meaning on an easel or overhead projector as they compose before them. The children become apprentices to the use of words.

When children write, they make mistakes on the road to communicating their messages. The teacher's first response is to the meaning. Before a piece is completed, the teacher chooses one skill that will enhance the meaning of the piece still further. From the beginning, the teacher works to build a strong history for writers through collections of all their work, some publishing, and the writers' effective sharing with other members of the class.

Most teaching of writing is pointed toward the eradication of error, the mastery of minute, meaningless components that make little sense to the child. Small wonder. Most language arts texts, workbooks, computer software, and reams of behavioral objectives are directed toward the "easy" control of components that will show more specific growth. Although some growth may be evident on components, rarely does it result in the child's use of writing as a tool for learning and enjoyment. Make no mistake, component skills are important; if children do not learn to spell or use a pencil to get words on paper, they won't use writing for learning any more than the other children drilled on component skills. The writing–process approach simply stresses meaning first, and then skills in the context of meaning. Learning how to respond to meaning and to understand what teachers need to see in texts takes much preparation.

The writing process places high demands on the teacher. The room is carefully designed for developing student independence: Decisions are discussed, responsibilities assigned and assumed. Routines are carefully established with writing becoming a very important part of the room's predictability. Initially, response to the child's writing is predictable with receiving of the child's text, followed by questions of clarification, and the child's next step in the writing process.

Teachers who use the writing process to greatest advantage spend time working with their own writing. They read and become involved in many of the National Institutes that are helping teachers use writing as a tool for their own learning. Soon they find their students' learning careers change as well.

18. IS THAT WRITING—OR ARE THOSE MARKS JUST A FIGMENT OF YOUR CURRICULUM?

by Carole Edelsky and Karen Smith, Arizona State University, Tempe

Carole Edelsky and Karen Smith emphasize the importance of students engaging in authentic writing activities. Too often, they point out, classroom writing activities are not authentic, but are contrived situations in which students write in response to a teacher's directions. These authors believe that if writing activities are to be authentic, the graphophonic, syntactic, semantic, and pragmatic systems must be functioning separately and yet interactively.

Edelsky and Smith give examples of authentic and inauthentic writing activities in one classroom. When students wrote letters to thank Mike, a karate expert, for visiting their class and showing his techniques, their correspondence was authentic, expressing the unique interests of individual writers. On the other hand, when students responded to a situation invented by the teacher, their letters were inauthentic, containing much the same information. The inauthentic writing was treated by both students and teacher in a perfunctory manner, while the authentic writing was generated with commitment and received with interest.

As the authors indicate, many times it is not easy to evaluate a writing activity as authentic or inauthentic. To help readers distinguish between the two, Edelsky and Smith give several characteristics of authentic writing: (a) the purposes for writing are the writer's, not the teacher's, (b) writers have a definite audience in mind, (c) writing is often initiated by the students, and (d) the degree of explicitness varies according to the purposes of the writer.

This chapter appeared in Language Arts, *vol. 61 (January 1984): 24-32.*
© *1984 by the National Council of Teachers of English. Reprinted with permission.*

Let's imagine a "creative" mother. Instead of simply putting last night's leftovers on today's lunch table, she prints prices by each container, gives her children pennies and lets them "buy" their lunch from her "cafeteria." It might look like it—money and goods being exchanged—but are her children making genuine purchases? Or let's say as a murderer in a play, you perform your dastardly deed with chilling believability; you give an authentic performance, but the murder was still not "the real thing." To come closer to our mutual interest in language, what if we non–Italian speakers memorize and recite a verse in Italian. Does that constitute "speaking Italian?"

While each of these examples may show important similarities to buying, murdering, or speaking, essential features of those acts are missing. And these missing features render the examples inauthentic. Writing in school is sometimes like that—an imitation, a facsimile, a substitute, "writing" rather that writing.

For a person to be engaged in genuine writing, she or he has to be using *four interacting systems* of written language to produce a *meaningful* text. The four systems—graphophonic, syntactic, semantic, and pragmatic—have to be operating interactively and interdependently. Thus, when the purpose of a piece is to aid in recall and the audience is the self, as in a grocery list, such pragmatic considerations would affect syntactic and graphophonic choices. In authentic writing, the pragmatic system is not separated from the other three; when really writing, a writer's purposes and intentions (part of pragmatics) have graphophonic, syntactic, and semantic consequences.

Putting pen to paper in school is usually an activity where a child writes out someone else's intentions, where prerequisite pragmatic conditions (like having a less informed audience when writing for the purpose of informing) are not met. In school writing, either one or more systems of written language are often missing altogether (as in workbook exercises) or the connections between the pragmatic system and the other three are distorted or severed. When either of these conditions obtains, what is engaged in and produced is not an instance of genuine writing because, to repeat, essential features are missing.

Given the pervasiveness of inauthentic writing in school alongside widespread desires for more able writers, there must be a widely held belief that inauthenic writing "transfers" to genuine writing. And given that so much research on writing has used "writing" (not authentic writing) as data, it seems reasonable to assume that professionals and policy makers believe that findings on inauthentic writing can be "generalized" to authentic writing. Whether these beliefs are correct will never be known unless researchers and teachers start distiguishing between the two.

Toward that end, we will present some characteristics of inauthentic as contrasted with authentic writing. Our samples come from a unique classroom. The teacher has a whole–language orientation to language and literacy, viewing any instance of real language–in–use as simultaneously tapping the four interrelated systems mentioned earlier and as having meaning and purpose at its core (see Goodman and Goodman [1981] and Harste and Burke [1977] for a fuller description of whole language vs. skills theoretical orientations). Thus, in contrast to many classrooms, much of the reading and writing in her room is authentic. There are few "instructional materials," no workbooks, no graded series of basals or texts, no grammar or spelling exercises. Instead, children read trade books and newspapers, use reference materials not necessarily written for school use, write stories for publication, receive spelling and punctuation instruction as it is appropriate to the piece of writing they are working on, and produce a variety of other kinds of writing. The teacher of this inner city sixth grade does not see the writing process as a mechanical sequence of steps (rehearsing, prewriting, writing, rewriting) but as a social, linguistic, and psychological enterprise children engage in to get a job done.

She reads literature and research, knows how a strong literature component enriches her science and social studies offerings as well as her writing program, and understands writer's block along with "dam overflowing writing" (writing through recess, lunchtime, and into the after school hours) because she is a writer herself.

This teacher is generally able to keep foremost in her mind the big purposes she believes writing can serve, refraining from "operationalizing" and thus losing the grand purposes with concrete short-term objectives which never add up to the ultimate goal. (Occasionally, however, she does lose sight, does operationalize—and some of the consequences will be presented as examples of inauthentic writing.)

Her conscious awareness of a reflectiveness on both theory and practice are combined with a crucial attribute: she is willing to discard practices (e.g., spelling lessons, writing exercises, a linear "writing process" program) that contradict her new information and evolving theory.

The characteristics of inauthentic and authentic writing to be discussed are based on samples of a variety of types—thank you letters, letters of information, business letters, invitations, dialogue journals, lists, outlines, notes, signs, stories, personal narratives, science logs, etc. Many of these were not and should not have been treated to prewriting and rewriting. With the exception of one sample elicited for research purposes, all others were official (related to school or classroom activities or interactions with the teacher); none, for example, were intercepted notes intended for another child.

DIFFERENCES BETWEEN INAUTHENTIC AND AUTHENTIC WRITING

Information

Letters written to carry out the teacher's or a researcher's intentions were different informationally from those written by the same child for the child's own purposes. When looking at letters the teacher had assigned (the inauthentic), we could see that most children included similar points in their letters. This was related to their frustrated wailings ("What'll I write?!"), their pumping the teacher and then sharing any suggestion given ("How about mentioning things you liked") with several others. By contrast, many children spontaneously wrote letters to thank Mike, a visiting karate expert, for a demonstration and to try to persuade him to return. Each of these letters had a unique approach (flattery, promises, appeals for sympathy, etc.) and focused on different content.

Inauthentic letters sometimes contained false information. Children had been assigned to write letters asking parents to come to an open house. David, whose father had not lived at home for several years, wrote to "Dear Mom and Dad." In other inauthentic pieces elicited for a researcher's purposes, children were to write how they felt about returning to school after summer vacation. Several told of partaking in what was probably their stereotype of "acceptable summer vacation activity"—swimming in their own pools and going on camping trips. Those particular children had not participated in such activities.

Information reflects purpose. At the start of the year, journals contained little authentic writing. The format, conditions for writing, and quality of the teacher's written responses to the child's entries were aimed at allowing child and teacher to get to know each other better and to assure each of them a daily personal point of contact. However, most children did not take on those purposes as their own until mid-fall. For over a month, they treated the activity as one of filling a page with "goody–goody" content to please the teacher ("I know I'll love this school," "I hope I pass," "I'll try hard," "You're a good teacher," etc.). Around the first of October, children started covering their journals as they wrote, seeking privacy for private moments with the teacher. The writing was now authentic—semantic and pragmatic cues operating in concert, some pragmatic cues not contradicting others. Kayla stopped gooing about how good sixth grade was and began to tell her side of playground arguments and to demand an explanation for why the teacher would tell her age ("Aren't you ashamed or nothing'?"). Freddie quit repeating line after line to fill the page, of how happy his brothers, sisters, mother, father, aunts, uncles, cousins, etc., would be to see the good report card he would get as a result of promised Herculean efforts and began to wonder in writing how his teacher could sign "Love, Ms. S." on every journal ("Do you really love us all?"). Later he penned his concern for her solitary living ("Maybe you should get a gun. I worry because you're home alone. Your should get good locks.").

Caring

When a child addresses an invitation to Mom and Dad though Dad is gone and Mom is called *mami* or *mamá*, it is clear that some pragmatic features for invitations are missing (e.g., at least one purpose is to invite; the invitee can receive the information). Most likely, David saw this as an exercise to be performed for the teacher's evaluation, changing the purpose from inviting to being evaluated. Efforts to please the teacher might account for his use of the teacher's, but not his own, address terms and for the inclusion of both parents. Once again, the relationship between semantic and pragmatic features was absent or distorted—and this simulation of writing appears to be something David did not care about.

Children in this classroom wrote many stories for possible publication. Like dialogue journals, this was a new venture for them and, at first, many treated the task as though they were beginning with story starters or other "creative writing" gimmicks—a task that, though not genuine writing, was at least one they were already familiar with. They looked to the teacher to evaluate and decide whether the piece was finished. When they realized such decisions were theirs, they pronounced a piece finished after the first conference. Illustrations and book covers were made hurriedly, sometimes without connection to the story. As they began to trust their work would really be read and discussed by their peers along the same dimensions other writing was discussed (character, plot, theme, believability, author's voice), they began to write about topics and characters they cared about.

While signs of not caring could be spotted in the written product, signs of caring were not as obvious. True, illustrations and book bindings took longer, were neater, and were clearly tied to the content of the writing. But more often, the signals that a child cared about what she or he was writing were more evident during the writing itself. During interactions with the student, the teacher came to know when a piece of writing was connected to a well of feeling and memory. At those times, the teacher had a rich piece to work with; the child would be willing to labor through multiple drafts and take part in numerous conferences to learn how to better craft a piece with significance for the writer. Caring, then, was a context for productive teaching and learning related to authentic writing.

Compartmentalization / Integration

Inauthentic writing was sometimes assigned to test whether certain content had been learned. Thus, when children produced pieces explaining digestion, for example, they were both carrying out the assignment and displaying knowledge for the teacher's evaluative purpose. ("Digestion starts before you eat. When you chew, the food it mixes with saliva. Then it slides down the esophagus and into your stomach...."). These pieces do begin to show syntactic and lexical attributes of expository writing about scientific topics but, while they have an informing style, they inform no one (the teacher audience is more informed than they are).

The children compartmentalized such inauthentic writing. They produced it, turned it in, and filed it away upon its return. They did not use inauthentic writing for anything other than evaluation/compliance. They did not discuss with other students points they made or substantive comments the teacher would write back to them.

Authentic writing on scientific topics was treated very differently. Children kept logs of their observations, mentioning whether these matched what they had read, explaining what they saw, and predicting future changes. They saw these logs and the teacher's returned comments as a way of helping themselves understand more about a topic. Spontaneously and informally, they consulted past entries to try to track changes. Children also initiated heated discussions with peers about substantive points. For example, "Do gerbils think?" was the teacher's response to Anna's notation "The mother gerbil thinks we're going to get her babies." Anna and four others argued and discussed for the greater part of a morning whether Anna was right to impute thinking to the mother gerbil. That is, authentic writing was integrated into other activities and became a part of interactions and contexts beyond the one for which it was intended.

Purpose

Children really wrote (instead of feigning writing) for many purposes. They wrote stories to entertain others. They wrote to help themselves plan (Grant listed illustrations he wanted in the book he was having published and assigned them numbers according to the chapters in which they would appear; Juan listed major story elements before he wrote; Manual itemized materials he needed for a puppet; Latrice and Noemi worried over a much-erased list of potential invitees to a movement and music show). They wrote to maintain order (Tami and Devvie made signs such as "don't touch" and "keep out of this desk;" Sonia and Dolores listed who brought which cans of soda pop for a picnic so that the contents of the cooler would be distributed honestly). They wrote to help themselves work out problems (Rosa wrote a story with herself as the main character who was being harassed by other children outside the room. She reported that as soon as she finished the story she realized how she could, in fact, get some help.). They wrote to invite people to visit, to order materials, to keep track of playground games, to help themselves remember details of events for later discussions, etc.

These were all the writers', not the teacher's purposes. Such variety of purpose in official, if unassigned, classroom writing stands in marked contrast to the more singular purpose with which children produced inauthentic writing—compliance with an assignment to be evaluated. Julian presents an interesting case here. Had he adopted as his own the teacher's purpose for journals, then his journal writing would have been authentic. Instead, he never wavered from the position he voiced the first week (*I don't want to say anything I'll be sorry for later*). Each of his entries was written to comply but not to "relate." Julian's expressed view of "studenting" was the learning and displaying of facts; good teaching, he felt, was the release of a steady flow of facts in a militaristic atmosphere. Given such beliefs, he wrote authentically when he gathered information and composed story after super–patriotic story about spies, satellites, and bombs. He delighted in the number of facts he learned and incorporated into these stories, seemingly writing for the purpose of learning facts and, in turn, living out the student role as he saw it.

If authentic writing conveyed the writer's (rather than the teacher's) purposes, it was also put to use by the writer according to the writer's intent. Children *needed* and, in fact, used the lists, letters, outlines, notes, stories, etc., mentioned earlier. When they wrote comments about books for literature study group discussions, they referred to those written comments during the discussions. Children who were reluctant to contribute without the written comment in hand were more active participants with them, seeming to gain confidence from *using* their own writing. The teacher's purpose for these comments had become their own and, thus, the effort constituted genuine writing and was *used*. If their purpose in writing the comments had been to comply rather than to help themselves think through in advance the contribution they would later make orally, we would consider the comments inauthentic writing and we would predict the children would not have referred to them later.

Children did not need or use inauthentic writing, although the teacher thought such assignments would be beneficial. Once, for instance, the teacher assigned children to list the steps and materials they would use to make a map on "land use" for a class social studies project. The teacher assumed the purpose of such a piece would be to help children organize their thinking, to help them know what to do as they carried out the task. However, the children's purpose in producing the lists was to comply. They did the assignment, had it checked, then treated it as nonexistent. Representative of pieces done for that assignment is the following:

Land Use

Supplies: tag-board, tissue paper, glue, scissors, social studies book, overhead projector, crayons, grease pen, acetate paper

Steps:
1. open social studies book to map of China in Land Use
2. get acetate paper and draw a map of land use in China
3. get overhead projector
4. get tag-board. Put acetate paper on overhead projector
5. get tag-board and copy the map on tag-board paper
6. get tissue paper cut in pieces. Get glue and tissue paper
7. dip tissue paper into glue. Glue on land forms
8. at the bottom of tag-board pick colors for each. Hand write the way it is used and its color.

Children filed such pieces away after producing them, never using them to help organize or think through what needed to be done next. By contrast, they did use the following pieces for their own purposes:

1. (plans for illustrations in book to be published)
   ch. 2, pg. 2 one boy throwing off another
   pg. 3 one boy turning ball over
   pg. 10 one boy throwing a pretty bomb on last down

2. (list identifying owners of soda pop cans in ice chest)
   David—1 cola
   Karla—1 welch strawberry
   Julio—4 pepsi

   Cynthia—1 orange

3. (labeled pattern/plan for puppet)

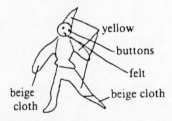

4. (planning sheet for deciding who to invite to a school program).
   Barton 32 kids
   Garza 29 kids
   —————
   61
   nurse   1
   principal 1
   library

At first glance, the Land Use piece looks superior, detailing as it does an entire process in more explicit fashion. However, if a more elaborate piece is simply not used, what good is it in the end?

There are good reasons why children discarded the "superior" Land Use, but put to intended use examples 1 through 4. Land use is inauthentic writing because at the outset, pragmatics made it hopeless to achieve any purpose but compliance/evaluation and because in the finished product, syntactic, semantic, and pragmatic cues are contradictory and confused. This assignment was supposed to help children think through and learn the steps of a process. However, in order to list the steps, children had to already know what those steps were. It was also supposed to be writing for oneself, writing for *self*-organization. In fact, it was for the teacher. Steps listed for oneself do not usually include so many verbs and articles. Nor would a piece for oneself include so many verbs and articles. Nor would a piece for oneself include information such as "open social studies book." Instead, much would be assumed and therefore deleted. Examples 1 through 4 were written *for the writer* to help the writer in self-organization—and the syntax and amount and kind of information provided are consistent with those pragmatic features of audience and purpose. Land Use pretends to be a particular audience and purpose but syntax and amount and kind of information reveal the pretense. It was really a retrospective listing for the teacher rather than a prospective or concurrent working plan for oneself. No wonder it was not used once completed.

Land use is like most book reports we have seen in elementary schools—written to fulfill the assignment, though supposedly to interest others in reading the book, never actually used by the others in choosing a book, actually written to prove to the teacher that the book was read.

Children's authentic writing gave straightforward, uncontorted signals regarding audience. Part of the inauthenticity of Land Use is that it gives a distorted and double message similar to the one Freddie gave in an early journal entry supposedly written to the teacher. During the time when Freddie's purpose was to comply and be positively evaluated and before he adopted the relationship purpose for journals, he produced "I am going to have a good day today and tomorrow and always have a good day Ms. S. or Ms. M. or whoever reads it." Authentic journal entries gave no hint that they might be meant for anyone other than the addressee; in fact, they most definitely were meant only for the addressee. Grant's journal entries were sometimes answered by the student teacher, Ms. M. After several responses from Ms. M. to entries addressed to Ms. S., Grant gouged a deep X over Ms. M.'s answer and wrote under it "Ms. S, I don't want Ms. M. to answer my journal. She's a very nice teacher but I put *to you.*"

Degree of explicitness varied appropriately in authentic writing. For example, William rewrote his Steps in an Experiment with Brine Shrimp so someone else could replicate the experiment. The rewrite had larger and neater handwriting and contained more verbs, articles, and information.

BEHAVIOR DURING THE ACTIVITY ITSELF

Children had to be coaxed and prodded when writing inauthentically. They asked frequent questions about form and procedures: "How long does it have to be?" "Do we write on both sides?" "How do you spell X?" "Does it have to be in cursive?" "Can I write it in pencil?" They whined and groaned "This is boring" and "I don't know what to write." Such complaining pleas for help with content were directed only to the teacher, though any answers she gave were shared with others so that, as described earlier, many papers were very similar.

Authentic writing was often initiated by the children themselves. They spontaneously took clipboards to football games, brought pencil and paper along to avoid boredom on days of indoor recess, and arrived notebooks with them when they went to watch the brine shrimp and gerbils. They assumed they would write several drafts of letters and stories. They expected to take notes on observations. That is, they did not have to be "motivated" to write by the teacher. Their questions were not about procedures and form, nor did they ask permission to stop ("Am I finished?"). Instead, they asked peers as well as the teacher for help with how to word something or for opinions about whether certain details in stories were believable. While inauthentic journal entries could be penned with a vistor looking over the child's shoulder, authentic entries were written with arm and body curved over to ensure privacy. Much authentic writing (certain lists, notes, signs) was dashed off, an investment of time and care appropriate to purpose and audience. Other authentic pieces were worked at, struggled with, but not chafed under. Like mature writers, these young writers sometimes blocked, paced and avoided. But they also talked about summer plans for capturing in print certain stories in their heads the way fishermen talk about going after elusive fish. And when the teacher gave them an extra period on some days to work on books they were writing for publication, they cheered.

We have provided contrasts from samples of authentic writing and its imitators from one classroom where the teacher has a whole-language orientation. It would be interesting to know whether the contrasting features presented here are characteristic of authentic and inauthentic writing for classrooms where teachers have other orientations. In any case, we urge teachers and researchers to consider that many popular and "approved" kinds of school writing may not be genuine writing at all and to begin to contrast and sort authentic from inauthentic writing. Maybe then we will begin to find out what relationships hold between the two and how language arts curricula might best reflect those relationships.

REFERENCES

Goodman, K. and Y. Goodman. "A Whole–Language, Comprehension–Centered View of Reading Development." Occasional Paper No. 1, Program in Language and Literacy, Arizona Center for Research and Development, University of Arizona, 1981.

Harste, J. and Burke C. "A New Hypothesis for Reading Teacher Research: Both Teaching and Learning of Reading are Theoretically Based. In *Reading: Theory, Research and Practice,* 26th Yearbook of the National Reading Conference, edited by P. D. Pearson, St. Paul, MN: Mason Publishing Co. 1977.

19. WRITE? ISN'T THIS READING CLASS?

by Marie Dionisio, Louis M. Klein Middle School,
Harrison, New York.

Marie Dionisio shows how the writing process supports the improvement of reading in remedial and developmental reading classrooms. She relates a convincing story about helping remedial readers become immersed in the reading process as they integrate writing into their reading program. As her students became involved in daily writing experiences with rereading of drafts and sharing of stories, their reading abilities naturally improved. When students selected new writing topics, they were motivated to choose readings that would give them background information about the new subject. In one instance, three students wanted to write a play, but did not know how to structure it. To solve their problem, they read a script together to help them understand plays. A fourth grade writing process teacher with whom the editors work recently had a similar experience. One of her students wanted to write a mystery, but did not know how to develop it. The teacher suggested that he read a mystery from the writer's point of view to find out how the author built the story. Then the teacher helped him find a mystery story that was very simply written so that the structure was clear.

This chapter appeared in The Reading Teacher, *vol. 36 (April 1983): 746-50. Copyright © 1983 by the International Reading Association. Reprinted with permission of Marie Dionisio and the International Reading Association.*

Another school year, another class of sixth grade remedial readers—reluctant, frustrated students who have been in special reading classes since second grade, who, after filling in thousands of phonics and hundreds of main idea worksheets, still score below grade level, hate reading, have learned that people read in order to answer a page of questions, and play the academic game of matching the words in the questions to those in the text in order to locate the answers. Too often these children can't read their own answers because they have no real understanding of what they have read.

Furthermore, these students are often deficient as writers. Rarely have they written any original compositions. More of the same frustrating instruction would further deprive them of a basic right—the right to develop reading and writing skills necessary for a meaningful role in the world.

Encouragement for changing my teaching strategies came from the work of Graves (Graves, 1983; Graves and Murray, 1980) who said:

> Children do extensive reading when they reread and revise their own texts. Just how much reading is involved in the writing process is just beginning to dawn on our research team. Large amounts of time have been taken from formal reading instruction and given over to time for writing in rooms where the study is being conducted. Surprisingly, reading scores did not go down; they went up...and significantly. Since writing is the making of reading, children may decode for ideas differently than if they had never written at all (Graves and Murray, 1980).

Disenchanted with traditional reading programs. I began to use the composing process in my own classroom. Not only did I enjoy teaching more, but I discovered that when reading is approached through writing, both skills benefit. The writing program I used valued the students' interest and focused on teacher–student–peer communication. Guidelines are few and simple to follow (see accompanying guidelines).

READING IN WRITING

The process of writing causes students to read for their varied purposes. Students read and reread their written drafts to insure clarity. They read to acquire additional information, discover style and form. learn organizational techniques, and insure correct usage of language conventions. Daily writing promotes and enhances reading.

In this program the first sign of the "reading" surfaced when my students sought response to their writing by reading their pieces to each other. Conferring, they heard their own writing and discovered the importance of reading and rereading what they had written. A significant change in the way students read their work to each other began to emerge. What started as reading to tell a story to a friend and receive praise became reading to be sure the words on the page clearly related what was intended without omissions or misunderstandings.

Initially, students approached a peer with, "Hey, listen to my story," anticipating "That's great!" as a response. But soon the writers began to ask more intelligent questions, such as "Will you listen to my piece and tell me how it sounds?" The reasons for reading their own writing apparently had changed in a way that could only increase their comprehension. When students began to interrupt their reading with "Oh, that's not right" and "This is confusing," I became further convinced that the writing and sharing provided them with the opportunity to improve their reading skills.

Starting out guidelines

Develop personal background
Acquire a personal understanding of your own composing process and investigate, through perfessional literature and workshops, the environments and approaches which enhance children's writing. This background is essential to support a shift from teacher-control to writer-control, the core of successful process-conference instruction.

Assess perceptions
Find out about your students' attitudes toward and perceptions of writing. Administer a survey using questions that provoke students' thoughts. Discuss the responses for each question with the class, compile them, and display the results in the classroom. (A survey is not useful below grade three.)

Explore possibilities
Help students generate lists of possible topics to write about, audiences to write to, and purposes for writing. Display the lists and add to them on an ongoing basis.

Model
Model the behaviors which the students are expected to exhibit. This is essential. You should write with the students, share your drafts and revisions, and seek as well as give meaningful response to the content of writing.

Choose the first topic
Have students list three things they would like to write about, adding why they would like to write about that topic or what they want to say about each topic. Model this process on the chalkboard, briefly explaining why you want to write on one particular topic. Ask the students to choose one topic from their lists and begin drafting.

An alternate strategy is to ask students to decide on a topic overnight and to be ready to write about it the next day. (Primary grade children should simply be asked to write about anything they want or about a personal experience.)

Circulate and respond
After writing for a short time, wander around the room and respond briefly to what individual students have written. Initially it is important to echo to the writer the content of what he or she has written. If appropriate, ask a question which causes the writer either to rethink or to expand the writing. Quickly move from one student to another. Encourage; don't interfere.

Materials
Develop a classroom library which includes a variety of good children's literature and basic reference books. Have a supply of lined and unlined paper of various types and sizes, different colored pens or pencils for editing, and folders in which each child can keep his or her writing.

Cautions
Remember that the process of writing takes time and that the amount of time needed varies from writer to writer and from piece to piece.

Consistent and regular time for writing is the cornerstone of growth in writing.

Leave the control in the writers' hands. Do not write for them. Resist temptation to insert your ideas. Allow the students to encounter and solve their own problems while writing.

Editing for technical control should be considered only after the content of the writing is finished.

Sharing very quickly expanded as students who previously read only under direct orders began spending time reading and critically commenting on or discussing each other's writing. One particular day, when a continuation of a popular mystery story was displayed, many students ran over to read it exclaiming, "Come on, it's part four. I can't wait to read it!" Seeing previously reluctant readers stop what they were doing to read with total concentration was very encouraging. One student's comment at the end of 10 weeks exemplified how reading played a part in her writing: "You can learn as much reading by reading our bulletin board. The board has stories just like the old reading books. I get ideas from reading the board."

READING TO EXPLORE NEW WRITINGS TOPICS

Writing regularly on topics of their own choosing created a need for students to read for many different reasons. The nature of their reading expanded as rapidly as the amount of reading increased. The need to know more about a topic led to reading for information they wanted to include in a piece of writing.

Frank and Fred, for example, were writing about the Elephant Man, John Merrick. After an enthusiastic start, they began disagreeing about certain facts needed for the piece. To resolve this problem, they requested some reading material and their research not only cleared up the disagreement, but provided new facts to expand the piece.

Gregg wanted to use real locations in his mystery "The Pick–Pocket Person," to make his story more credible. He decided on Nevada but, not knowing the names of any cities in Nevada, searched through his social studies book. Serious examination of the map in his book led to the choice of Carson City as the most desirable locale. While inserting the name in his draft, Gregg told a friend, "I even got the spelling right this way."He had not only read for the needed information, but discovered another editing reference as well.

Bernadette came to a writing conference with a short piece on the sun, but was concerned because "There isn't enough in it." Our conference stimulated some reading.

Teacher: What are you trying to say in this piece?
Bernadette: I think the sun is nice.
T: Why do you think the sun is nice?
B: It helps us.
T: How does the sun help us?
B: It gives us heat and light.
T: Is there anything else the sun does for us?

B: I guess, but I don't know what.
T: How could you find out?
B: I could read about the sun in the library.

Using the information she had discovered in the library, Bernadette revised her piece, adding three ways in which the sun is helpful. In this case the teacher conference generated reading, but in every case the students read for information that was important to them and directly used that information in their writing.

Even more significant is the fact that these students related that same information to peers weeks later. Since these students could not remember details, this recall indicated an obvious increase in their reading comprehension.

READING TO ACQUIRE STYLE

Students also used reading as a method for developing style and form, especially when they attempted to write in new genres. Valerie wanted to write a poem, but each attempt closely resembled a paragraph. After several abandoned drafts, Valerie asked with desperation for a book of poetry—"Maybe if I read some poems, I'll see how to write one." After her reading, she expressed satisfaction with knowing "how poems look different from paragraphs." Her subsequent draft of a poem still gave her some difficulty but her problems were resolved in a teacher conference.

Three girls came into class and enthusiastically announced that they were going to write a play based on a story one of the girls had written previously. I refrained from making discouraging remarks about such a difficult task as they happily ventured off to produce a play. In their first attempt, they added character's names followed by a colon to the original narrative. It was obvious that the girls were totally unaware of a play's unique format.

"How could you find out what a play looks like?" was all the teacher prompting they needed. "Hey, we could read one, like in the Macmillan reader or from the library." Since multiple copies of the reader were readily available, they decided to read one play together to familiarize themselves with the format. Conferences were used to compare their work to the play they had read in order to eliminate the problems of uninteresting or flat dialogue, excessive use of a narrator, and lack of stage directions. Although the year ended before the play could be completed, the success of the venture could not be denied nor could the part played by reading.

198

READING TO ORGANIZE

While writing, students, particularly remedial readers, have difficulty developing coherent organization. One student discovered that this problem could also be solved through reading. Freddy was writing a book on his hobbies and his first organizational decision was to divide the book into three chapters. In chapter two, "Foreign Stamps and Money," he wrote about both simultaneously. Freddy corrected this problem by recognizing material of a similar organizational nature in his earlier reading.

Teacher: What is the first sentence about?
Freddy: Stamps
T: What is the second sentence about?
F: Money.
T: What is the third sentence about?
F: Stamps.
T: What is the fourth sentence about?
F: Money.
T: Would you consider telling all about stamps and then all about coins?
F: Hey, that's just like in my social studies book. One chapter is on India and China. First it tells about India on this side and then about China there. I could do the same thing.

Although the reading was not the result of need for his writing, Freddy certainly was using previous knowledge of reading to improve his writing. The nature of his reason for reading had changed. He, perhaps, was reading for more than one purpose at a time, for useful organizational patterns as well as for meaning.

READING TO EDIT

As a direct outgrowth of their writing, these students began to spend more time reading their work to ensure correct usage of language conventions. At this editing stage, students used dictionaries, English grammar books, and numerous other sources to correct the errors they found in their completed drafts. Editing requires an entirely different focus from reading for meaning and in my previous experience, remedial students had always been unable to make this shift.

The ease and success with which these students changed the focus of their reading to fulfill their own purposes suggested that perhaps what had been lacking was the reason, not the ability. Just as Gregg checked the spelling of Carson City in his social studies book, Joann checked the punctuation of dialogue in an English text. As Freddy read one of his compositions that I typed, he complained loudly about an error in agreement: "You made a mistake in my piece; it should be *chase* not *chases.*" No longer did I proofread and correct; the students began checking the typing of their work.

READING TO UNDERSTAND

It was a pleasant surprise to find these remedial students reading voluntarily and to discover that the nature of their recreational reading was changing. They were moving from surface understanding to immersion in the reading process. A good example is Valerie's report on the books of Laura Ingalls Wilder. This was an unsolicited report. Valerie wrote, "I really enjoyed her creating books. It probably took her a long time to write all those books. I think she did very well. She probably had to keep on throwing her piece of paper away until she got the one she wanted to write about."

Clearly, Valerie's reading went beyond literal understanding and reflected a feeling of kinship with other writers. Furthermore, she had overcome the intimidating notion that written language is unchangeable which Thomas Newkirk (1982) calls "Plato's Challenge." Valerie had recognized that written language can be questioned and is the result of authors' choices. Valerie now reads Laura Ingalls Wilder and other writers with greater understanding and perhaps even empathy. For a reluctant reader, this outcome is, indeed, an incredible bonus.

These students did not have any traditional remedial reading instruction. Instead, they wrote every day, and in the process were driven to read. They were no longer reading to answer questions in a workbook or teacher's manual. They were using reading and writing as a unified tool for learning; they became willing and able readers and writers.

REFERENCES

Graves, Donald H. *Writing: Teachers and Children at Work.* Exeter, N.H.: Heinemann Education Books, 1983.
Graves, Donald H., and Donald H. Murray. "Revision in the writer's Workshop and in the Classroom." *Journal of Education*, vol. 162 (Spring 1980), pp. 38-56.
Newkirk, Thomas. "Young Writers as Critical Readers." *Language Arts,* vol. 59 (May 1982), pp 451-57.

20. DIALOGUE JOURNALS: A TOOL FOR ESL TEACHING

by David L. Wallace, Researcher, Center for the Study of Writing, Berkeley and Carnegie Mellon, Pittsburgh

David Wallace reviews the literature concerning dialogue journal writing as it applies to English-as-a-second-language (ESL) classrooms. He provides characteristics of journal writing, features of dialogue journals, research concerning journals, and several suggestions for their use. Further information on this topic may be found in several of the works cited by the author, especially those of Ruth Spack and Catherine Sadow, and Vivian Zamel.

Although Wallace focuses on ESL classrooms, other teachers will also find helpful suggestions for using dialogue journals with their students.

This chapter appeared in the Educational Resources Information Center (ERIC), 1987, ED 280 316. Copyright © 1987 by David L. Wallace. Reprinted with permission.

For a number of years, teachers have been quietly using dialogue journals in their teaching of writing. These journals differ from other student journals in that the teacher responds in writing to each entry by the student. Until recently, the use of dialogue journals has not been widely publicized. The increased attention given to them as a teaching technique is largely due to the work of Jana Staton and her colleagues at the Center for Applied Linguistics, Washington, D.C. She says:

> The concept of dialogues in writing between teacher and student is a sound idea in terms of both theory and common sense. Dialogue journals are a teacher–developed rather than research–initiated practice which has only recently been studied. (1983, p.1)

As Staton suggests, dialogue journals have grown out of the common-sense need that teachers felt was necessary for interaction with their students. Staton herself became interested in researching dialogue journal writing in 1979, when she was made aware of a sixth–grade teacher, Leslee Reed, who had been asking her students to carry on a daily written conversation with her for a number of years.

Dialogue journals also share the heritage of general journal writing in the teaching of English. Journals are often used in English courses as a means of promoting writing fluency and development of ideas. Fred D. White calls journals "an indispensable writer's tool," and adds that for this reason they "should be taught in first-year composition courses" (1982, p. 147). Sherry Banks describes journals as "an extraordinarily valuable adjunct to improving student writing (1982, p. 159). Journals serve an expressive function in a language course. They allow students freedom to experiment with language. Dan Kirby and Tom Liner list three characteristics of journal writing which make it a valuable learning activity: (1) the journal is less structured and more subjective than most school writing, (2) students use journals to write about things that they are interested in, and (3) the audience of the journal is the students themselves (1981, p. 46). Dialogue journals, however, add a new dimension of real communication to journal writing.

As the name implies, interaction is a defining feature of dialogue journals. Kirby and Liner see the consideration of audience as highlighting an important difference between journals in general and dialogue journals. While both types attempt to help students learn to express themselves in writing by reducing the demands of the rhetorical situation, dialogue journals have an audience, the teacher. Thus, while dialogue journals share the general benefits of journal writing, they have developed beyond general writing to provide for interaction.

There is no clear-cut definition of dialogue journals, but Staton identifies four essential features:

1. A dialogue journal is a conversation in writing carried on over an extended length of time, with each partner having equal and frequent turns.
2. Each writer is free to initiate conversation on any topic of mutual and personal interest, expecting the other partner to comment on it.
3. The writers share external frames of reference and boundaries which determine the topics each feels free to bring up, as in any mutual conversation.
4. A wide range of topics (not limited to academic topics) can be used. (1982, p. 4)

The dialogue journal is a safe practice ground in which beginning writers can experiment and develop their writing abilities in a situation which is meaningful to them. As James Moffett says, "Ideally, a student would write because he was intent on saying something for real reasons of his own and because he wanted to get certain effects on a definite audience" (1968, p. 193). Dialogue journals allow students to do this. They foster a growing interaction which generates real topics for a real audience (the teacher), and yet because the teacher focuses on communication not correction, dialogue journals allow the student to concentrate on meaning instead of form.

RESEARCH SUPPORTING THE USE
OF DIALOGUE JOURNALS

Recent composition research for native speakers supports an approach to the teaching of writing in which beginning writers are given the opportunity to focus on meaning by limiting rhetorical concerns. Because ESL composition has been almost nonexistent until very recently, Ruth Spack and Catherine Sadow note that ESL teachers have "looked for clarification and guidance to those writers, teachers, and researchers in native English–speaking contexts who were challenging the traditional method of teaching composition" (1983, p. 576). As early as 1976, noted researcher Vivian Zamel argued that ESL teachers could learn from research about native speaker composition; until that time the teaching of writing in ESL was still seen from a behaviorist perspective. She proposed that the act of composing needs to become the result of a genuine desire to express one's feelings, experiences or reactions, all within a climate of encouragement. Dialogue journals are one method in which teachers can limit rhetorical concerns of writing for students and allow them to focus on meaning.

In the past five years, there has been significant research to verify the use of dialogue journals as a teaching method for both native speakers and students in the ESL setting. Two studies of dialogue journal writing have been conducted by the Center for Applied Linguisitics (CAL). In the first study, Staton and her fellow researchers analyzed the text of 26 student/teacher dialogue journals from Leslee Reeds' sixth–grade classroom from July 1980 to January 1982 (1982). The study attempted first to determine how students reacted to the freedom from constraints provided by dialogue journal writing over traditional classroom writing exercises. The study was also designed to see if dialogue journal writing had any negative consequences on the grammatical correctness of the students' writing.

Perhaps the most important conclusion of this study is that dialogue journals can serve as a natural and functional bridge for young writers to begin to make the transition from oral speech to written communication. "Our strongest recommendation for the *use* of dialogue journals," says Staton, "is as an initial developmental step for beginning writers to provide extensive opportunity for successful communication in written language before asking them to try a more complex form" (1982, p. 133). By focusing attention on communication, dialogue journals limit rhetorical concerns to the minimum needed for communication. They allow fledgling writers to have extensive writing experience which is at their own level and yet is a real communicative experience. Roger Shuy, who also participated in this study, concludes that dialogue journals are an ef-

203

fective tool for learning to write because they mimic conversation better than any other type of school writing and because the tasks and topics are both real and student-generated (1982, p. 20). Joy Kreeft, another participant in the CAL study, adds that dialogue journal writing incorporates both "the interactive aspect of oral face-to-face communication and the solitary aspect of expository writing" (1982, p.8). In the area of surface correctness, the study focused on spelling. Although no corrections were made in the students' journals, the spelling in their journal writing generally improved while performance on spelling tests remained constant (1982, p. 121).

The second CAL study focused mainly on ESL students. The 27 participants were pre-adolescents. They represented 12 countries and 10 languages with only two native speakers of English. The subjects had from zero to six years of classroom exposure to English. By analyzing the journals of these 27 students, taught by Leslee Reed, Kreeft discovered that the journals allowed Reed to monitor the progress of each student daily (1983, p. 3). She also notes that the journals allowed Reed to adjust to each student's level individually instead of starting at some predetermined level of language competence (1983, p. 10). In short, dialogue journals allowed the teacher to individualize instruction in a way which is impossible in teacher-fronted situations. Summarizing both CAL studies, Kreeft says that the process of journal writing—

> allows students learning a second language to learn in a manner very similar to the way that a first language is learned—by discovering the rules of language form and use in the context of real, learner-generated communication. (1983, p. 12)

DIALOGUE JOURNALS IN ESL METHODOLOGY

The use of dialogue journals is consistent with a communicative language learning approach to teaching ESL. By definition, dialogue journals are a communicative language event since the focus is always on meaning. Both parties in the dialogue generate and respond to real topics.

The communicative nature of dialogue journal writing is most clearly seen in the examination of the student and teacher roles. Staton explains that in the journals:

> Student and teacher both drop for a moment their customary roles. Through searching for and finding a mutually interesting topic, they are able to talk directly as friends do . . . Mutual conversations are clear evidences of the 'co-membership' status of student and teacher in the journals. (1982, p. 101).

When the teacher focuses only on communication and does not correct errors, the students see that the teacher regards communication as the priority. Thus, the traditional teacher/student roles are deemphasized in the dialogue journal experience.

Dialogue journal writing also shares a holistic understanding of learning with communicative language learning. Shuy (1981) describes this type of teaching approach as constructive, based on the Kantian assumption that people come to know their world by actively constructing it rather than passively taking it in. As they write in their journals, students are actively engaged in creating meaning through language. This corroborates James Moffett's belief that students need to have an active role in the learning process. He argues that any type of teacher feedback about the student's performance will not be effective if the student's "will is not behind his actions, for will is the motor that drives the whole process" (1968, p. 191). Dialogue journals encourage students to take control, to become actively engaged in interaction with a supportive friend, thus allowing students to acquire language in the context of their own communication.

While dialogue journals do not emphasize learning discrete language skills, they do teach vocabulary, grammar, spelling, and word usage for the students. The teacher's entries in the journal provide a wealth of comprehensible input for the students. Because the focus of the journals is communication, the teacher must adjust his/her input to the level of each student. Instead of circling errors in red ink, the teacher elicits change by modeling correct usage in his/her response.

SUGGESTIONS FOR USE

In this section, the suggestions and procedures of teachers who have used dialogue journals are discussed in the following four areas: introducing journal writing to the class, evaluation of students' journal writing, protecting the privacy of journal entries, and limitation and variations of dialogue journals for specific purposes.

It is almost always necessary for the teacher to first introduce journal writing to students. Fred White advises that for most students any type of writing is unnatural, therefore "students must be guided into the journal, must become aware of its immense possibilities, its traditions, and its usefulness" (1982, p. 147). White's suggestions about journals apply to dialogue journals, which are even more unfamiliar to students. Students need to know from the outset the purpose of these journals. Spack and Sadow warn that some ESL students do not feel that writing on personal topics is appropriate for school writing (1983, p. 579). Thus the teacher must not only make the communicative nature of the dia-

205

logue journals clear, but he/she will also often have to sell the student on the value of this kind of writing. Even if the teacher does a good sales job, he/she should not be surprised to find that students do not feel comfortable writing about personal topics at first. It takes time to build relationships in which students feel comfortable initiating personal topics.

Because dialogue journals are a communicative event, they cannot be graded in the sense that essays can. Any evaluation should enhance rather than deter students' motivation to communicate. In short, if any type of grade must be given for dialogue journal work, it should encourage and reward consistent effort to communicate and not pass judgment on content or grammatical correctness.

Privacy is another issue which should be discussed with students when dialogue journals are introduced. In the first CAL study, absolute privacy between teacher and student was guaranteed from the beginning. Staton says, "This guarantee of privacy becomes an essential element in sustaining and deepening the communication as the year progresses" (1982, p. 19). Trust is essential to the development of a real communicative relationship between the student and the teacher. However, there will also be times when the teacher wants to share students' journal entries with the entire class. A simple solution is for the teacher to make it clear to the students he/she will always ask a student's permission before sharing any of the student's writing with the class or anyone else. Students' privacy may be further protected by having entries typed and deleting names and other identifying elements.

In a variation of dialogue journal writing proposed by Spack and Sadow, privacy is not really an issue. They suggest that journal writing in the ESL writing class can be limited to topics related to the class. They argue that personal writing can become too egocentric to be of value and that it can become too personal and thus difficult for the teacher to make adequate responses (1983, p. 579). This limitation is worth considering because it focuses the activity while still allowing it to be a communicative event.

Marsha Markman (1984) suggests using dialogue journals as a means for students to air their feelings about the course. This is another example of using this journal as a communicative event on a focused theme. If topic limitations are placed on such writing, it is important to allow enough latitude so that students feel in control of the subjects on which they write. Also, since by definition dialogue journals require frequent interaction, topics cannot be so limited that students feel that they have nothing to say.

CONCLUSION

In summary, dialogue journal writing is a communicative language event which can be used effectively in the ESL classroom. It is a low–cost writing fluency activity that is relatively easy to initiate and yet can provide an important bridge into the adult, English discourse community. It fosters student acquisition of writing skills in a controlled atmosphere with individualized attention. Dialogue journals are a flexible fluency tool which can be used on a daily basis for intensive student/teacher interaction or less frequently in specified areas. Staton says that dialogue journals are "not a method of instruction in literacy for language learners, but...a valuable component in developing writing and reading competence in both first and second language classes" (1983, p. 1).

WORKS CITED

Banks, Sherry. (1982). The Journal–Tool for Developing Writing Skills. *The Writing Instructor, 1* (4), 159-61.

Kreeft, Joy. (1983). *Why Not Really Communicate? In Dialogue Journals?* Washington, D.C.: Center for Applied Linguistics. (ERIC Document Reproduction No. ED 214 197)

Kirby, Dan and Liner, Tom. (1981). *Inside Out: Developmental Strategies for Teaching Writing.* Boynton/Cook.

Markman, Marsha C. (1984). Personalizing Composition Instruction Through Dialogue Journals. *Dialogue, 2* (3), 5–6.

Moffett, James. (1968). *Teaching the Universe of Discourse.* Boston: Houghton Mifflin.

Shuy, Roger W. (1982). The Oral Basis for Dialogue Journals. In *Analysis of Dialogue Journal Writing as a Communicative Event. Final Report* (Vol. 2). Washington, D.C.: Center for Applied Linguistics. (ERIC Document Reproduction Service No. ED 214 197)

Shuy, Roger W. (1981). A Holistic View of Language. *Research in the Teaching of English, 15* (2), 101–111.

Spack, Ruth, and Sadow, Catherine. (1983). Student–Teacher Working Journals in ESL Freshman Composition. *TESOL Quarterly, 17* (4), 575–93.

Staton, Jana. (1983). Dialogue Journals: A New Tool for Teaching Communication. *ERIC/CLL News Bulletin, 6* (2), 1–3.

Staton, Jana. (1982). *Analysis of Dialogue Journal Writing as a Communicative Event. Final Report* (Vol. 1). Washington, D.C.: Center for Applied Linguistics. (ERIC Document Reproduction Service No. ED 214 196)

White, Fred D. (1982). Releasing the Self: Teaching Journal Writing to Freshmen. *Writing Instructor, 1* (4), 147–56.

Zamel, Vivian. (1976). Teaching Composition in the ESL Classroom: What We Can Learn for Research in the Teaching of English. *TESOL Quarterly, 10* (1), 67–76.

21. THE AUTHOR'S CHAIR

by Don Graves and Jane Hansen, University of New Hampshire, Durham

Don Graves and Jane Hansen show how first graders benefit from a writing and reading process classroom. They advocate the use of an author's chair, a special place for students to use when they share their own published or trade books. Classmates listen to the student in the author's chair and then respond with comments or questions about the material.

Graves and Hansen collected research data in this community of readers and writers, examining students' concepts of authorship and the relationships between reading and writing. They explain how students develop the concept of authorship, delineating three phases: replication, transition, and sense of option. In the replication phase, students imitate and invent as they struggle to put their ideas on paper. The young authors also engage in social interaction about their writing and reading. During the transition phase, oral composing becomes unnecessary and authorship becomes real as students publish books. In reading, there is an observed increase in sounding out words and a great deal of rereading in an effort to make sense of the text. Students move from the transition phase to the option-awareness phase when they begin to realize that authors make choices when they write. They see that the reader must supply some of the information and become aware that, as readers, they have options in making sense of what they read. Graves and Hansen make reading and writing connections very clear as they describe young students' development in these areas.

This chapter appeared in Language Arts, *vol. 60 (February 1983): 176-83. © 1983 by the National Council of Teachers of English. Reprinted with permission.*

The Author's Chair is where the reader sits. Randy, a first–grade author, reads a page from one of his published books: *I Went Bottle Digging.* Then he turns the book to show the pictures to the class assembled on the carpet in front of him. When he finishes the book he places it on his lap, "Now."

The acceptance begins, "I liked the part where you get dirty. I like the part where you found the pottery."

The questions follow, "What do you do with the money when you sell them?" "Why did you choose this topic?" "How do you feel about being an author?"

Each day in Randy's classroom the children take their turns reading from the Author's Chair. They read their own published books and trade books from the same chair. Of the four situations, in only one case is the real author on the chair. But, it is always the Author's Chair.

Whether the story is about Anatole, or Jeremy's new piece on his dirt bike, the process of responding to each work is the same. First, the children receive the work by stating what they think it contains, then they ask questions of the author. When the child–author is present, the child answers the questions. For the authors of trade books, the teacher and children together speculate on answers the author might give. The prestige of the chair grows throughout the year.

The author's chair is in the first–grade classroom of Ellen Blackburn in Great Falls School, Somersworth, New Hampshire, a working–class community. The two of us interacted with the children in Ellen's classroom at least twice each week throughout 1981-82 and will continue during 1982-83. Our intent is to formulate hypotheses about the development of the children's understanding of the relationship between reading and writing. We started by giving the same definition to both reading and writing: They are composing acts.

Then, because no study had ever been done with beginning writers and readers on the two composing processes simultaneously, we used case study as the principal method of investigation. We studied three children who represented low, middle, and high achievement levels. This meant biweekly data collection through video, audio, and hand recordings of the children composing and conferencing in reading and writing. Also,we asked the children questions from ten different protocol sheets. When the case study children were not composing, we gathered data on the other twenty children in the classroom. The Author's Chair became an important point to examine children's concepts of authorship as well as the relationship between reading and writing.

THE CLASSROOM

The children read and wrote every day. They lived in a community of authors who were constantly reading and writing. They viewed other children composing books, and reading the words of Freddie, Jennifer, Ezra Jack Keats, Dr. Seuss, or Holt, Rinehart and Winston. They were both audiences and writers.

They kept all their writing in their writing folders and published in hard cover about one out of every four pieces. These published books are placed on the bookshelves in the classroom library along with the published books of professional authors. Each published book has a biographical statement about the author at the end. This writing, in both its invented spelling form and published form, is the center of instruction for reading.

Most of the children's writing is done at one time of the day with reading handled at another time. But the distinction is misleading; much reading is done during the writing, or writing during the reading time. For example, one day when Charley came to the writing table to illustrate his newly typed book waiting for publication, he spontaneously reread his book before coloring. Joey, seated next to him, asked, "Will you teach me to read it?" Soon Robbie, seated on the other side of the table, got up, walked over and asked, "Will you teach me too?" When Charley finished teaching, Robbie said, "Now do you want to learn how to read mine?"

Each week a child is chosen as Author of the Week. This means the child's photo is placed on a bulletin board along with a list of the child's published book titles. The books are in pockets and other children post comments about the author's books. The author chooses his or her own published, favorite book and the teacher makes five copies for the other children to read during reading time. During this week the child reads his or her own books, basals, and/or trade books to the class.

Whenever anyone reads a trade book to the class the children are interested in the authors. When Ellen reads to the children she first gives background about the author, including other books composed. She doesn't separate the person from the work—the same procedure used for the children's own books. Soon children become known for the books they have written, for the territory they have established, and are capable of defending it under the questions of the other children.

The prestige of the Author's Chair led to satellite chairs during the reading time. Children would gather their own copies of books, readers, trade books and read to clusters of children. Reading was a time for sharing, receiving the content of the selections and asking questions of the reader. During this reading time the teacher moved about listening, questioning the work of children, working with reading tools in phonics, and meeting with groups, but above all, focusing on the meaning of what the children were doing.

DEVELOPMENT OF THE AUTHOR CONCEPT

Three phases marked the children's growing understanding of the author concept: (1) Replication, (2) Transition, and (3) Sense of Option. We will give background for changes in the author concept in light of the children's composing in both reading and writing.

Phase I: Replication Phase
   "Authors Write Books"

"Authors write books," answered most of the children when asked, "What do authors do?" We asked Ellen's students this question during September 1982 as part of a series of questions about their concepts of reading and writing. We followed it with, "Well if authors write books, how do they do that? What do they do?" The answers followed no pattern; they varied from, "I don't know," to "Make a cover, then pages in there then they typewrite it, staple it together," to "Probably print up words." The author's process is invisible to the beginning first–grade child.

Earlier in this same interview we asked, "Can you write?" All the children answered, "Yes," and showed what they meant by drawing, making numbers, writing their names, writing letters or, for a few, even writing sentences. But after each child had written and we asked, "Are you an author?" few of the children felt they were authors. They knew their own ability to write was different from that of an author.

We also asked, "Can you read?" Several of the children surprised us by answering, "Yes," and showed what they meant by telling stories as they paged through familiar books, by mixing in repetitive words as they told a story, or by reading from early basals.

The children "play" their way into an understanding of reading and writing. They both invent and imitate their way into reading and writing. They observe and interact with the other children and Ellen as they read and write. They borrow certain conventions but demonstrate their own renditions of how to compose in each process.

They invent and imitate versions of writing through drawing, spelling and various uses of the page. Their words change from erratic placement on blank spaces and around drawings to more orderly lines reserved for the print. Children also share their version of oral reading by imitating the intonation of others. They hold their book, "read," and share the pictures from a pseudo–author's chair when they are reading alone and they take part in impromptu sharing sessions during the reading period.

They imitate the appearance of writing when they invent the spellings for the words they want on the pages they write about their personal experiences. They imitate the appearance of reading when they invent their retelling of a story they have heard. They imitate the general processes and invent their own renditions.

In this phase the concept of authorship is a vague one. But they begin the long process of advancing toward a richer understanding of the concept by doing what writers and readers do: As writers they struggle to put their thoughts on paper and they talk about these thoughts with other writers. As readers they compose messages and ask questions about published stories. They play, they invent, they mimic when they compose in reading and writing and sitting on the Author's Chair.

Phase II: Transition Phase,
     "I Am an Author"

The author concept follows the publishing cycle in the classroom. The first published book appears during the first week of school and by October many of the children have had their first writing published in hard cover. Whenever a child publishes a book he or she reads it to the class. The author concept begins to become real as more and more children publish books.

As the children take part in the publishing cycle from drawing, to writing, to the making of the book, and sharing it with the class, they begin to understand the chain of events that leads to authorship: "Cindy is an author. She just got her book published."

The children start to identify with professional authors when they become aware of the prominence of topic choice. They think about what they know and make a decision. Usually they write about personal experiences. Professional writers choose their own topics and these children do likewise. They look at the content of trade books with the assumption the author is relating personal experiences. After reading a book to the class, Ellen frequently asks, "How do you suppose the author chose this topic?" One day she had read a factual book about barber shops and the answer to her question was by now predictable, "Rockwell must have just been to the barber shop."

The children project more than experience to the professional writer. One day Don Graves was not at the research site and one of the children asked, "Where is Mr. Graves today?" Jane Hansen replied, "He is at home writing his book." "He's doing the same thing we are," the child said casually.

The children think they know authors as persons. For example, Bill Martin becomes a early favorite because of his collection at the listening center. His books are some of the first ones they learn to read: "I can read my own book and Bill Martin Junior's book about the brown bear."

During this phase the children gradually show greater precision in their use of print. Although art work in reading and drawings in writing are still important, the transition phase is marked by more interest in print. Their decoding and encoding skills mature so they view the information in the illustrations as an extension of the text, whereas in the inventive phase the drawing was of primary importance. Now the child sees the print as a necessary adjunct to the drawing. Whereas the drawing (when writing) and the illustrations (when reading) were dominant in the inventive phase, now there is a more complementary connection between the two. In their published books they draw a picture for every thought they express in words. The child sees pictures and print as an organic whole, a necessary precursor to seeing the distinctive functions of each.

The reading and writing in this phase take on different forms. The writing become more internalized. There is less oral composing during writing; they can write some words without producing every sound orally. The reading process evidences itself in just the opposite way. More and more sounding is heard. When we ask the children what they do when they read and write in this phase the response is the same as in the inventive phase, "Sound out the letters," even though it is less true of what they do when they write and more true of what they do when they read. A further query produces a glimmer of their process awareness, "Some kids still memorize their books, but I sound out when I read."

Gradually, more of their attention shifts to broader units of involvement in the composing processes. Rereading may go back several words and even several sentences in order to decide which word comes next. When they write, they reread before almost each new word. When they read, they reread when the message is interrupted by sounding out a word. The children do an abundance of rereading as they strive to make meaning.

This context broadens because of the events around the Author's Chair. As they receive and question books their questions involve the information in the stories. They ask, "Why didn't you tell why you still love your sister? Why didn't the author explain the way the goat felt?" In short, as the time–space units expand with the process moving back and forth between current word and broader text, the child begins to develop a sense of option. And as the child develops a sense of option, the authorship concept for self, other children, and professional becomes more distinctive.

Phase III: Option-Awareness Phase
"If I Wrote This Published Book Now, I Wouldn't Write It This Way"

The children's books no longer end with, "I feel sad," or "I feel happy." They can understand stories when authors write implied messages. Although they still expect most information to be explicit they now portray the mood of a story in their overall message. They expect their readers to compose a message when they read. They start to do this on purpose. One day Susan was reading a draft to us, "Do you like gym?" As she read she inserted, "Yes," and explained to us, "I won't put 'yes' in the published book. The kids will have to say that when I read it."

And one day when Steven read a new published book to the class someone asked him why he hadn't included a certain piece of information, "I thought you could figure it out." It is unlikely Steven had made this conscious decision as he was composing, but he does know that this is an acceptable assumption. Authors have the option of leaving some of the composing up to the reader.

In time they also learn how to handle the option of fictitious information. Jessica has sat in the Author's Chair both as a reader of her own books and trade books. She has heard different points of view about content and author's intentions from the other children. One day when she read her piece about the death of her grandfather, her book sounded like a first person account. Richie asked, "Is this a true story?" Jessica replied, "Some of it is not. Most of it is true." Richie continued, "Which parts are fake?" Jessica replied, "The part where I said I went to the funeral." At this point the teacher asked Jessica about her options, "Why did you put it in if it's not true?" Jessica asserted, "I thought it made the story better." The teacher wants to reveal Jessica's option, the right of any writer.

At this phase the children are wrestling with such polar issues as true–untrue, imaginary–real, and explicit–implicit. As each becomes more distinctive, children develop a sense of option in interchanging them in their writing and reading. They learn that child authors and professional authors have options.

Children also discover that authors publish different versions of one story. "Hey, look, here's the same story but the words are different. I wonder why the author published it both ways."

The sense of option becomes real to the children because of the changes in their own reading and writing processes and because of the Author's Chair. Children both exercise and experience the effects of audience. When they share their own pieces and view the reception of the works of both classmates and professionals, they recognize the variance of opinion. Ellen encourages children to provide information to back their opinions, "Why do you suppose the author rewrote this book and published it again?" "Because the first one was sad." As children experiment, adapt, change their opinions they become open to options during the reading and writing process.

In the previous phase children read more for fluency. They read in order to share their accurate reading of words. The effects of the story on the listener were not as important as an accurate rendition of the print and the sharing of illustrations. The children read the book or rewrote the piece until it was "just right." The children already knew what the message was going to be because in reading they almost always chose stories they had heard before and in writing they related incidents that had happened to them. They didn't read and write to find out the product. They read and wrote because the process of putting together an already known message intrigued them. Now, the children reread and rewrite for altered meanings.

The children reread not with the conscious view of going after different levels of comprehension. Rather, the children reread to reenjoy characters, plots, and actions. But in doing so the child gathers a sense of option about the interaction of various components of the story. New meanings appear in successive readings. In short, the child "revises" the content of the piece read.

The actual reading performance changes as well. The children go back and forth within the paragraph or story in order to juxtapose part–whole relationships in the whole piece.

The writing process also involves an exercise of option. The children reread with more than a view of reorienting themselves in their emerging texts. Now they reread with a view to making the part under construction consistent with the overall intention in the piece. The child discovers inconsistencies and will choose to cut and paste for reorganization, choose to organize a story by chapter in order to make it more clear, or write a complete second draft that includes, "a lot more information." The child rewrites with a sense of what the class will ask when he or she reads the piece from the author's chair.

When children are asked about how they read and write, their answers now show more separation between the two processes, "When I write I choose a topic. That's the hard part. Then I write drafts. Then I might publish it. When I read I choose a story, sometimes I can read it without lots of practice, then I might read it to the class." In both reading and writing, the children have a sense of process and are especially free of the "sounding out" component so dominant in earlier statements. Such freedom lifts the children into more thinking about information and the content and organization of what authors actually do in writing.

The children do have options. They do make decisions. They decide whether to put information in their pieces or not. They defend their pieces when the class asks questions. They question published authors. They respond to a story by accepting it and asking questions. Their responsibility as a writer is to anticipate questions from readers. Their responsibility as a reader is to ask questions of authors. They become assertive readers who expect authors to defend the choices they made when they wrote.

215

HYPOTHESES ABOUT AUTHORSHIP

We did not know where the 1981–82 year would take us. We certainly did not know the Author's Chair would come to symbolize the relationship between reading and writing. Somehow, readers who are also writers develop a sense of authorship that helps them in either composing process. The above observations lead us to the following hypotheses about the relationship between reading and writing as it develops in beginning readers.

1. Children's concept of author changes from a vague notion about some other person who writes books to the additional perception of themselves as authors to the realization that they have choices and decisions to make as authors.
2. Children's concept of authorship becomes more pronounced as their concepts of reading and writing become more differentiated.
3. Authorship concepts become more differentiated because children actively compose in both reading and writing. Composing in each of these processes consists of imitating and inventing during encoding, decoding, and the making of meaning.
4. Children change from imposing their own understandings of process and content upon authors, to realizing various authors can use process and content differently.
5. Children realize authors have options because they do the following in both the reading and writing processes: exercise topic choice, revise by choice, observe different types of composing, and become exposed to variant interpretations.
6. Children who learn to exercise options become more assertive in dealing with other authors. At first an author is distant, then an author is self, finally the self–author questions all authors and assertive readers emerge.

The data for this [chapter] came from the first year of our investigation of the relationship between reading and writing. We could not have gathered these data if we had not been in a classroom in which the children had ample opportunity to both read and write. Our recognition of the importance of the author concept came because of the uniqueness of our field site. Since the significance of the author concept did not emerge until the second half of the year, we have started a new yearlong study with a new group of children to examine the author concept in greater depth.

22. BEYOND BASAL READERS: TAKING CHARGE OF YOUR OWN TEACHING

by Kenneth S. Goodman, University of Arizona, Tucson

Kenneth Goodman offers several helpful ideas concerning reading programs in the schools. He points out that with the emphasis on basal readers, accompanied by such impressive terms as "skill hierarchies," many teachers are led to distrust their own professional judgment. Even when the recommendations in the commercial materials do not make sense to teachers (or students), they often follow suggestions because they trust the "experts" who wrote them. The situation with basals is getting worse, according to Goodman, because with the current emphasis on test scores, basals have "become even more atomistic and arbitrarily sequential." In addition, basals require more time to complete as there are more materials and suggested activities. Thus, less time is available for actual reading.

Goodman offers hope when he says whole language is countering the skills movement. He emphasizes that whole language is research-based and "tries to integrate, not fragment the reading process." Three research findings have had the greatest impact on the development of whole language: (a) children possess knowledge about written language before entering school, (b) prior knowledge influences children's reading comprehension, and (c) an interrelationship exists between learning to read and to write. Goodman concludes with the reminder that teachers influence students' learning, materials do not.

Most school systems today require teachers to use basal readers and to spend considerable time teaching according to the manuals for them.

In recent years, however, these teachers' manuals have become thicker and more detailed. Mastery systems built into basal programs require explicit testing of skill sequences, and many teachers have come to feel like technicians administering a predetermined curriculum. They feel they have little power to use their professional knowledge and insight to meet the individual needs of their students.

LEAVING THE TEACHER OUT

How did we get to this point? Modern basal readers developed from the allure of technology in the 1920s. Even human problems like teaching reading, it seemed, could be solved "scientifically." But the basal technology, with the weight of time, has come to have a life of its own.

Generations of teachers were awed by impressive terms such as readability, readiness, grade-level equivalents, controlled vocabulary, word-attack skills, scope and sequence, and subskill hierarchies. Some came to mistrust their own professional judgment. If the tests showed that the kids weren't good readers, then of course they weren't—even if they were reading everything they could get their hands on. And if the skill drills didn't make sense, some teachers still had faith that those anonymous experts who wrote the workbooks knew what they were doing.

Lately, though, in response to back–to–basics pressures and accountability demands requiring narrow test–teach–test methodologies, contemporary basals have generally become even more atomistic and more arbitrarily sequential. All the required testing can take time away from actual reading and real reading development. In fact, students who read widely and comprehend well may be underestimated on these isolated skill tests. Those who perform well on them but who can't or don't care to read may be overestimated, and so both these students and their teachers may begin to feel complacent about their reading "ability."

THE OTHER TREND IN TEACHING READING

Countering all this is another trend, most often referred to as "whole language." Based on the latest reading research, this approach tries to integrate, not fragment, the reading process. And it acknowledges the skill and intuition of teachers as critical.

Essentially, it follows the principle that students read best when they can choose what they read—when good teachers help them match stories, articles, novels, and other print to their interests and experiences. Three important research findings influencing the whole-language approach are:

1. *Kids already know a lot about written language before they come to school.* They learn it in pretty much the same way they learn oral language—and for the same reasons, to communicate and understand. This has confirmed for many teachers what they always suspected: If what students are expected to read is meaningful, functional, and relevant, they'll learn it easily and well.

2. *The knowledge children have* before *they read strongly influences how much they will understand* when *they read.* Thus teachers are learn-

218

ing techniques to find out about students' prior knowledge and to get them interested in a story or passage *before* they begin reading.

3. *Reading and writing help each other to develop.* Teachers have a new awareness of the writing process and have revived the use of thematic units as they've come to realize that children learn language while they use language to learn.

The whole–language approach stresses choice by the learner and the importance of learners feeling ownership and power in their reading and writing. The kids read what they need and want to read.

POWER TO THE TEACHERS

Whether you're familiar with the new research or not, you know your students. And you know that it's *you* not the materials that make the difference in their learning. The textbook publishers may know kids in general, but you know Tim and Jose and Leroy. You know Shoshana and Jennifer and Althea. You know their homes and cultures, the experiences they have and haven't had. You know their likes and dislikes, their fears and fantasies. You know where they are in skill development and how to move them along. You know these things as a caring human being—as a professional kid–watcher. It's just not possible to build that sensitivity into even the most sensitive set of materials.

If there are well–written stories in the basal, appropriate and relevant for some of your students, they'll be useful to you. You can make the basals work for you, not the other way around.

Many teachers (you may be one of them) have already made some adjustments in their use of basals. They've followed them—more or less. They've made them the central part of their instruction. But they've used their own judgment about how to augment them with trade books, when to use the test scores, which workbook pages to skip over. They've used the manuals, but not slavishly. Others have quietly set the basals aside entirely or used selected stories from the student books. *Whatever has worked for them.*

TRUST YOUR JUDGMENT

So why don't you put the basals in their proper place and organize a classroom in which *you* are the professional in charge, directed only by the strengths, needs, and abilities of your students? Ask administrators to recognize that teachers, not materials, will make the difference in their schools. And ask them to support your taking responsibility for the literacy of your students.

23. RESTORING POWER TO TEACHERS: THE IMPACT OF "WHOLE LANGUAGE"

by Sharon J. Rich, Reading Consultant, Board of Education, London, Ontario

Sharon Rich writes with power and persuasion about the triumphs and tribulations of whole-language teaching. Through brief scenarios she introduces readers to two whole-language teachers and the challenges they faced from other teachers, administrators, and parents. Sometimes the two teachers were able to enlighten others about their beliefs and practice; in other instances they were not. For example, one teacher helped her principal become convinced about the worth of whole language. In another situation, however, the teacher was not able to help her superintendent understand its value. As a result, she planned two lessons; one for the students and one for the superintendent.

Rich describes her view of teaching as "a delicate balance between freedom and control." She defines whole language as "an attitude of mind which gives a shape for the classroom." The whole-language teacher rejoices as each student's approximations in reading and writing lead toward independence. Materials are used to meet students' needs rather than serving as a means of placing and processing students according to predetermined standards of performance. Whole-language teachers do not let students make all the decisions, but they see the student as central in the process. They also see themselves as learners as well as teachers. According to Rich, whole-language teachers empower students to shape their own learning and reality. These teachers know their students, and are knowledgeable about child growth and development. They also understand learning theory and are informed about current research, but they do not accept every idea they read or hear without evaluating it. Rich emphasizes that teachers are theory builders as they formulate hypotheses based on experience with their students.

This chapter appeared in Language Arts, *vol. 62 (November 1985): 717-24. © 1985 by the National Council of Teachers of English. Reprinted with permission.*

There has been an increasing interest in whole language over the past few years. Many school districts are actively promoting whole language in local curricula, teacher support groups have developed in other areas, and publishers have begun to develop whole language teaching material.

Unfortunately, much of what is called whole language is simply a generic offering of some specific teaching/learning strategies which are delivered according to a "whole language formula." Such an approach denies the best of whole language. Whole language in its essence goes beyond the simple delineation of a series of teaching strategies to describe a shift in the way in which teachers think about and practice their art. In essence the term "whole language" outlines the beginning stage of a paradigm shift. As a movement whole language encompasses prior research information, then goes beyond to extend thinking about language and learning into new realms. Whole language as it develops in schools, with teachers and children, can be most aptly described through an actual story about teachers, children, learning, and dreams.

Once upon a time . . .

In one school not so very long ago one teacher decided that the only way to survive with a grade one class of twenty boys and six girls, seven of whom were born in December, was to abandon the basal reader lessons and begin planning with the children's interests in mind. There was begging, borrowing, and pleading to get sand and water tables. There were raids on the library for children's books; the reader workbooks were packed safely in boxes; there was work, laughter, tears.

The teacher next door came by and said, "I've just run off these dittos. Perhaps they'll help you organize your phonics program." The first teacher smiled sweetly, accepted the offering, filed the dittos, and went on reading.

The principal came by with visitors from central office. "Please close your door. It's much too disturbing for our visitors." The teacher smiled sweetly, closed the door and went on writing.

A parent came by asking, "Why isn't Johnny in the same reader as Mary from Mrs. Smith's class?" The teacher talked quietly to mom for some time. Mom looked at the books the children were reading; mom listened to Johnny read on tape. The parent left. The teacher smiled sweetly, nodded, and the children went on dancing

One day children began to leave the room. Quietly they headed towards the teacher next door, the principal's office, the custodian, and Mr. Hopeful, the area superintendent who just happened to be visiting. Quietly, insistently, the children read the stories that they had written. Day after day children left the room to demonstrate for the school that they were, indeed, readers and writers.

The principal called the teacher to his office. The conversation was long. Doubts were expressed. The teacher showed writing folders. The principal was uncertain. The teacher played tapes of children reading. The principal wavered. The teacher led the principal back to the classroom where a little girl came rushing up saying, "My God, would you look at what I have just written! It's humongous!''

The principal said,''I am beginning to learn and there is so much more to know. Let me share what I am learning with my colleagues. Help me to understand.''

The teacher smiled and invited him to join the local support group.

In another school not so very long ago a teacher, much like the first teacher, was experimenting. Basal readers provided security but something was missing. The teacher began to try corporate reading with big books. The teacher began to experiment with children's literature. One day the teacher even let the children write—and they did. The teacher was excited! The teacher called the principal who called the superintendent, Mr. Basic. After all, these children had been identified as the potential special education candidates. They were the late birthday boys. They weren't expected to do so well this year. The superintendent arrived. The teacher engaged the whole class in reading *The New Baby Calf*. The children were enthralled. They wanted to reread the story. They wanted to write. They wanted to talk. They wanted to sculpt. They were interested, alive, reaching out.

The superintendent called the teacher aside. ''You have had these children involved in a single task for forty–five minutes. That is beyond their attention capacity! It would be better if you ran your regular reading program, especially since I noticed that some children didn't really know all the words. They just said what their friends said.''

The teacher tried to explain.

The superintendent said, ''Now, now, my dear. This new approach is too much work for someone like you. You do have a young family and I know that you work hard at home too. You can run an effective program the old way and the children still learn.''

The teacher sighed, closed the classroom door, and began to plan two lessons for the next day. One for the superintendent and one for the children.

WHOLE LANGUAGE: AN ATTITUDE, NOT METHODS

The actual situations just described reflect what can and does happen to teachers as they begin to move towards using whole language in their classrooms. It could be suggested that the teachers mentioned in this story were whole language because in their classrooms children read and write daily. There are opportunities for children to interact. Talk is important. Children's literature is present. Both teachers belong to a support group. The teachers and the children keep journals. There are library and creative corners. These are the surface features that make a whole language program. There are many classrooms which incorporate all of the above features and then some, but which are far from being whole language in its best sense.

What is whole language? There is no formula for whole language. There is no published material, whether it be newsletter or reading text, that can literally be whole language. Certainly such material can be supportive of whole language but then an article by Jerry Harste or Ken Goodman, a local newspaper, or a neat story written by a child is supportive of whole language. Some material conscientiously attempts to delineate techniques which are by their very nature whole language. These techniques are obviously beneficial for all teachers because our teaching can always improve, but the whole language teacher is much more than a technician. The true whole language teacher demonstrates that the answers to the theory–to–practice question do not reside in a text but within the self. In classrooms which are truly whole language one can almost hear an echo of Frank Smith (1981): ". . . The decision to be made is whether responsibility for teaching children to write and read should rest with people or programs, with teacher or technology. This is not a matter of selecting among alternative methods of teaching children the same things . . . The issue concerns who is to be in control of classrooms, the people in the classrooms (teachers and children) or the people elsewhere who develop programs. Different answers will have different consequences." Whole language teachers have made a conscious choice to opt for people. The answer to the question "What is whole language" is that it is an attitude of mind which provides a shape for the classroom.

Who is the whole language teacher? In whole language classrooms there is a sense of caring for children and childhood. Teachers engage with children carefully, cooperatively so as to help the children enter the literacy community. Just as the children's parents assumed that each squalling, mewling infant would become independent and rejoiced at each approximation towards independence, so the whole language teacher assumes that each child will become literate and celebrates each approximation. Materials are used to fit the needs of children rather than the children being put through the material to accomplish someone's identified objective.

True, there is a certain insecurity in this. I receive numerous calls from teachers saying "Sharon, it's February and Theodore's still only memory reading," or "Sharon, it's February and Maria keeps reading the same books over and over. What should I do? Last year these children would have been in *Toy Box*."

"Would they be reading any better?"

"No, and I would hate listening to them and they wouldn't like to read."

223

"What can Theodore and Maria do?"

"Well they are writing stories. The spelling is coming in their writing. Theodore wrote a whole page yesterday. He had all initial and final consonants but no vowels. I guess you could say he is taking risks with writing now. Theodore can read all of the signs around the school and Maria reads to a buddy in Junior Kindergarten but they don't know many words in isolation."

My final question, "What have you learned from Theodore and Maria?", usually leaves the teacher reflecting on her program both present and past and resolving to move ahead in her present manner.

Because whole language teachers choose people over programs, they reflect a belief in the learner that must be central to any real education. Basic to whole language is the idea that children are intrinsically motivated to learn, to make sense of the world. Whole language teachers know that using language helps children make sense of the world and of language. In their classrooms they arrange the environment so that children have opportunities for interaction. The priorities have been firmly established as being supportive of language and children. There are no questions about "Where do I find the time to read to the children?" "How do I accommodate children's writing?" The simple truth is we make time for those things we perceive to be important.

No two whole language teachers are likely to have identical programs although there will be a common thread running through every program. The classrooms will be comprehension-centered and child-centered, but the methodologies will be as varied as the teachers and the children.

The teachers may well be eclectic in their approach to teaching but that eclecticism is informed by their knowledge of the child and the situation. For example, one teacher in an open area school in responding to children's demands to do workbook pages like the other grade two recognized that this group of children had particular needs. Instead of throwing up hands in despair, the teacher cheerfully cut up two workbooks and put the pages out for the children to use. The children who had made the request picked up the pages, looked at the worksheets, and responded disdainfully. "This isn't really reading!" and went back to their reading corner. The teacher had recognized a need expressed by these children, provided them with the experience they wanted, and allowed the children to make a choice.

Now, it should not be interpreted that the whole language teacher abdicates the teaching role or leaves the children to make all of the decisions or find their own way. Instead, whole language teachers put the child at the center of schooling and learn with the children. In so doing they discover much about the way learning goes. They provide children

224

with the power to shape their own learning, to shape their own reality. This means that the whole language teacher may decide upon a broad topic or theme with which to work in a class but then will provide many opportunities for negotiation within that so that individual needs can be met. The teacher may establish a framework because the teacher has a greater experience with life. There are, however, plenty of opportunities for the children to share in decision making and incorporate their personal experiences into the curriculum. Because of the way learning goes for children, no one program or set of materials will satisfy the whole language teacher. There is always more to share, more to discover, and more views of reality than that of the teacher.

WHOLE LANGUAGE, INSECURITY, AND LEARNING

Not only does the whole language teacher trust the child's desire to learn, the whole language teacher is a learner who remains open to new experiences, new learnings. This teacher has engaged in a clarification of beliefs. Previous assumptions about the way learning goes have been questioned and the belief system underlying these old assumptions examined. (As the Wiz said to Dorothy when she tried to find her way back to Kansas, "It ain't enough to know where you're goin'; you gotta know where you're comin' from.") The whole language teacher knows where she is coming from. The process of discarding the old beliefs was a painful one for many whole language teachers. For a time many of them clung to the whole language teaching strategies they were learning and applied them without much thought. Sometimes when all didn't seem to be going well they had doubts and questions but like children pretending their way into literacy, they were pretending their way into whole language teaching. One day the surface structure of whole language was in place. The teacher began to analyze the nature of this peculiar phenomenon of whole language in the classroom. The teacher read, asked questions, learned, and began to construct a personal reality of whole language. Inspired by some of the language process research, the teacher looked to the children for demonstrations. The teacher found that sometime what had been read and heard reflected the reality of the classroom, but at other times reality was different. The teacher asked questions and always wondered, "Is all this as it seems? Is this really how learning goes?" Yet the essentials remained and the teacher was always struck by the power of children to construct meaning. The teacher had changed. Like the children the teacher had become a learner. Now when attending workshops or lectures, the teacher listened, questioned, and shaped personal meaning. The teacher no longer came back from a con-

225

ference saying "my life has been changed—I now have the formula to make everyone literate." Instead the teacher took that which was useful, which fit a developing belief system and personal knowledge of children and learning. Confidence grew along with willingness to share knowledge with others. The teacher presented workshops, shared children's work, but always suggested that everything was in process, that today's conclusions were tentative and that there were many more questions to ask. Sometimes the teacher would laughingly suggest that the light that sometimes seemed to flicker at the end of the tunnel was a train coming to challenge assumptions once more. Then the teacher paused, reflected, and discarded the tunnel image as inappropriate for learning. Learning was multidimensional, a kaleidoscope rather than a tunnel, a view from the mountain tops, not the valley.

WHOLE LANGUAGE: A POLITICAL ACTIVITY

Whole language teaching, in its best sense, can be seen as a political activity since a true whole language notion returns power where it belongs—to the children and teacher in the classroom. Whole language is radical in that it assumes that everyone is a learner and everyone can become an expert. Because the curriculum is shaped by teachers and children together, sometimes central offices become uneasy, concerned that there is not sufficient attention paid to accountability. At other times, central offices mandate whole language, even to the extent of developing whole language curricula. It takes time to come to understand that whole language cannot be mandated. It is an idea, a concept that must be gently nurtured, facilitated. A booklet of whole language techniques can come from a central office, but the booklet remains cold, a slab of black on white until the reality of live people takes the concept, shapes it and develops ownership. The teachers must take the techniques and using these, determine the ambiance of classrooms, the degree of collaborative negotiation that must ensue, the nature of group work, and the freedom to learn without fear of error. Whole language in its best sense is frightening because it implies a restructuring of traditional schools and an opening of the curriculum with parent education as a part of the total school package.

There is a second sense too in which whole language is political and that is the sense in which whole language teachers are not content to be quiet about those beliefs which are imperative. Whole language teachers believe that they must speak for those things which they know to be true about children, learning and language. They know that each child is unique, full of language, and eager to learn. They recognize that all too

226

frequently schools abuse children by taking from them their natural instinct to question, to make sense of their environment. This abuse is a subtle one, but in its own way just as damaging as physical or sexual abuse because it takes away the child's potential. Children need foundations, the basics, the roots. But they need wings more because wings encourage the children to soar, to think, and to test what they might become. Whole language teachers try to sustain the child's intrinsic motivation. They recognize and try to fulfill the ideal that the primary purpose of teaching is to help children claim kinship with humanity.

In achieving that goal whole language teachers are deliberately, quietly assertive, sometimes verifying beliefs through simple demonstrations of children's ability. At other times whole language teachers refuse to be subjected to the complaints of teachers next door and the cries of "What do your children really know?"

When confronted by those who suggest that school as it used to be did not do them any harm, that they hold jobs and are productive members of the community, whole language teachers do not react defensively. They simply ask, but what *might* you have become if you had been given the power to ask questions, to shape your own learning? Whole language teachers want to open doors to children so that the children can dream better dreams than we have ever known. Whole language teachers want to give children the power to become literate, the power to learn, the power to dream.

Whole language teachers know their children. They are well versed in child development, understand learning theory, and keep up to date with research. Yet, they do not accept everything that they encounter in print without question. They risk challenging the theorists, the experts, because in their own classrooms they are in the business of theory making. They shape reality together with their children and filter their developing knowledge through the screen of prior knowledge discovered by others. The whole language teacher is above all a responsible, caring human being who knows about theory, children, people, and, above all, life.

Whole language teachers believe in political action if political action means returning power to children. Not the power to dominate, to destroy an environment, but the power to learn. In giving that power teachers ensure that children have ownership of the program, of the learning. They create a classroom ambiance in which children can make choices, make mistakes, and learn the consequences of those mistakes. The environment created by whole language is one characterized by trust, security, and interaction. There is a community of colearners in each classroom who help each other move towards claiming a full human identity.

WHOLE LANGUAGE: FREEDOM AND CO.

The above beliefs should not be taken to mean that the whole language teacher believes in total freedom. The responsibility of the teacher extends to establishing a broad framework of curriculum planning which allows for negotiation. The framework is necessary because children cannot make intelligent choices without knowing the full range of choice available. The whole language teacher establishes a delicate balance between freedom and control. Children learn the delicate art of accepting responsibility for their own actions, of shaping their own lives and of caring for others.

The whole language teacher then is somewhat like nine-year-old Maria who, when asked of her response to creative dance, said, "In dance, you put joy together, take someone's hand, and move to the beat."

In whole language classrooms teachers engage in a similar dance. They start with the belief that learning is joyous and that they too are learners. They provide daily demonstrations of themselves as members of humanity, of the literate environment. They stretch out their hands to the children, inviting them to join in the dance. At times they slow their steps to accommodate their young partners, at other times they must dance faster to follow where the children lead. The joy is in the dance. The reward is in claiming the potential of humanity.

REFERENCE

Smith, Frank. "Demonstrations, Engagement and Sensitivity: The Choice Between People and Programs," *Language Arts* 58 (1981): 634–642.

24. A REFLECTION ON REFLECTIVE PRACTICE IN TEACHING READING AND WRITING

by Bernice J. Wolfson, University of Alabama at Birmingham

Bernice Wolfson presents ideas about her experiences in teaching reading and writing to individual students. The focus of her chapter, however, is not on teaching reading and writing. Rather, she focuses on her increased awareness of the importance of reflection-in-action and reflection-on-action. Wolfson describes her growth as a teacher as she reflects on her actions, on the research regarding the teaching and learning of reading and writing, and on her own views of reading and writing development. As she writes, "My reflection-in-action, my tacit knowledge about the student and the reading process, and my intuitive reactions all entered into my actions while teaching." Now formally retired from teaching, Wolfson continues to work with students and teachers.

The author presented a different version of this chapter at the 1987 Conference of Curriculum Theory and Classroom Practice in Bergamo, Indiana, sponsored by The Journal of Curriculum Theorizing.

Teachers reflect on their teaching practices at different times of the day or night. For example, they think about other ways they might have responded to one student; they wonder what kinds of books might interest another; they puzzle over the activities that didn't work out as anticipated. No doubt some teachers are more reflective than others.

As Donald Schon (1983, 1987) has described it, professionals also reflect–in–action, making multitudes of decisions and trying out various actions. Of course, teachers act spontaneously and intuitively, too. These actions and their consequences become material for subsequent reflection–on–action.

In order for reflection to move teachers to more satisfying practice, they need to have some vision in mind of what is desirable. Of necessity, they have their own assumptions and beliefs, both conscious and tacit, about the purpose of schooling, how students learn, and what should be taught. They also have their own personal histories and future expectations, which affect their reflections. And to clarify their thinking, teachers need to talk with others about their ideas and practices.

Recently I became particularly aware of the reflective process that Schon (1983, p. 280) describes as an "interaction of thinking and doing," as I used Marie Clay's Reading Recovery Program (Clay 1985) in teaching second graders. From her research, Clay (1985, p. 7) concluded that a proficient reader "operates on print in an integrated way in search of meaning, and reads with high accuracy and high self–correction rates. He reads with attention focused on meaning." Readers bring their prior knowledge of the world to reading. They use a variety of cues to construct meaning, including the content of the text, the structure of the sentences, and graphophonic relationships. Clay's program is not designed as a total reading program; it is an intensive tutoring program that includes a half–hour of individual tutoring a day in both reading and writing. The purpose is to accelerate the progress of students who are having difficulty in learning to read.

This chapter discusses my tutoring experiences in autobiographical fashion. I hope teachers will find the report of interest and value as they think about meaningful reading and writing experiences for individual students.

REFLECTION–ON–ACTION

A few years ago I studied in London at the Centre for Language in Primary Education and practiced under the guidance of Moira McKenzie, who was then the director of the Centre. I took a course, observed a reading tutor, and then tutored Ben, a five–year–old, in a school in northern London. At the very beginning, I found myself saying things that were inconsistent with Clay's theory as well as with my own beliefs. For example, when Ben got stuck while reading aloud, I heard myself saying, "Look at the word; how do you think it sounds?" I had long believed that such an approach was the least useful strategy for getting meaning from print. Becoming aware of this inconsistency, I noted some responses suggested by Clay that I wanted to use such as, "What do you think would make sense there?" or "Can you read on and then go back and try again?" I had reflected on my response and found alternatives that were consistent with Clay's theoretical framework and my own views.

Another time when working with Ben, I realized that I was encouraging him to depend on me to verify his responses. Whenever he read or wrote a word that he was not sure of, he would look at me with a smiling and questioning look. I would reassure him that he was correct or assist him if he was incorrect. Reflecting on this practice led me to stop responding in this way. Even when he asked directly, I would say instead, "What do you think?" or "What might fit there?" He gradually came to depend more on himself and to become aware that he knew more than he thought he did.

Reflection–on–action led me to more changes in my actions to make them more consistent with my intentions, a process that I will necessarily continue a long as I teach. My intentions as a tutor were to focus on meaning and to allow the child to figure out things with little or no intervention from me. Dr. McKenzie's suggestions, my own reflections, and videotapes of my teaching helped me to revise my actions.

On returning home from London, I started working with a few teachers who were interested in the procedure and with some second graders. As I worked with the teachers and the students I continued to reflect-on-action. I tried to move toward making my actions more and more consistent with my beliefs about the reading process and about how students construct meaning from text.

As I worked with students, I was frequently surprised. For example, I was amazed when a boy, who spoke little and seemed timid and unsure of himself, told in sequence and great detail the story he had read the previous day. When given the opportunity and not constantly questioned and corrected, students often reveal that they can do more than we imagine. I saw how they tried to make sense of reading and writing, each in a unique way.

I began to understand better the significance of the particular text being read and of the student's prior knowledge. In one case, I was working with a boy who could not tell me anything about the story he had read the day before. I realized that he did not have the necessary background knowledge. The story was about soccer, which I had mistakenly thought was an interest of his, since he had mentioned that his older brother played soccer. We then selected a different story to read. After that, I began to provide two or three stories from which students would select one to read.

Following Clay's suggestions on writing, I asked students to say a word aloud slowly and then to write the beginning letter or any other known letters in the word. I then filled in the remaining letters. This procedure, according to Clay, allows students to become aware of what is already known, and also prevents them from seeing incorrect spelling. Furthermore, the procedure is designed to help students become aware of the linear relationship of the sound–symbol system.

As I worked with students, I was struck by how differently they responded to the writing task. Some only used words they thought they could spell correctly. Many expected me to spell each word for them. Others did not ask for help or refused help when they were writing. Recent studies (Ferreiro and Teberosky, 1982; Kamii and Randazzo, 1985) of the spelling of young students suggest that, using invented spelling, they construct the relationship of sounds with symbols by first developing a coherent system of sound–symbol correspondence that may not be correct but that enables them to move to a higher level, and, eventually, to conventional spelling.

I reflected on my actions and the students' responses as I used Clay's suggestions about writing. I also reflected on the recent spelling research and my own views of students' spelling and writing development. In so doing, I had to alter my actions to make them more consistent with my own views and the research and theory about spelling. Therefore, I began to encourage students to do the best they could, using their own spelling systems. I accepted their spelling and did not correct the errors. If they noticed they had misspelled a word and wanted to correct it, I encouraged them to do so.

REFLECTION–IN–ACTION

Gradually, I came to see that the teacher's role involves a series of judgment calls or reflections–in–action. For instance, the teacher has to decide how long to wait for a student to respond, when to intervene, and what intervention might be helpful at a particular point. I became aware of how uncertain I was about how to respond. I believe that my reflection–in–action, my tacit knowledge about the student and the reading process, and my intuitive reactions all entered into my actions while teaching. Uppermost in my mind was the desire to strike a balance between being too helpful, which could make the student dependent, or holding back too long, which could cause the student to feel frustrated and incompetent.

As I continued to teach, it became increasingly clear to me that reading is not about learning words. It is about thinking. I observed Billy reading a story he had written. The first two times he read *house* for *home*; the third time he read *home*. How could I explain this? No one had corrected him; he had not analyzed the word sound by sound; he had not practiced the word over and over. It seems obvious that as Billy got his story more under control, he was able to coordinate better his awareness of the cues available to help him as he read.

In another session, Don was presented to me by his teacher as a problem. He was not responsive in the tutoring session, or elsewhere for that matter. "Is there something wrong with him?" the teacher asked. "Is he learning disabled, dull–normal, or fearful?

I worked with Don, mixing conversation and questions, and tried to make contact. I suspect I intimidated him but I tried to show him that I am gentle and friendly. I waited a long time for his responses. Sometimes he nodded; sometimes he said a word; sometimes he just sat with

232

his head down. I made a joke and he looked at me and smiled. I could feel his intelligence.

In one session, Don reluctantly wrote a story. It was the same as a story he had written on the previous day, but I accepted it and worked with him as usual. In another session, I read a new story to him and watched him as he tried to read it after me. I saw his eyelids lower, as he sat unmoving, and in a while he looked up again and responded briefly.

I concluded that I would continue to work with him in the same personal way, giving him lots of time to respond, watching carefully for any changes and continuing to try to join our worlds. This year I have worked with Don twice a week. He has been labeled learning disabled and is getting special help. Our relationship now is friendly and he is more open and cooperative, most of the time.

Tutoring turned out to be a continual inquiry into the student's process of reading and writing, and, at the same time, into my own responding and thinking during and after the teaching sessions—into my own teaching actions. As Schon (1983, p. 280) pointed out, "It is the surprising result of action that triggers reflection, and it is the production of a satisfactory move that brings reflection temporarily to a close."

FINAL REFLECTIONS

Working with students in reading and writing is a fuzzy, tentative, nonlinear process. Yet I try to be aware of how I am thinking and feeling as I teach and of how the students are thinking and feeling. As I work with students over time, I have a better chance of identifying the strategies they use and the thoughts they have about reading and writing. Yet assuming one knows what a student is thinking, or what will work is also a danger. One needs to look for small changes as well as big surprises.

In reflecting on the entire experience, I reached several conclusions. First, as a teacher I need to inquire into how students think about reading and writing. Some think reading is remembering words or sounding out words. One student I taught believed that she would be a good reader if she could read with her eyes closed. Others think that writing consists of getting the words spelled correctly. Second, I need to observe carefully and try to understand what students are doing—how they process reading and writing. Third, I need to respond to students more appropriately—that is, to make my actions more consistent with my theoretical framework and intentions. Also, I need to keep in touch with what the student is doing.

I was amazed at how difficult it was, while teaching individual students, to change my old habits and to act more consistently with my convictions. But I did change. My style and my relationship with students became more conversational and more genuine.

Most of all I was fascinated by the journey with each student as we discussed ideas and feelings and as he or she constructed meaning in the process of reading and writing. Maxine Greene (1986, p. 80) described the process in this way, "To reflect in the course of situated teaching is consciously to attend to what is happening and to those who are present with the teacher in a shared moment of lived life." In fact, my experiences in working with individual students consisted of such "shared moments of lived life."

REFERENCES

Bussis, A. M., and others. *Inquiry into Meaning: An Investigation of Learning to Read.* Hillsdale, N.J.: Lawrence Erlbaum, 1985.

Clay, Marie. *The Early Detection of Reading Difficulties.* 3d ed. Auckland: Heinemann Educational Books, 1985.

Ferreiro, Emilia, and Teberosky, Ana. *Literacy Before Schooling.* Exeter, N.H.: Heinemann, 1982.

Greene, Maxine. "Reflection and Passion in Teaching." *Journal of Curriculum and Supervision* 2, no. 1 (Fall 1986): 68–81.

Kamii, Connie, and Randazzo, Marie. "Social Interaction and Invented Spelling." *Language Arts* 62 (February 1985): 124–33.

Schon, Donald. *The Reflective Practitioner.* New York: Basic Books, 1983.

Schon, Donald. *Educating the Reflective Practitioner.* San Francisco: Jossey–Bass, 1987.

Smith, Frank. *Understanding Reading.* 3d ed. New York: Holt, Rinehart, and Winston, 1982.

25. IN THE PROCESS OF BECOMING PROCESS TEACHERS

by Gary Manning, Maryann Manning, and Roberta Long, University of Alabama at Birmingham

Gary Manning, Maryann Manning, and Roberta Long give the views of four effective teachers who abandoned the traditional curriculum to provide students with more natural reading and writing activities. The authors met regularly with these teachers and worked with them in their classrooms. During this period, the teachers also read professional material about emerging literacy. The teachers describe how they began by focusing on strategies and materials to use with their kindergartners. As they developed in their understanding, however, they arrived at a balance between the need for strategies and materials and the use of their own ability to think, supported by an understanding of and a rationale for such activities. In other words, they became increasingly interested in and knowledgeable about how students learn and develop. They followed up their readings and conversations with the authors by testing their ideas with their students. Before long, they were generating their own strategies by using their developing whole-language theory.

The chapter provides a number of ideas for implementing practices that reflect whole language. But, most importantly, it provides insights into the growth and development of teachers in the process of becoming process teachers. An encouraging development—more and more kindergarten intructors in the Birmingham City Schools are becoming process teachers in their views and practices. The kindergarten supervisor, Janice England, continues to support these teachers as they focus on how young children emerge into literacy.

This chapter is reprinted with permission of the publisher Early Years, Inc., Norwalk, CT 06854, from the February 1988 issue of Teaching/K-8.

Worksheets! Workbooks! Paper and pencil activities! They've filtered down to kindergarten and comprise much of the school day for many young children. Kindergarten teachers are spending children's time to learn isolated bits of language that have little or no meaning for young children. It's time to rethink what we are doing to young children's thinking and development.

A number of kindergarten teachers we know have done just that; they questioned the structured approach they were required to use and now are exploring ways to help young boys and girls develop literacy in more natural and meaningful ways.

In this [chapter], we provide views of four kindergarten teachers who, with our support and that of their supervisor, abandoned the traditional curriculum of the school system and allowed children to explore written language through a process or whole language approach to literacy development. We met with them monthly and exchanged ideas, and also worked with them and their children in their classrooms throughout the year. Their goal became one of helping young children develop their knowledge of written language in a natural way. Again, the focus of instruction, as related by one of the teachers, Delyne Hicks, is one of process, not product. Three of the teachers work with all low-income children who are primarily minority children; the fourth teacher, Kay Lee Wright, teaches in a magnet school with both low–income and middle-income children.

These four teachers are fortunate because they have the support of their kindergarten supervisor, Ms. Janice England. She, too, realized young children construct their own knowledge of written language just as they construct knowledge about the world. Construction occurs from within, not by having it "poured in" from the outside. Let's listen to the teachers as they share their ideas.

THE NEED TO CHANGE

Lynn Douglas began to question many of the practices in the suggested curriculum. As she says, "Kindergarten has become more structured each year. Performance on tests has become the goal." Searching for a better approach to help her children, Lynn realized a process approach was for her.

Another teacher, Becky Davidson, states, "Many times I would see another class of quiet, well–behaved children coloring or doing worksheets and then I would return to my own room, where I saw lots of different and noisy activities going on. I sometimes questioned what was best, but intuitively I felt I was right." Becky makes an excellent point and we learn from it. Good teachers, like good parents, often use good practices based on their own good intuition. Sometimes teachers abandon their own good intuition for structured materials and approaches "pushed" by other well–intentioned educators.

Kay Lee says she notices that children who develop easily as readers and writers have several things in common: "They come from homes where there are many reading materials and they have been read to frequently. If this is so, then I should teach this way, rather than teach isolated and separate skills in an unnatural way."

All four teachers agree that they see children as more competent written language users. Delyne puts it this way: "The children know a lot more than I ever gave them credit for. I used to think they had little knowledge of reading and writing. Now I view them as knowing a lot about written language, and I realize we have to begin with what *they* know, not with what *I* know."

SHARING BOOKS

It's important for teachers and children to share in the joys of literature. Thus, the four teachers have many good children's books available for children to read independently or together; the children can also listen to books read aloud. They enjoy talking about the books they read before, during and after the reading episodes.

In addition to reading and sharing regular–sized children's books, the children read and share big books. Kay Lee says, "Big books are wonderful for the children and for me. All of the children can easily see the text as we work together in a group." Kay Lee and the others use a number of activities with big books, such as getting children to predict what will happen next, using a cloze procedure by covering a word or phrase and having them predict the covered words, and getting children to talk about the story.

PREDICTABLE BOOKS

These teachers realize children can "read" predictable books very early in the year. Predictable books share several common features including rhythm, repetition of vocabulary and repetition of story structure. These books, read over and over, enable children to remember the text and thus they predict and "read" along with the teacher, with other children and by themselves. Delyne says that in the beginning she had difficulty identifying books that were predictable. "As I got more into it," she notes, "I realized that predictable books had to have a rhythm to them and there had to be a kind of 'sing–song.' There had to be something to help children figure out what was coming next."

Becky declares, "I wish I had realized the value of predictable books years ago. We read them every day and discuss the stories. It's exciting to see how many children can read their predictable books." In other words, predictable books help children realize that much of what readers read is what they predict or expect to read.

237

JOURNAL WRITING

Although the teachers had started some writing in recent years, an increase has occurred in the amount of daily writing, including journal writing. Becky says, "We write daily in our journals. I staple five sheets of paper together every week. We start on Monday and the first thing the children do when they come in is write in their journals. I treasure their writing and delight in watching progress in their writing abilities."

The teachers remind us of the importance of accepting and valuing children's writing, whether it consists of scribbles or a string of letters, as we support their development to higher levels. We are not reinforcing scribbling by accepting it—but, rather, supporting the child's development as a user of written language.

GROUP DICTATION STORIES

The teachers also use group–dictated stories. In this activity, children collectively compose a story, with the teacher serving as a scribe. The group stories are read and may be enjoyed by the children for the remainder of the year. Kay Lee often takes the group story into bookmaking and the children illustrate the pages.

The dictation of a story where the teacher writes and serves as a model helps some children learn how written language works. According to Lynn, children profit from dictated stories, especially those children who have little experience with written language. The teachers caution us, however, not to overuse it or let it replace opportunities for children to do their own writing.

READING ALOUD

All four teachers have read aloud to children for years, but they say it is now a more integral part of their curriculum. Delyne says, "The big thing I have always done is to read to my children. They love it. I use a lot of different kinds of literature, and I now have a stronger literature program because I see a greater need for it. Before, I would read to them right before a nap or squeeze it in at other times during the day, whereas now it is a more natural part of what I am doing."

BOOK–EXTENDING ACTIVITIES

In these kindergartens, there are many book–extending activities: puppet plays based on favorite books, dramatic presentations, murals, collections of pictures and author studies, to name a few. These teachers have always included book–extending activities, but now they emphasize them to a greater extent.

INDEPENDENT READING AND WRITING

It's important to have books readily available for children. As Lynn says, "The books need to be accessible so the children can read them at self–selected times during the day. There should be different kinds of books for children to explore and to select for their own independent reading." A reading area in the room provides a space for books and for children to read. The areas differ from classroom to classroom: a carpet in Lynn's room, a bathtub in Kay Lee's room, a corner with pillows in Becky's room and a reading loft in Delyne's room.

Independent writing also is encouraged. Sign making and card writing are two popular activities in Kay Lee's room. Whenever children want to give directions to others, such as not wanting classmates to play with a clay figure, they make a sign for the others to read. Card making includes the writing of get–well cards, family and classmate birthday cards, and thank–you notes. In addition, the children write their own individual books and group books. The teachers have a writing area in their rooms which emphasizes the importance of writing and provides a place for the storage of writing materials.

DIFFICULT OR EASY?

Is using a reading and writing process approach difficult or easy? Delyne says, "I think it's difficult because there's no 'cookbook' or guidebook to go by. You really have to know the processes of reading and writing, and you really have to know your children and what they can do so that you can respond appropriately."

Becky thinks the process approach is easier. She says, however, that she still has to work very hard. Kay Lee indicates that for her, the approach is harder but more interesting. Lynn agrees with Delyne and Kay Lee about the difficulty of implementing such a program. However, she notes that she has a better feeling about her teaching because she now has children who view reading and writing as meaningful and pleasant activities.

IN THE BEGINNING

These kindergarten teachers say they learned by doing. It's a gradual developmental process, and one makes mistakes in the process. But teachers can learn from those errors and continue to improve the learning environment. Says Lynn, "You must be willing to take risks as you try new things, and then learn from what you and the children do." However, she emphasizes, "Even though I know things on a conscious level, I have to work at not falling into the teaching traditions of the past and into what I see still being done by teachers who are using a skills–oriented approach." It's difficult to stop following practices one has been using over a period of time, but it can be done, as demonstrated by these four teachers.

AND IN THE END

The following comment by Becky summarizes well what all of the teachers feel: "The more I'm involved in the reading and writing process, the more I want to learn. I'm constantly trying to make each day worthwhile, considering appropriate responses I should make to children as they use the processes of reading and writing. I'll continue to develop a community of readers and writers in my classroom, a place for meaningful explorations of written language."